RELIGION

RELIGION

The Modern Theories

SETH D. KUNIN

EDINBURGH UNIVERSITY PRESS

Edinburgh University Press is one of the leading
university presses in the UK. We publish academic
books and journals in our selected subject areas
across the humanities and social sciences, combining
cutting-edge scholarship with high editorial and
production values to produce academic works of lasting
importance. For more information visit our website:
www.edinburghuniversitypress.com

Transferred to digital print 2016

Edinburgh University Press Ltd
The Tun – Holyrood Road
12(2f) Jackson's Entry
Edinburgh EH8 8PJ

Typeset in Goudy Old Style
by Norman Tilley Graphics, and
printed and bound in Great Britain by
CPI Group (UK) Ltd, Croydon CR0 4YY

A CIP record for this book is available
from the British Library

ISBN 9780748615216 (hardback)
ISBN 9780748615223 (paperback)

Contents

Introduction

The question of the nature of religion has interested scholars from a wide range of different disciplines during the course of the last two centuries. In each generation definitions and discussions of religion have been closely related to the predominant understandings of humanity and human nature. Thus, in the nineteenth century most of the theories were influenced by or were responses to Darwin's theory of evolution by natural selection. This is also true of models and theoretical perspectives discussed here; some are shaped by concepts of market relations associated with capitalism, others with psychological complexes associated with the theory of Psychoanalysis, and others by views of the relationship of religion and reason, and the assumed associated rise in secularisation. It is thus important to note from the outset that theories of religion or of any other subject are not unmotivated. They reside in a particular social context and in some sense are a reflection or a response to that context. This is not to suggest that such theorising has no value, rather it argues that the theories must be seen in a provisional or relative sense, rather than as expressions of some final or essential truth.

This provisional nature of theory, seeing theory as a basis for argument rather than the end of an argument underlies the choice of material include in this volume. We have chosen not to include those approaches to religion that are not based on empirical analysis. Thus, we have excluded theological approaches and included the social scientific approaches. We are not suggesting by this that theological approaches are not significant; rather, this volume seeks to develop an argument about a certain type of analysis, one that interacts with and analyses social facts. Theological approaches ultimately rest on belief and therefore on assumptions that are not testable or verifiable. From the perspective of social science, beliefs should not be the basis of analysis (that presupposes their truth), they should be included among the data that is analysed. The discourses of the social sciences and theology may overlap, but due to their different presuppositions they are mutually exclusive and should remain so – we would not advocate reducing theology to a humanist perspective, nor reducing the study of religion to a transcendental one.

This volume is divided into three parts: setting the agenda, continuing the discussion and taking the discussion in different directions. The first part lays the groundwork for the theories developed in the twentieth century. It touches on some of the significant theorists who established some of the main avenues of discussion. The second part introduces the approaches of the social scientific disciplines that study religion. Although each discipline is examined separately, we attempt to raise some general questions about the nature and problems associated with definitions. The analysis of the theories suggests that we need to problematise the understanding of definitions and move to a new more dialectical and analogical model. The third part looks at religion through a microscope, examining elements that are often seen as being constituents of religion. This discussion is based on a similar argument to that developed in the second part. It suggests that all of the constituent elements and their respective definitions need to be problematised in the same way as the more general category of religion. The book concludes with suggestions of how new definitions of religion might be framed, to provide more culturally sensitive and open-ended methodologies for understanding.

PART I

Setting the Agenda

Introduction

This part examines several major approaches to the study of religion. The significant theorists, primarily from the early part of the twentieth century, are discussed as a means of establishing the important issues for the study of religion, which continue to be of relevance in discussions today. We have selected those thinkers whose ideas, even if highly modified, still underlie current trends in the study of religion. Thus, for example, the Marxist approach has three modern offshoots: a specifically Marxist critique of religion, carrying on the main threads of Marx's analysis; the tradition in anthropology of cultural materialism, which uses materialism as the primary explanatory feature for understanding different aspects of culture including religion; and aspects of the Feminist critique of religion, which continues the Marxist argument seeing religion as a form of exploitation and false consciousness.

Most of the approaches that are presented share a common attitude towards the study of religion. This attitude can be specifically distinguished from that of theology. Each of the thinkers, with the exception of Rudolf Otto who was essentially a theologian, examines religion from an external perspective. Religion is an object of study rather than an object of belief or faith. In spite of this external approach, it should not be assumed that the study of religion is unconcerned with faith or belief; these, however, rather than being seen as forms of explanation or analysis, are seen as data for study. Study of religion examines both the observable aspects of religion and the unobservable ways that insiders express and relate to their religious constructs.

As discussed below, Otto is the major exception to this common theme. He speaks as an insider, basing his analysis ultimately on his own religious experience. As an adherent of a particular tradition, he also uses that tradition as the basis of judgement of all other traditions, thus his comparative analysis is part of his theological enterprise. Otto's work, however, is significant to the development of the study of religion in several respects. First, it reveals the problems associated with a theological analysis of comparative religions: it allows us to see some of the problems associated with an emphasis on the insider's point of view, delineating the need for an analytical framework that resides outside of a particular theology. Second, it forms the intellectual basis for one group of essentialist approaches to religion, that is, it approaches viewing religion as qualitatively unique and distinct from other cultural phenomena. Many of these themes and issues become the building blocks from which the phenomenological study of religion is built.

The other approaches discussed here share an additional theme, to a greater or lesser extent, that of the role of human beings in the creation of religion. Arguably all of the non-theological thinkers address religion as a human construct without the need for a supernatural or transcendental other. This humanistic approach leads the thinkers to address the role played by religion as a social or human artifact.

This role of religion is seen to work on two distinct levels: that of the individual and that of society. The psychological approaches of Freud and Jung emphasise the role played by religion in individual development: a positive role in the case of Jung and a negative one in that of Freud. They also see religion as emerging from the individual psyche. Otto can also be seen to fit into this category, because he sees religion as emerging from individual experience.

The sociological approaches focus on the function of religion in relation to society. Marx sees religion as playing a dual role; on the one hand, it plays the positive role of expressing and challenging alienation, on the other it plays the strongly negative role of validating economic structures and particularly exploitation – both of these roles are ultimately one, in that both are forms of false consciousness. Durkheim and the anthropologists who followed him see religion as playing a more positive societal role, creating different levels of societal cohesion, with the object of religion, god, representing society.

One of the other significant and related themes shared by the non-theological approaches is that of the nature of religion as an institution. If human beings either for individual or societal reasons create religion, then it can and must be examined as part of its cultural context. This is clear on the societal level; it is also true on the individual level. Individuals do not exist outside of their communities. Our thoughts and ideas and ways of understanding the world are constructed in relation to the community in which we live and must be analysed in that context. Thus, even if religion arises from individual needs, these needs are shaped in relation to a specific community or culture. If religion is part of culture, there is no reason to separate it from other cultural constructs. This suggests that far from being something essential and qualitatively distinct, religion should be analysed using theoretical approaches that are relevant to other areas of society.

If religion is not qualitatively distinct we might also be correct in asking whether the concept of religion is a social construct, which relates to the way our society divides itself up, but may not reflect the way that other societies structure themselves. Although this question is not directly addressed in the analysis of the thinkers in this part, some of their discussions allow us to move in this direction. This permits examination of elements that are from our perspective part of religion, that are outside the confines of the religious rubric, and in the context of their role and relation to other aspects of culture.

CHAPTER 1

Karl Marx and Cultural Materialism

Marxist thought, which has its roots in the writings of Karl Marx (1818–83) and Frederick Engels (1820–95), has been highly influential both on the political and theoretical levels in the understanding of society and the role of religion within society. Although the statement that religion 'is the opium of the people' is well known, perhaps the most quoted statement from Marx's writings, the emphasis on the negative interpretation of religion does an injustice to the subtlety of Marx's wider discussion of the subject.

Before we examine the Marxist approach to religion it is necessary to touch on some aspects of the wider understanding of society. A fundamental aspect of Marxist analysis is that it gives priority to the material aspect of human experience over the ideal. Although Marx does focus on the material components of experience, his theory does not create an antithesis between mind and body. Rather, Marx sees the mind as part of the body and therefore part of the material. This element is closely related to Marx's emphasis on the need to see both aspects together in the concept of praxis, the nexus of thought or theory acting in the material world.

At a more simplistic level, Marx can be understood as emphasising the economic component of social experience as the formative element. The relationship between the economic level and other societal institutions, for example, art, religion, science and law, is encapsulated in the model of structure and superstructure. Economics is the underlying structure. It alone of all societal institutions is not derivative. All other elements are superstructure; they are derived and shaped by the underlying economic structure. Thus religion cannot be seen as something essential and separate from economics but rather is derived from and related to its specific economic structural context.

Although when depicted in this way society may be seen as static, Marxism incorporates an essential aspect of dynamism. Marx takes up the dialectical aspect of Hegelian thought, thesis, antithesis and synthesis, and moves them from the ideal to the material sphere. In Hegel it was ideas or the ideal that developed in a dialectical process, in Marx it is the economic relations within society.

Marx's model suggests that a motor for change is built into any economic system. This motor is at times presented as the conflict between classes. As an economic system develops the contradictions associated with the exploitation of one class by another become more and more powerful until they lead to the dissolution of one economic form and its transformation into another. This process continues until the basic contradiction of exploitation is removed. Superstructure plays a secondary role in this process. Its main role is to validate the particular economic system, but as will be seen respecting religion it can also serve as an expression of exploitation or alienation, and be part of the dissolution rather than the support of the system.

One of the recurrent themes in Marx's thought and one that is directly related to religion, is that of consciousness. Marx continually emphasises that humanity is a knowing species. A key aspect, as suggested above, of this knowing is that it is not merely knowing, but knowing in relation to the material world and acting upon the material world. Consciousness is not being inward or absolutely reflexive; it is awareness of 'men in their actual life process'. For Marx being conscious and productive are essentially identical.

For a full understanding of consciousness, Marx contends that it is necessary to distinguish between true and false consciousness. Although labour or production is part of true consciousness, the degree to which the worker is alienated from his production and to the degree that there is exploitation, false consciousness emerges. In regard to society and labour as a whole the worker, in order to gain true consciousness must take control over his labour. False consciousness accepts the nature of the world uncritically; it thus supports or validates the system of exploitation. Religion, as is true of other forms of ideology, can in certain contexts be a vehicle for false consciousness.

Many of the themes mentioned thus far are encapsulated in Marx's discussion of religion in the 'Critique of Hegel's Philosophy of Right':

> *Religious* suffering is at one and the same time the expression of real suffering and a *protest* against real suffering. Religion is the sigh of the oppressed creature, the heart of a heartless world, and the soul of a soulless situation. It is the *opium* of the people. (2002 [1844]: 171)

This quotation indicates a duality in Marx's thought respecting religion.

It is both an expression of alienation and, at least in part, a means of perpetuating alienation, and thus false consciousness. It also suggests that religion is a form of protest. It protests against the interrelated phenomena of alienation and exploitation. To the degree that it is a form of protest, it can be seen as having positive aspects. Religion at this level can also be seen as indicative. It reflects the existence and the degree of alienation found within a particular economic structure. In spite of this positive aspect, Marx does not see religion as necessary within society, or as an essential part of human nature. Religion as a reflection of alienation is only needed when alienation exists. As alienation is a feature of the exploitation of one class by another (e.g. the workers or proletariat by the capitalists) when this exploitation ends the need for religion will also end.

The above quotation, particularly in the statement 'it is the opium of the people' and the discussion that follows it develop the other side of Marx's evaluation of religion. This aspect is hinted at in the statement that it is the 'heart of a heartless world', which suggests that although religion is a means of expressing distress, it is essentially illusory. Marx suggests that religion rather than leading to real happiness creates 'illusory happiness'. He argues that we need to give up these illusions in order to move towards real happiness. Thus we need to critique religion as it prevents us from seeing where our real happiness lies. This change involves praxis, though expressed in action, as the removal or critique of religion necessitates a change in economic structure.

Religion as an illusion plays a dual role in false consciousness. On the one hand, as suggested by the above discussion, religion creates an illusory form of happiness and thus makes those who accept it equally willing to accept the conditions of the world as they are. It can also play a more ideological role in creating false consciousness. Religion is part of superstructure, reflecting the economic structure of society. As such, it plays a role in validating and justifying that economic structure. This role is further enhanced because religion in an ideological sense is controlled by the ruling class and used by that class to sedate the ruled majority.

Although Marx's theory provides a useful critical tool for understanding the role of religion within society, there are several problematic areas that need to be addressed. Three significant areas upon which the theory has been challenged are its use of a unilinear model of cultural evolution, determinism and materialist reductionism.

Both Marx and Engels accepted the basic presupposition that society evolves along a single path, progressing towards a singular end. To a great extent they accept the evolutionary models developed by Edward Burnett Tylor and Lewis Henry Morgan. One of the features of many evolutionist theories was the view that cultural level was related to the level of tech-nology; this aspect fit well into the emphasis on the economic and the material as the driving forces of society. Although many examples might be cited, one of the clearest uses of this model is found in Engels' discussion of the origin of the family. He states, for example:

> We have, then, three chief forms of marriage, which, by and large, conform to the three main stages of human development. For savagery – group marriage; for barbarism – pairing marriage; for civilisation – monogamy, supplemented by adultery and prostitution. (Engels, 1972 [1884]: 744)

The sequence used by Engels, savagery, barbarism and civilisation come directly from Tylor. The only essential difference between Marx and Engels on the one hand, and the evolutionists on the other, is that Marx and Engels looked forward to a future stage of evolution beyond civilisation.

Marx and Engels' use of an evolutionary paradigm is also implied in their discussion of religion. In *The German Ideology* (1972 [1846]) they introduce the concept of 'natural religion' as an early form of consciousness. It arises due to a sense of duality between man and nature, with nature appearing 'alien' and 'all-powerful'. Although this is the common basis of religion, it goes through a process of development and evolution. Since people's relationship with nature is determined by the economic structure of society, the form of society also shapes religion. It should be noted that this dis-cussion also includes the aspect of false consciousness. The duality, which is inherent to the beginning of religion, is a false duality, for Marx and Engels man and nature are one.

Evolutionary theories, particularly the unilinear evolutionary theories developed in the nineteenth century have been challenged on a number of different levels. Most significantly the ethnographic evidence does not support them. The theorists who developed these models had little or no direct knowledge of the cultures that they categorised; they relied on rather dubious data, often collected by missionaries and colonial administrators, and took this data out of context to construct their models.

Empirical data developed by anthropologists suggest that there is no single path of cultural development – each society develops along a unique path. Equally important, there is no one selection of technology or other artefacts associated with particular forms of society, this is primarily because societies do not invent their entire cultural repertoire; much of it comes to them through diffusion. Their acceptance of these artefacts is also as much a question of choice as availability.

Both the unilinear model and the data that supported it can also be challenged as a form of ideology. As we have suggested, much of this data was collected by missionaries or colonial administrators. In both cases these individuals came out of an imperialist system that viewed its cultural forms and beliefs to be superior to those that they were describing. Thus an implicit or explicit qualitative distinction was built into their descriptions. The theory itself, which arose in expansive colonial empires, also served as an ideological justification for the actions which were performed by the missionaries and administrators – justifying their right to convert and rule over peoples who were seen to be at earlier stages of development.

The unilinear evolutionary model, which underlies Marx's analysis, also introduces an often implicit and occasionally explicit sense of determinism into Marx's concept of history and historical development. The cultural evolution model is highly deterministic; with each culture moving progressively through the same historical stages. The dialectical aspect of Marx's theory also seems to have an inbuilt deterministic motor. Marx's theory does, however, through his concept of revolutionary transformation and praxis add a degree, albeit relatively weak, of human agency.

Although unilinear evolution underlies much of Marx's discussion, Marxist analysis does not require it for its explanatory power. The Marxist critique of society and the role of religion within society can still be applied outside unilinear evolutionary system. The relationship of economics to other aspects of society and the role of class struggle as a motor for change are still relevant to the understanding of both society and religion. If a developmental aspect is needed, and Marxism does suggest change and development within society, then it can equally be found in multilinear evolutionary models; the development of materialist multilinear evolution forms part of the discussion in the next section of this chapter.

One of the consistent critiques of Marxist analysis is that it is reductionist. It is accused of reducing all social phenomena to the material or economic level of structure. Although, as we have suggested, Marxism does consider the economic level to be structure with all other aspects and societal institutions being superstructure and therefore derivative, Marx's materialism is not simplistic. Marx emphasises that mind must be understood in interrelation with body, that it too is part of the material. Marx also emphasises the role of consciousness, albeit consciousness in relation to praxis in the transformation of societal structures. Although economic and material structure are clearly significant factors in shaping human institutions; and, exploitation and alienation are motivating factors in societal transformation, it seems likely, particularly given the wide variation in social forms, that the interrelationships between the different aspects of society are more complex than can be explained in either a simple or even a more complex materialist model. This aspect is developed in the work of

Weber (discussed below). Weber attempts to analyse a more complex set of interrelations between the material and the ideal.

Marxist analysis of religion has been challenged from one additional perspective; it is seen as over-emphasising the negative aspects of religion and ignoring its potentially revolutionary aspects. This approach sees Marx viewing religion purely as an ideological tool by which the ruling class prevents the working class from either realising that they are being exploited or from acting against the structures that enable that exploitation. Although it is agreed that many established or mainstream religious structures act in the negative way suggested by this reading of Marx, various counter-examples are cited demonstrating that religion can be a form of protest. The rise of Islamism is a particularly useful example for this type of argument. Islamism, except in rare cases, is not the established form of religion in the states in which it is found. It is often associated with challenges to totalitarian authority structures. It can also be said that the rise of activist Islamism is also a response to neo-colonialism and Western imperialism or globalisation. Thus it seems to be a protest movement challenging rather than validating economic relations. Catholic Liberation Theology, particularly in South and Central America, has also been presented as providing a voice for the poor in totalitarian dictatorships supported by the United States. Adherents of Liberation Theology in these states have fostered, in contradistinction to the usual practice of the Catholic Church, left wing challenges to right wing policies and governments. Thus, like radical Islamism it can be seen as challenging economic relations rather than supporting them.

These movements can be seen, in part, as a cry of distress against alienation and exploitation. As such, they are good examples of Marx's first analysis of religion, that it is a reflection and expression of alienation. In spite of this positive spin, it is also possible to see how both examples feed into false consciousness. The answers given by the two religious protest movements would be seen by Marxists to be a form of delusion. Although they are responding to and reflecting actual distress, their answer will not ultimately resolve the problem, which is fundamentally economic. Although radical Islamism has aspects of revolutionary praxis, neither it nor Liberation Theology is fundamentally revolutionary; they might tinker with aspects of economic structure but they do not seek to overthrow the capitalist system. Thus, ultimately they are a form of false consciousness, which uphold capitalism rather than being revolutionary movements that could topple it.

– CULTURAL MATERIALISM –

Marxist and materialist analysis have been highly influential in many analyses of the role of religion in society that have been developed during the twentieth century. One of the most significant of these developments, the feminist critique of religion, is discussed in detail below. This critique focuses specifically on the role that religion plays in validating and expressing the exploitation of women by men. A more direct line of influence is found in the anthropological tradition of cultural materialism. This tradition, most significantly represented by Marvin Harris, emphasises the deterministic materialist features found in some aspects of the Marxist paradigm.

Professor Harris' work is the culmination of a chain of anthropological theorists who took up both the materialist emphasis and also attempted to develop multilinear models of cultural evolution. As suggested above, both materialist reductionism and evolutionary models share a degree of determinism. The multilinear models attempt to include this deterministic element while introducing the possibility of several alternative lines of evolutionary development.

Leslie White's book *The Evolution of Culture* (1959) is an instructive example of how these theorists tend to approach the subject of religion. White distinguishes between technological, sociological and ideological aspects of culture. The first two areas relate essentially to the materialist aspects of culture and the third to the ideal. His discussion of this third area is found in a thirteen-page section of a volume that comprises three hundred and seventy pages of text.

White presents a theory of ideas that is directly related to the material component of our existence. Beliefs emerge from experience of the sensory world. These experiences may be internal, sensory experiences of bodily states, for example tiredness, or sensory experiences of the external world. He organises a particular system of beliefs under the heading of philosophy – the term religion is not found in the index of the volume.

White distinguishes between two types of philosophy: naturalistic and supernaturalistic. The difference between the two is the belief in the second that there are supernatural beings who direct the course of the world which we experience. It is presented as a projection of the self onto the external world. He suggests that this projection is due to a 'failure to distinguish between the self and the not-self' (White, 1959: 262). Thus religion, or supernaturalistic philosophy, is ultimately based on illusion or error; nonetheless, both the naturalistic and the supernaturalistic refer to the same set of human experiences and are thus rooted in the material.

White develops some aspects of functionalist theories of religion, that is philosophy (religion) serves specific functions in society. It provides a way of acting upon the world – philosophy in the naturalistic sense acts upon it through science, and in the supernaturalistic sense through ritual and magic. It also provides a means of resolving fundamental questions of existence. Philosophy also serves a social function, specifically related to integration into society and acceptance of its norms and values.

White also discusses the relationship between philosophy (religion) and technology. His discussion mirrors that of Marx; it suggests that since philosophy emerges from experience, and experience is shaped by technology, the specific technological level of the society ultimately determines philosophy. White states:

> As the culture, so the experience; as the experience so the philosophy. And since every cultural system rests upon a technological basis, as of course it must since it is here and with these means that man and culture are articulated with earth and cosmos, both experience and the philosophy that reflects it will depend upon the technological component of the culture. (1959: 273)

As technology changes, so culture evolves and the religion or philosophy that arises from that technology will reflect those changes. White challenges Ruth Benedict's argument that religion is separate from technology; that any form of religion can emerge from any form of society. He argues that the gods created by a society that feels superior to animals will be very different from one that does not. He closes his argument by arguing for the coherence of society; culture, technology and philosophy all work together.

Marvin Harris further develops the interrelationship between the material or technological and the ideal or religious components of culture. He presents two indicative examples of his method in a popular book: *Cows, Pigs, Wars and Witches* (1975). This book examines a wide range of enigmatic cultural phenomena, explaining them from a cultural materialist perspective.

The first substantive chapter of the book examines the role of the cow in Hindu society; asking what is the materialist reason for the veneration of the cow? Harris introduces his argument with empirical data that seems to argue against any practical (read materialist) reason for the cow to be venerated. He cites scholars who have suggested that cow veneration, far from serving an economic purpose, has impoverished India.

Harris argues that in spite of appearances, the cow serves an essential economic function in Indian society. He points out that rather than an excess of cows in India there are too few; this shortage is specifically found regarding oxen needed for ploughing. Thus at one basic level cows are essential because they produce oxen for ploughing in a society that cannot afford to provide mechanical means for ploughing. Cows also serve two additional and perhaps even more significant economic purposes; they provide milk and most importantly they provide dung, which is a necessary fertiliser for successful agriculture. He concludes this part of the argument by observing that cows used in beef production produce fewer calories than needed for that production, thus if that plant food is eaten by humans rather than beef cows it will provide a greater amount of food value than would the beef. The religious rule prohibiting the eating of cows therefore reflects the essential economic needs of a subsistence society with a huge population in which the cow was more efficiently used as a tractor and petrochemical plant on hooves than it would have been if eaten as beef.

Harris presents a similar argument to explain the prohibition in Judaism and Islam against the eating of pork. Given, he argues, that the pig is an excellent transformer of tubers to high-grade protein and fat, why is it forbidden in certain societies? He first examines the traditional explanations for the prohibition, for example health, but concludes that none of these stands up to historical analysis. As in the case of the cow, he argues that there must be a materialist reason for the prohibition. Based on a somewhat problematic literalist reading of the bible, Harris develops an argument based on the presumed economic/technological structure of proto-Israelite culture, that is, they were pastoralists living in very arid country. He argues that given this environment and technology it would have been inefficient to raise pigs for food. Pigs were inefficient for pastoral nomads in two main respects. First, pigs require a large amount of water for their proper husbandry; water in the arid land in which they lived was a scarce resource, which was needed by humans, and thus not efficiently available for pigs. Second, pigs were not able to survive on the types of grass that could sustain cows and goats. They required tubers and other foodstuff that given the scarcity of resources were also needed by people for food. Thus pigs were in direct competition for food and water and did not provide an efficient source of food to justify this competition.

Harris also points out that in most pastoral societies the animals are only rarely used for food; they provide other resources, for example, wool and milk. Using them for meat would not be an economically efficient use of their resources. The pig, however, does not serve as an efficient source of anything other than meat, and thus can only serve as a luxury food source in societies where resources are plentiful. Harris' arguments suggest that for essentially materialist or economic considerations the pig was deemed to be both inedible and unsacrificable, while the cow and other similar ruminants were considered to be both edible and sacrificable.

Although in his arguments Harris emphasises the materialist aspect of these traditions, he does allow for other considerations as well. Thus, he suggests that the aspect of boundary maintenance and identity can also play a part. This concession to other forms of explanation, however, forms only a relatively insignificant part of his discussion.

As suggested above this trend in materialist analysis is much less subtle than traditional Marxist analysis. It ignores the ideological aspects of Marxist analysis and the role that these particular symbolic constructs might play in systems of exploitation and control. The analysis is also limited in its narrow focus. Both the cow and the pig are taken out of context. There is little attempt to relate them to other aspects of either their own symbolic systems or the wider context of social institutions. Thus, in the case of the pig, Harris' argument ignores the fact that the pig is only one small part of a larger system of food rules, many of which cannot be explained in simple materialist terms. The food rules themselves need to be looked at in relation to concepts of purity and sacrifice, and on a wider level to an understanding of nature and the animal world as a whole.

Harris' arguments are also an example of the genetic fallacy. They confuse the supposed origin of a practice with the reason for its continued practice. Although it is possible that there were good materialist motivations for rejection of the pig as a source of food – though it is unlikely that the Israelites were ever pastoralists as described in Genesis – many of these motivations no longer exist and have not existed for most of Jewish history. Most Jews today live in communities where there is no materialist reason for rejecting the pig; there is plenty of food and water. Given that the food rules are still practised by many observant Jews the reason for the practice cannot be a simple materialist equation as suggested by Harris. In order to understand the practice today we need to move well beyond mere speculation about origins and look at the practices in the context of a wide range of sociological and symbolic factors.

CHAPTER 2

Emile Durkheim and Functionalism

The Elementary Forms of Religious Life (2001), first published in 1912, was a groundbreaking work, which presents an extended argument examining the relationship between religion and society. Although, as indicated in the conclusion of this chapter, there are problems with both the nature of Durkheim's analysis and the ethnographic material from which he built his arguments, his work has been influential throughout the twentieth century and arguably into the twenty-first century. Durkheim's work raises issues relevant to a wide range of theoretical perspectives on religion. His work has influenced or addressed issues of functionalism, materialism, idealism and structuralism, to name just a few.

The primary goal of *The Elementary Forms of Religious Life* is suggested by the title of the work. Durkheim (1859–1917) is seeking to establish the basic structures of religion, and argues that the best way to do this is through the analysis of the simplest form of religion found in the ethnographic literature. Like Freud, Durkheim sees totemism as the most elementary form of religion. The interest in totemism is emphasised by the original French subtitle of the volume, *Le système totémique en Australie*. This emphasis, however, belies the main argumentative thrust of the work. The *Elementary Forms* presents a sociology of religion, not merely an ethnographic study of totemism, in Australia. As Carol Cosman points out in her introduction to the English translation, the study of totemism is in effect a thought experiment for the study of a much broader range of more complex religious phenomena.

Although Durkheim's analysis has an underlying acceptance of evolutionary models of societal development, a fact suggested by his understanding of the relationship between totemism and other 'more complex' forms of religion, he does not on this basis see more complex forms as qualitatively better. He states: 'We turn to primitive religions, then, not with the ulterior motive of depreciating religion in general, for these religions are no less worthy than others. They answer the same needs, they play the same role, they issue from the same causes. They can effectively serve, as a result, to show the nature of religious life ...' (2001: 5). The equivalence of the different forms of religion, whether simple or complex, arises not from their specific content or beliefs but rather from the fact that they all arise from a common source, society, and fulfil a common range of functions in relation to society.

Durkheim also rejects the normative evolutionary assumption that earlier forms are less true than later forms. In fact, Durkheim was not interested specifically in the truth or falsity of particular religious doctrines. He argues that there are no false religions. All religions are a response to a specific societal form and thus all are true representations.

This does not mean, however, that he avoids the evolutionary pitfall of suggesting that there are ways of establishing a hierarchy of religions. Rather, he suggests that they might be ranked in terms of the quality of their structure or content. Nonetheless he strongly maintains that they are all still essentially part of a unitary phenomenon. The evolutionary argument, though problematic, does not devalue Durkheim's analysis, as it does not intrinsically depend on it. Whether or not all religions arise from totemism, if Durkheim is correct that religion arises in relation to society, in whatever type of society, then it is possible the common issues will be found whether we examine totemism or any other religious form.

Durkheim specifically addresses the nature of religion and religious truth in his discussion of two alternative theories of religious origin: animism and naturism. In both cases the theorists were also working within an evolutionary paradigm, and viewed the origin of religion as being rooted in a misunderstanding of reality. Durkheim contends that the misunderstandings, which animism and naturism suggest underlie the origin of religion, cannot explain the persistence of religion once they are no longer relevant (see particularly the conclusion of his arguments against animism, 2001: 62, and his arguments against naturism, 2001: 70).

The animist approach, specifically associated with E. B. Tylor, suggests that religion arises from a misunderstanding or confusion between dreams and reality, and the associated problem of death. It suggests that the soul is the primary constituent of religion, and that its existence was derived from the experience of dreams in which a spirit separable from the body seemed to exist. The soul is extended into a concept of existence after death, and then further extended into inanimate objects or processes, which are also understood to possess souls and thus be conscious agents.

The naturism approach, which Durkheim attributes to Max Müller, views religion as arising from the human response to or experience of nature. It arises from the feeling of awe experienced by people upon seeing a sunrise, and culminates in the deification of specific forces of nature. The error or misunderstanding, which underlies the naturism position, is the move from the abstract inanimate force to the particular and animate. This transformation occurred though the medium of language, that is, the transformation of figurative speech into personalised reality.

Durkheim's critique of animism and naturism raises several issues that are relevant to his own discussion of religion. In regard to animism, he challenges the logic of the extension from dreams to the concept of a separable soul and also argues that the theory rests on a view that people will spend mental energy on something that does not pose a real problem. He suggests that it is illogical to assume that 'primitive' people would spend a lot of time meditating on their dreams, rather than on the more pressing issues related to their existence, both social and individual. He also touches on an issue which he considers particularly decisive in relation to naturism – the distinction between sacred and profane – what makes a soul sacred after death such that it can become part of an ancestor cult?

The distinction between sacred and profane is the essential argument against naturism. As suggested below, this distinction is an essential feature of Durkheim's own definition of religion. He argues that even if it is accepted that people marvel at these natural occurrences, this does not logically or necessarily lead to religion. His argument rests on the essential duality of his own definition. When we experience nature, even if we find it immensely powerful, he argues that we do not perceive it as an idea of duality, rather we see it as essential, unified and one. Thus, there is no basis in the mere experience of nature for the origin or concept of the sacred and thus not basis for the origin of religion.

This discussion leads to one of the key elements of Durkheim's definition of religion, that is, the distinction between the sacred and the profane. As seen in his discussion of naturism this duality is fundamental to Durkheim's understanding of religion: it is equally fundamental to his conception of society, which also depends on the ability to conceive of the world in fundamentally distinct categories. This interrelationship between religion and society underlies all of Durkheim's analysis. While religion, as argued below, emerges as a reflection of society, it is also a key building block in the development of society.

Durkheim suggests that all religious beliefs share the duality of the sacred and the profane. Sacred things are those that are in some sense set apart and protected. As suggested by his analysis of totemism, in which the totemic object represents the group, Durkheim argues that the sacred is also a representation of the group. The sacred is not limited to any specific object;

in fact anything, whether it be an object, a gesture or a word, can be perceived as sacred. He suggests that although it is possible to move from the profane realm to the sacred, this can only be done through an elaborate process. The one necessary element in establishing the distinction between the two realms must be that it arises from society and not the individual. This last point is necessitated by the fact that as a transcendent representation of the group it must arise from the group.

The emphasis on the social that is seen in the discussion of the sacred is a feature of both Durkheim's methodology and his understanding of religion. Durkheim argues that the sociological study of religion or indeed any aspect of society should be concerned with the analysis of social facts rather than factors specifically relating to the individual. Social facts arise from society rather than the individual and at least in part control the individual's ways of thinking and acting. Durkheim's concept underlies a persistent theme in sociology and anthropology, which sees much of our behaviour and ways of thinking as being socially constructed.

The connection between religion and the social is also a fundamental aspect of Durkheim's understanding of religion. This emphasis is particularly illustrated in his distinction between religion and magic. He suggests that the nature of religious beliefs as social facts is that a specific group holds them – and more than being individually believed, they are something that defines the group and expresses the group's unity. In essence, this group or church, hold and are held by common views of the nature of the sacred, which as suggested above arises from the group's representation of itself. Magic, while sharing many elements with religion, for example, rites and beliefs, and growing out of religion, is specifically oriented to the individual rather than the group. While it may be practiced by large numbers of individuals within a particular society, it remains individual and never brings a group together. As Durkheim suggests, 'a magician has a clientele, not a church, and his clients may well be entirely unrelated and even unaware of each other; even their relations with him are generally accidental and transitory, like those of a patient with his doctor' (2001: 43). Unlike religion, which relates to a moral community, he argues that magic never creates a moral community.

Bringing these elements together, Durkheim suggests the following definition of religion: 'A religion is a unified system of beliefs and practices relative to sacred things, that is to say, things set apart and surrounded by prohibitions – beliefs and practices that unite its adherents in a single moral community called a church' (2001: 46). This definition brings together the primary elements of the sacred/profane dichotomy and society. The conclusion of the paragraph, which includes this definition, is highly indicative of Durkheim's emphasis and relates as much to the distinction between sacred and profane as to the concept of church; it states that religion, as a church, is 'eminently collective'.

Durkheim's emphasis on the distinction between the sacred and profane, and on the collective as the essential aspect of religion should be seen as interrelated. As suggested above, the sacred/profane duality must be understood in relation to group identity. If the sacred, as seen in totemism, is a representation of the group as well as the divine, then propitiation of the sacred is nothing more than propitiation of the group. The profane, in opposition to the sacred, becomes a marker for those who are not members of the group.

Using the analogy of totemism, Durkheim makes a very strong association between the personified aspect of the sacred, god, and society. His understanding of totemism was derived from the early ethnographic work of Spencer and Gillin in Australia. It was understood to be a form of social organisation in which large groupings, called clans, had a name, which was taken from a plant or animal, that is, the totem. The totem represented the group, being their identifying marker, and was also sacred, representing the divine. The totem, as a sacred object, was hedged with prohibitions; members of that particular clan were usually forbidden to eat their totemic object.

He suggests that in totemism the totemic object is a material form of the divine and at the same time the symbol of a specific group. He then asks: 'if the totem is both the symbol of god and of society, are not these one and the same' (2001: 154)? He concludes that all three, the society, the sacred object, and the divine must all represent the same thing, that is, society itself. This analogy, he suggests, can be extended to all religions.

One of the significant aspects of religion is the area of religious practice, that is, ritual. Rituals are defined as those formalised practices that are associated with a sacred object. Ritual is particularly significant in Durkheim's analysis as it is the social forum within which religious beliefs, and the distinction between the sacred and the profane, are embodied and enacted. Ritual provides the public space where a group can reaffirm the tenets of religion, and thus revalidate the unity of their particular church.

Ritual, however, in its creation of effervescence becomes a particularly strong vehicle for the affirmation of collective identity. Effervescence is an intermittent state created by the group experience. It is found in a wide range of group activities, for example, political rallies, provided that those activities are practices aimed at establishing some type of group identity. He suggests that effervescence arises from the very act of coming together as a group: 'their proximity generates a kind of electricity that quickly transports them to an extraordinary degree of exaltation' (Durkheim, 2001: 162). Effervescence causes individuals to lose their sense of individuality and to feel united with god and thus the group. Ritual practice serves the social function of validating and strengthening group cohesion.

In Durkheim's discussion of effervescence we see the elements of a myth of religious origins. He states: 'Therefore it is in these effervescent social settings, and from this very effervescence, that the religious idea seems to be born' (Durkheim, 2001: 164). Durkheim seems to be suggesting that effervescence spontaneously occurs when a number of individuals come together and, that out of that effervescence, a sense of the sacred and group identity emerge.

Durkheim's analysis of ritual and effervescence highlights another aspect of his sociological approach, which is social function. As indicated in the discussion above, ritual and indeed religion can be seen in part to have a specific social function, that is, of maintaining and strengthening social solidarity. This aspect of function is a key part of his sociological theory of society and is interrelated with his understanding of different forms of society.

Durkheim distinguishes between two forms of society, each of which is based on a different form of solidarity. The form found in 'simple societies' is called 'mechanical solidarity' and that which is found in complex societies is identified as 'organic solidarity'. Mechanical solidarity is found in societies that have no division of labour and equal access to material resources. It can be characterised as societies in which solidarity is based on similarity. Individuals share a sense of group because their life experiences are essentially the same. Durkheim suggests that punitive sanctions are used in this form of society to maintain collective values.

Organic solidarity characterises societies that have complex social structures and a high degree of division of labour. In these societies individuals will have varied access to societal goods and varied life experiences. Thus, solidarity is no longer based on similarity; rather it is based on interdependence. The different elements of society must work together because cooperation is needed if the society is to continue. The organic metaphor is used to illustrate that such a society is like a living organism that needs all of its organs to function together in order for it to survive.

In his understanding of the relation of religion to society, Durkheim sees an indirect relation between religion and complexity. As society becomes more complex, as it breaks down into an increasing number of units, the smaller role religion will play. In societies based on mechanical solidarity, where there is little or no internal distinction between different groups, religion will be strongest as religion and society are in effect the same. As societies become more complex, functions will be taken up and carried out by different organs, for example, by law or economics, and religion will become less pervasive.

Durkheim's theories raise several issues that need to be addressed. While problematic, several issues do not directly challenge his findings. Thus, although the evolutionary model, which underlies his discussion of religion, has been shown by subsequent anthropological research to be deeply flawed and based on an ethnocentric understanding of society, it is not intrinsic to his arguments. His distinction between forms of solidarity or 'elementary forms' of religion can be taken out of their evolutionary context and seen as descriptive rather than developmental. This rereading of his text is made possible by his suggestion that religion plays the same function in whatever form of society it is found.

Similarly his analysis has been attacked for relying on ethnographic material that was already being challenged in his own time. Many of his specific uses of Australian totemism, for example, no longer fit the ethnographic data. In spite of this, his discussion of the nature of religion does not absolutely depend on the specific data he employed – he was using the data in effect as a thought experiment, and thus is perhaps more challengeable on that basis rather than on the basis of poor ethnographic material.

There are, however, some more substantial issues that arise in relation to his theories. The first of these, and perhaps most fundamental, is found in his strong distinction between the sacred and the profane. As suggested above, he argues that this is present in all religions and that the two spheres are distinct, with movement between them necessitating elaborate rituals. This strong distinction is not supported in the ethnography. While some societies do make a clear and unbridgeable distinction of this kind, other societies do not necessarily distinguish between the two categories. And, even where such a distinction is made, movement between the categories may be relatively easy.

Brian Morris, in *Anthropological Studies of Religion* (1987), challenges Durkheim's argument that in societies based on mechanical solidarity, religion and society are one and the same. In societies with this form of solidarity no distinction is made between any social institution or function, thus while society and religion are one, so too is it one with the other social institutions. Thus, one could argue that society was originally entirely economic or political, on the same basis as he is arguing that it is religious.

Evans-Pritchard, in *Theories of Primitive Religion* (1965), highlights the problems found in theories that claim to explain the origin of religion. He argues that all of these theories are essentially conjectural and thus cannot or should not be seen as scientific demonstrations. He challenges, for example, the assumption, which is taken up by Radcliffe-Brown (see below), that religious entities conform to social structure, and are in effect no more than society, suggesting that the reasoning behind this is no more than plausible, and often in contradiction to the ethnographic evidence.

Although Durkheim's emphasis on society and the social construction of the individual is a very important building block in the understanding of religion and society, it does, perhaps to too great an extent, devalue the importance of the individual as a mediator for social facts. Shared conceptions are thus not because they exist in some collective consciousness outside of the individual but because they are instantiated in each individual through that individual's use of them.

Religion is clearly in part a social phenomenon, but it is also an individual experience and functions on levels that are not directly related to the group. Some of these levels may indeed be anti-structural or anti-hierarchical, and thus challenge rather than support social structure. Many scholars have highlighted the fact that this individual aspect undermined the distinction between religion and magic. The distinction is further challenged by many ethnographic observations, which emphasise that magic is often a means of defining self in opposition to other or a means of redressing issues within a group and thus at some levels is indistinguishable from Durkheim's concept of religion.

Despite these and other criticisms, Durkheim's theories have been highly influential in both the anthropological and sociological study of religion and culture. The immediate influence of his work was the concept of function. This concept became a dominant characteristic of theories of religion and culture. His work also contains the roots of both structural-functionalism and French structuralism – this is specifically seen in his ideas about categorisation and his myth of societal development, which share many features with that of Lévi-Strauss (see the chapter on anthropological theories). The emphasis on religion as a social fact, and the role of society in shaping our experiences and understanding of reality is a significant feature of the work of Berger and Luckmann (discussed in the chapter on sociological approaches). Most of all, Durkheim moves the discussion away from issues of truth and allows us to explore in a non-judgemental way how and why religion works within different social settings.

– THE FUNCTIONALISTS –

Functionalism was one of the most significant approaches to religion and culture that arose from Durkheim's work. In anthropology, functionalism is most specifically associated with the work of Bronislaw Malinowski

(1884–1942) and A. R. Radcliffe-Brown (1881–1955). Both of these anthropologists took up the organic metaphor found in Durkheim's concept of organic solidarity and developed it in related, though divergent, directions. Functionalism has also continued to be of great influence in sociology. It was particularly associated with the work of Talcott Parsons (1902–1981), viewing society as an almost self-sustaining ecosystem with different elements functioning to maintain the whole. More recently Bryan Wilson has continued to explore the social and psychological functions of religious institutions.

Bronislaw Malinowski, one of the pioneers in long-term participant observation, focused on the functions of societal institutions in relation to the individual. Although he used an organic model, its functions were understood to fulfil individual biological and social needs – which ultimately could fulfil societal needs as well as the individual needs, which were their primary function.

He argued that individual needs could be divided into three main areas: basic needs, instrumental needs and integrative needs. Basic needs, of which there are seven, were those associated directly with our biological nature. They include our need for food and the need to procreate. Instrumental needs were those that were necessary for the individual to fit into society and for society to work to fulfil individual's basic needs. These needs included a legal system and some process for education or enculturation. The integrative needs were those needed to provide a conceptual integrated framework within which the other needs could be met; these included a sense of security, both physical and psychological. Malinowski suggests that religion primarily arises from our biological needs, but also plays a role in the other individual and social arenas.

One of the significant features of both Malinowski's and Radcliffe-Brown's concepts of function was that all aspects of society served at least one specific function. This is encapsulated in the term 'universal functions'. This concept specifically challenged previous theories, which saw some features as survivals with little or no functional value. A second significant, and interrelated, element was the functional unity of society. This principle argued that all aspects of a society and its respective functions were interrelated. Sociological functionalists, particularly Robert Merton, have challenged both of these elements; they suggest that the level of inter-relatedness is not as complete or significant as suggested by Malinowski or Radcliffe-Brown. Merton also argued that not every cultural item necessarily has a specific or useful function.

As suggested above, Malinowski argues that religion primarily arises in response to specific biological needs. He argues that religion is not essentially about speculation or reflection. Like Durkheim, he also rejects the idea that religion arises from error or misunderstanding. Rather, he suggest that it arises from the pain and trauma of human existence, 'the tragedies of human life'. Although his argument suggests that religion in part arises from the anxieties and issues that arise from man's acting in society, Malinowski places the root of religion at a more basic and fundamental human experience, 'the fact of death'. It is not merely the existential trauma of death, but the fact that death undermines and challenges all plans and intentions. Religion is the response to this fundamental fact, and its essential characteristic is its denial of the finality of death.

Malinowski suggests that through its resolution of the problem of death, religion serves an essential individual and social function. For the individual it becomes a means of resolving the existential problem of one's own death. This is done both through belief systems, learned through enculturation, which enable the individual to 'confirm their hope that there is a hereafter' and through repeated rituals that connect the belief in immortality with those who have gone before. The resolution also serves an essential social function through which the bereaved, who due to their extreme emotions may present a danger to themselves or society, are brought back under social control.

He argues further that all other aspects of religion also serve diverse functions in relation to other needs of both the individual and society. He highlights the fact that most religious practices are associated with points of crisis, for example, birth, puberty, marriage and death, and thus serve to resolve the issues created by these crises. The significant point in his argument linking these factors is that each crisis creates strong emotion, which is potentially dangerous to the individual and society. The function of religion therefore is to positively channel these emotions and thus relieve the dangers posed. Religion should thus be seen as a means of social control, controlling individual emotional response and maintaining social order and cohesion.

Like Durkheim, Malinowski distinguishes between religion, magic and science. He suggests that all three modes of thought are present in all societies. Science, he suggests, relates to the empirical knowledge that is necessary for survival. All societies must possess a high degree of empirical knowledge in order to properly function within their environment. This knowledge arises from forms of trial and error, which are in effect the same as our model of scientific experimentation. Magic, while including many elements that make it similar to religion, has a narrower purview. It is a practical way of thinking that comes into play in those areas that we are not able to fully control. Magic is a means through which we can attempt to control the accidental. Magic is not science or misunderstood empirical knowledge; it is the recognition of the limits of such knowledge and the attempt to control things that are beyond the limits of that knowledge. Where magic and science work on the practical sphere, the ranges of functions associated with religion work on the integrative sphere and are not specifically concerned with practical ends.

Radcliffe-Brown brought together both the functionalist and structuralist aspects of Durkheim's approach in structural-functionalism. Unlike Malinowski, who emphasised the individual and individual needs, Radcliffe-Brown emphasised society and social structure. Of the functionalists, Radcliffe-Brown most strongly stressed the organic metaphor for the understanding of social processes. His approach emphasised the need to understand the interrelationship between three related elements: the structure of society; the social processes, which acted within that structure; and most importantly the social function of those processes. He contended that the main role of the latter, the social function, was to maintain the unity and continuity of the system as a whole.

Unlike Durkheim, Radcliffe-Brown does not attempt to discover the origins of religion. In line with his general organic metaphor, he sees religion as a social institution with the function of maintaining social order. And through doing so, it reflects that order and is thus an expression of society.

One of the main differences between Radcliffe-Brown and Malinowski is found in their understanding of the role of religion, and particularly ritual in relation to anxiety. Malinowski argued that religion arises to a great extent in response to anxiety. Thus rituals are performed due to and reflect the actual anxieties of their performers. This emphasises the focus on the individual characteristic of Malinowski's approach. Radcliffe-Brown, however, saw ritual as a means of attributing feeling or value rather than expressing feeling or value that was already present. This argument is much closer to Durkheim's concept of social fact. Feeling does not arise in the individual, it arises in the group and is created by or expressed in the ritual.

Radcliffe-Brown also takes up a second aspect of Durkheim's thought, the models of categorisation, and begins to develop along lines that would culminate in the structuralist analyses of Lévi-Strauss, Leach and Douglas (see the chapter on anthropological theories below). For a more detailed discussion of this issue see Morris, 1987: 125. In his discussion of myth and legends in *The Andaman Islanders* (1964) Radcliffe-Brown begins to outline a triadic system of categorisation, which underlies the different myths and legends. He states:

> This is, I think, what the legend really means. Thus the story of the flood gives a picture of a three-fold world, the waters below with their inhabitants the fishes and turtle and other marine creatures, the solid earth, and the upper region of the top of the forest where the flowers bloom and the butterflies and other insects pass their lives. (Radcliffe-Brown, 1964: 347)

His discussion presents a depiction of the world in which all elements are categorised and placed in a specific special location. The significant aspect of this analysis is that he is beginning to outline a general pattern or structure of thinking that is an organising feature of Andaman thought. This point is emphasised in a footnote in which he indicates that the same three-fold division is also found regarding spirits who are associated with one of the three spaces.

E. E. Evans-Pritchard takes up many aspects of the structural functionalist theoretical tradition developed by Radcliffe-Brown. Like Radcliffe-Brown he rejects the possibility of determining the origins of religion or particular religious practices, seeing such discussion as merely speculative. He also challenges the discussions of the truth of religion. He suggests that the anthropological study of religion, as suggested by Durkheim, should be concerned with social facts, which can be observed and analysed empirically, rather than questions of theology, which cannot. The role of anthropology is not to determine truth, it is to 'determine their meaning and social significance' (Evans-Pritchard, 1965: 17).

Evans-Pritchard emphasises that society must be analysed as a coherent system. No element, be it religion or any other, can be analysed on its own. Each element should be studied in relation to the other elements. Thus particular beliefs and religion as a whole should be studied in relation to other social institutions, for example, social structure, legal and economic systems. In part he is challenging any notion of reductionism. Society cannot be reduced to any one element, be it religion or economics, each element is both significant and interrelated.

Evans-Pritchard was also interested in the logic or patterns of thinking which underpinned these coherent social systems. He argued that although these patterns of thinking were different from those of western societies, their logic was as coherent and consistent. A fundamental aspect of his argument was that such systems of thought were not independent of their cultural context, but rather arose and were coherent with that specific cultural context.

This way of approaching culture and the role of religion within culture is exemplified in Evans-Pritchard's *Witchcraft, Oracles, and Magic Among the Azande* (1976). The analysis examines the belief and practice associated with witchcraft among the Azande of central Africa. He demonstrates that Azande beliefs form a coherent system in which the understanding of witchcraft forms the basis of an explanatory system and functions in relation to points of tension or crisis within Azande society.

Among the Azande, all events, particularly death or accidents, were attributable to witchcraft. However, far from being a replacement for empirical knowledge, witchcraft was used to explain the why, not the how, of events. This distinction is clearly seen in Evans-Pritchard's analysis of the collapse of a granary:

> In Zandeland sometimes an old granary collapses. There is nothing remarkable in this. Every Zande knows that termites eat the supports in the course of time and that even the hardest woods decay after years of service … People sit beneath it [the granary] in the heat of the day … Consequently it may happen that there are people sitting beneath the granary when it collapses and they are injured … That it should collapse is easily intelligible, but why should it have collapsed at the particular moment when these particular people were sitting beneath it … It was due to the action of witchcraft. (1976: 22)

As Evans-Pritchard suggests, the beliefs in witchcraft provide the link between the two sides of a coincidental event, and provide an explanation for why the event happened. His analysis makes it clear that there is no confusion over the empirical nature of the events; termites were the proximate cause of the granary falling. The proximate cause, however, is not a sufficient explanation; the Azande is interested in the primary cause, why the event happened.

This logic, however, needs to be understood in the broader context of Azande society and social institutions. Witchcraft is understood to be a process that occurs within the immediate community, often the immediate family. It is at least partially unconscious and is caused by an individual who possesses the potential, having socially inappropriate feelings. The process of determining who is the witch brings out the points of social tension, and through a ritual process allows them to be resolved. Witchcraft is also related to patterns of social hierarchy, as a witchcraft accusation could never be made against someone of higher social status. Evans-Pritchard's detailed analysis of the workings of this system among the Azande demonstrates his argument that the system is both coherent and logical in its own terms, and that in order to understand one area of society, that area must be examined in relation to other social facts.

Evans-Pritchard's analysis of Azande witchcraft has influenced the study of magic and witchcraft from a functionalist perspective. He demonstrates that accusations of witchcraft fit into a coherent system in Azande society and function to resolve points of social tension within the immediate community. The system of witchcraft and oracles also fits into a wider system for the administration of justice within Azande society. Both developments of this type of argument and challenges to it are examined below in the chapter examining anthropological approaches to elements of religion.

Talcott Parsons, a major figure in American sociology, developed aspects of both Durkheim's and Malinowski's application of functionalist theory. In 'The Theoretical Development of the Sociology of Religion' (1954), Parsons evaluates the contribution of Malinowski, Durkheim and Weber. He accepts Malinowski's argument that magic relates to the practical sphere and religion to that area of experience in which 'no practical goals can be pursued'. In his analysis of reactions to death, Parsons highlights the fact that it will have a greater emotional effect on those who experience it because of the impossibility of practical action. He also agrees that although magic and science are both within the practical realm, they are distinctive; that is, magic is not inadequate rationality and has different social function. He argues, however, that Durkheim went further than Malinowski, as the clear distinction between the sacred and the profane was essential in seeing the categorical distinction between science and magic.

In taking the argument further Parsons draws together elements that were found in the work of the earlier theorists. He suggests that the cognitive patterns associated with religion must be seen in relationship with other sociological facts and understood in relation to sentiment, particularly sentiment associated with significant events in life, that is, death and birth. Parsons framed the understanding of both in terms of continuity and solidarity of the society or social group as a whole. Although Parsons does suggest the need to look at society in abstraction from the individual, his thesis is closer to that of Malinowski's than Radcliffe-Brown's. He then shifts his discussion to Weber, particularly in relation to the variability seen in different religious systems. He suggests that in addition to emotional resolution there is also the need for cognitive resolution, a need for an explanation of why something, perhaps the death of a child, happened. Although this need for cognitive resolution is similar in all human societies, he suggests that Weber demonstrates that there are different logical ways through which this resolution can be found (this relates closely to the arguments made by Evans-Pritchard). These cognitive responses will be closely integrated with the socially constructed values in other social spheres.

In this discussion we find the essence of Parsons' understanding of the social function of religion. He suggests that events like death create frustration on two interrelated levels: the emotional (Malinowski) and the cognitive (Weber). Religion is a response and resolution of these two levels.

These aspects are succinctly developed in the following definition found in 'Religious Perspectives in Sociology and Social Psychology':

> A religion we will define as a set of beliefs, practices and institutions which men [sic] have evolved in various societies, so far as they can be understood, as responses to those aspects of their life and situation which are believed not in the empirical-instrumental sense to be rationally understandable and/or controllable, and to which they attach a significance which includes some kind of reference to the relevant actions and events to man's conception of the existence of a 'supernatural' order which is conceived and felt to have fundamental bearing on man's position in the universe and the values which give meaning to his fate as an individual and his relations to his fellows. (1979: 63)

His discussion also takes up in detail the nature of these frustrations, which relate directly to the problems of meaning both in respect of how and why. As suggested, the first category of frustration (in reverse order to his discussion) relates to the uncertainty. This is the case when, despite all human endeavour, uncertainty as to outcome remains. This category is identical to that suggested by Malinowski as the basis for magic. The second category of frustration relates to that which arises when we are hit by events that we cannot predict – in these cases we find the problem of meaning. Why did this happen? Although Malinowski touched on this aspect, he focused on the emotional issues. Parsons focuses instead on the issue of meaning itself that was addressed by Weber.

Parsons develops Malinowski's and Durkheim's arguments in an additional and perhaps more significant direction regarding the distinction between religion and magic. It is clear from Parsons' discussion that he considers the two areas to be essentially the same – in his discussion he applies the category of the sacred to both religion and magic, and thus underlines their distinction from science. This merging resolves some significant issues raised in relation to both Malinowski and Durkheim. The emphasis on Weber's 'problem of meaning' also becomes a significant feature of more recent discussions of religion, particularly those of Spiro and Geertz.

Robert Merton further developed the sociological analysis of functionalism. His analysis of functionalism, while challenging some of the presuppositions of earlier functionalists, develops the application of the model both in general and in relation to religion in several new directions. Merton challenges three of the main postulates of anthropological functionalism: the functional unity of society, universal function and the indispensability of institutions.

He suggests that the concept of functional unity, that all parts of a culture work together in an integrated way to maintain the whole, can only be supported in the 'pre-literate' societies studied by anthropologists. Merton suggests that, although some integration of function is necessary in a society, almost by definition, some societies are not integrated to the degree that all elements are functional for both the society and the individual.

He specifically focuses on the analysis of religion, challenging the view that religion necessarily has the integrative function ascribed to it by most functionalist analyses. He highlights the fact that in certain social systems religion is disintegrative and thus dysfunctional rather than functional. This type of disintegrative aspect is specifically found in societies that are composed of more than one religion. Although for the specific religious group it might have an integrative function, this function very rarely moves beyond that level. Thus, on a wider societal level, religion can divide rather than unify the group. He also highlights the possibility that religion can have a more active level of dysfunction, as for example, the Inquisition or religious wars.

As already suggested in the discussion of functional unity, Merton also challenges the concept that every activity or institution must have a function, must play some 'vital function' in society, that is, the principle of 'universal function'. He suggests that this principle arose as a response to the evolutionists, denying the possibility that there might be survivals from earlier stages of development. Merton argues that the concept of universal function is over-ambitious. He argues for a more limited approach: that cultural elements have 'a net balance of functional consequences' for maintaining society; some elements may have no function and others may indeed be dysfunctional.

Merton also takes up the issues of the assumption of the indispensability of institutions and the functions related to them. He suggests that under-lying this proposition is an essentially circular argument. The specific institutions are seen to be pre-requisites for the persistence of society and at the same time pre-requisites for the existence of society. Merton suggests that this proposition needs to be rethought, arguing that items can have multiple functions, and that multiple items or institutions can perform the same specific functions.

One additional point, which is highlighted in Merton's general discussion of function, is the distinction between latent and manifest function. This distinction relates to both the functional role or the item or institution, and the perception of that item or institution:

> The concept of latent function extends the observer's attention beyond the question of whether or not the behaviour attains its avowed purpose. Temporarily ignoring the explicit purposes, it directs attention *toward* another range of con-

sequences: those bearing, for example, upon the individual personalities of the Hopi involved in the ceremony and upon the persistence and continuity of the larger group. Were one to confine himself (sic) to the problem of whether the manifest (purposed) function occurs, it becomes a problem, not for the sociologist, but for the meteorologist. And to be sure, our meteorologists agree that the rain ceremonial does not produce rain; but this is hardly the point ... But with the concept of latent function, we continue our inquiry, examining the consequences of the ceremony not for the rain gods or for the meteorological phenomena, but for the groups which conduct the ceremony. And here it may be found, as many observers indicate, that the ceremony does indeed have functions – but functions which are non-purposed or latent. (Merton, 1964: 64)

Manifest function is the purpose that those who are using or performing an activity attribute to it. Thus, one manifest function of a ritual dance may be to bring rain. The latent function is that which is attributed to the activity by the observer. The observer may suggest that its function is to integrate a particular group, breaking down normal patterns of hierarchy. This distinction is particularly relevant to the study of religion, as there is often a clear difference between the function perceived by the performer and the ethnographer.

In relation to the functionalist analysis of religion, Merton makes a useful comparison between the approach taken by functionalists and Marxists. He suggests that the two perspectives share several key elements:

(1) Both approaches agree that specific religious systems have specific effects on sentiment and action. Although both approaches usually suggest that religion leads to a validation of norms and therefore passivity, some scholars, for example, Weber, have argued that religion can modify behaviour and lead to changes in social structure.
(2) Both approaches also see religion as a partially independent determinant of behaviour, though this aspect is less pronounced in Marxist analyses.
(3) Both approaches examine the role that religion has within the different classes or strata of society, recognising that it can validate or mobilise different strata to different forms of behaviour.
(4) The functionalist concept of reinforcing social integration and the Marxist concept of 'opium of the masses' are not analytically different; both are statements of the principle that religion reinforces and validates social structure.

Merton suggests that the essential difference between the approaches is not their analytical framework but rather the evaluation placed on the analysis. The functionalists focus specifically on the level of integration created, without examining the consequences of the integration. In their discussions integration is presented almost as a good in and of itself. The Marxists see religion as, by definition, creating negative integration, allowing the exploitation of one class by another. In effect both approaches are functionalist, the differences arise purely in relation to the evaluation not the analysis itself.

Although functionalist theories were an important development in the understanding of culture, and the role of religion in culture, there are some significant issues that need to be addressed. These problems include reductionism, lack of development or transformation, and circularity. Functionalism is sometimes seen to be a form of reductionism, focusing on one particular area or need. Thus, in the case of Malinowski, individual biological needs become the underlying foundation for all cultural constructs, with higher-level functions being seen as derivative from specific biological or basic needs. Although Parsons presents a more developed theory, he can still be accused of reducing religion to the resolution of a very narrow range of individual frustrations. On the societal level, Durkheim's reduction of religion to society, and all social facts to religion and society in mechanical solidarity, can be seen as an extreme form of reductionism. Similarly, Radcliffe-Brown can be understood to be focusing too narrowly on societal needs, particularly those of social control and maintenance of social structure, which become the sole or significant motivators for all cultural constructs.

Although the elements under discussion clearly do play a significant role in shaping cultural forms, just as the Marxist emphasis on economics is an essential feature, none of these elements is a sufficient explanation for all cultural beliefs, forms or practices. Many different factors come into play, and no one factor seems to be the structural basis upon which all other elements are developed.

One of the most significant challenges to functionalist theories is that they present a picture of culture that ignores historic development or transformation. The organic model suggests that like a body, culture will attempt to remain essentially static, emphasising continuity rather than change. The systems they present may have tensions, but rather than including transformative mechanisms, those that they describe resolve the tension and return the system to its normal steady state. Recent studies of these mechanisms suggest that they can serve a significant transformative function as well as resolving crisis to maintain the system. It is possible that this ahistorical model arises from two problems with previous approaches that attempted to incorporate history and change: the need to avoid the implications of cultural evolution and the problems associated with speculating about the origins of particular forms of culture or religion.

The final criticism relates to the structure of functionalist argumentation. Many functionalist analyses seem to present a circular form of argument. Function is both the explanation of the ritual and the cause of the ritual. Such a circular argument undermines both its explanation of function and more seriously its explanation of origins by its circularity – it does not advance the argument, it merely uses the object to explain itself.

In spite of these problems, functionalism and structural functionalism continue to influence discussions of religion. Although many theorists have moved away from using function either at the individual or societal level as the sole motivating factor for culture, function remains a significant factor in explaining the persistence rather than the origin of cultural and religious action. In some cases function is moved to the level of cognitive or psychslogical need, as suggested by Parsons, in others it is implicitly present as an underlying validating structure. In some recent sociological discussion, conscious function and perception of function become significant motivating factors in religious choices.

CHAPTER 3

Max Weber

Max Weber (1864–1920) was a contemporary of Durkheim who examined the nature of religion in complex societies. His analysis takes up some of the themes examined by the idealists and the materialists, the relationship between the material or economic and the ideal, but rather than reducing societal and cultural process to one sphere or the other, Weber develops a more subtle analysis examining the complex interactions between the two. Although Weber's most influential work examines the relationship between Protestantism and capitalism, Weber also extends his arguments into the area of comparative religion, examining, for example, Hinduism, Confucianism and ancient Judaism. Weber's analysis also examines the development of institutions within religion and particularly the role of charisma as a motive and potentially transformative force in religious systems.

Weber, like Marx and Durkheim, analysed religion as part of a wider network of societal institutions, which constituted society. His analysis focuses on the individual as part of society, and argues that the individual is shaped by the societal institutions, particularly religion, of which they are part. Weber, however, unlike Durkheim emphasised the need for sociology to be the study of individual agency; he argued that although individuals act in groups, groups themselves do not act.

Like Marx, Weber analysed the relationships between different groupings within society; rather than focusing on class, which had its roots in the inequalities of economic access and power, Weber focused on status groups, which had their roots in differentials in status rather than economics. In status groups the primary motivating factors are prestige and the feeling of social cohesion. In emphasising this aspect of social cohesion, and seeing religion as, in part, serving this purpose for a particular status group, there is a clear similarity to the theories of Durkheim and the functionalist schools.

The status groups do, however, share an essential commonality with

Marx's concept of class; different status groups have different access to prestige and privilege, and indirectly to economic opportunities, and thus are in conflict with each other to gain access to these differentials. Religion and religious ideas are relevant to Weber's analysis in as much as they lead to common action, which enables groups to gain access to prestige and economic power.

Although the social aspect, and the role of status groups, are significant aspects of Weber's analysis, as suggested above, he also laid a very strong emphasis on the individual. A basic aspect of his sociological method was the need to study human action in relation to the subjective beliefs of the actors. This aspect was also a significant part of his discussion of religion. He suggests that the continuation of beliefs and institutions has as a significant component the beliefs of the individual social actors in relation to those conventional beliefs and institutions. Unlike Durkheim, Weber suggests that culture is ultimately vested in the individuals rather than in some external collective construct.

Although Weber understood the role that religion had as a conservative force, maintaining and validating particular forms of stratification, he also saw religion as a motor for change in society. Protestantism, for example, was not merely the child of capitalism, but was one of a complex set of processes that enabled the very development of capitalism. The two phenomena, Protestantism and capitalism, are intertwined, but not in the simplistic way suggested by historical materialism. Thus, Weber's analysis brings together material and ideal considerations. Worldview, rather than being solely a response to either material conditions or ideas arises as an interaction of the two spheres.

Weber examines the dynamic interrelationship between Protestantism and capitalism in *The Protestant Ethic and the Spirit of Capitalism* (1958 [1904/5]). Rather than seeing one as necessarily secondary or derived, Weber examines the underlying ethos of each of these social phenomena, focusing on how they interrelate. Although capitalism is not a new phenomenon, indeed it has always existed, modern capitalism or rational capitalism is of recent origin. This type of capitalism is characterised by large capitalist enterprises with long-term rationally planned investment of capital, a complex division of free labour and a market economy. The ethos that underlay this economic structure was one which validated work as a good or a value in and of itself:

> And in truth this peculiar idea, so familiar to us to-day, but in reality so little a matter of course, of one's duty in a calling, is what is most characteristic of the social ethic of capitalist culture, and is in a sense the fundamental basis of it. It is an obligation which the individual is supposed to feel and does feel towards the

> content of his professional activity, no matter in what it consists, in particular no
> matter whether it appears on the surface as a utilisation of his personal powers, or
> only of his material possessions (as capital). (Weber, 1958: 54)

This economic ethos was in direct opposition to what Weber saw as the normal human tendencies, and thus, an explanation was needed as to how this new ethos originated and came to dominate society. Weber argues that far from merely reflecting the material order, that is, this ethos arising from the material structure, at least in some cases, for example, as in New England, the ethos pre-existed the rise of capitalism.

Weber suggests that, at least in part, the source of this ethos may lie not in the material constraints but rather in the ethos of Protestantism. In spite, however, of language, which at times suggests origins, Weber is not suggesting a simple relationship between the ethos of Protestant and the rise of capitalism:

> We have no intention whatever of maintaining such a foolish and doctrinaire
> thesis as that the spirit of capitalism … could only have arisen as the result of
> certain effects of the Reformation, or even that capitalism as an economic system
> is a creation of the Reformation … On the contrary, we only wish to ascertain
> whether and to what extent religious forces have taken part in the qualitative
> formation and the quantitative expansion of that spirit over the world. (1958: 91)

The Reformation is not seen as being necessary for the origins of capitalism; it is, however, essential in the spread and success of capitalism. The inter-relationship between the two is somewhat indirect. It lies in the development of or correlation between a secular ethos and the religious ethos of Protestantism. Weber demonstrates the somewhat paradoxical relationship between Protestant asceticism and the interrelated ethos of 'everyday economic life'. He suggests that the features of this ethos include: seeing time wasting as a sin; work is a sign of grace; enjoyment of wealth is a sin; the nature of calling, each person is called to a specific role or task; profit is a sign of election – but must be seen in relation to a person's obligation as a trustee of God. He suggests that these elements came together in a form of worldly asceticism, enabling both the building up of capital and the investment of capital necessary for the development of capitalism, through the rejection of consumption and at the same time made acquisition and profit positive godly values.

In drawing together the ethos of capitalism and that of Protestantism, Weber is suggesting that Protestantism was one among many causal factors which enabled the successful development of capitalism as an economic and social institution by giving individuals an ethos which enabled them to work within a capitalist framework. He concludes his discussion by suggesting that an equally fruitful analysis could be carried out examining the ways in which Protestant asceticism has been influenced by other factors, particularly economic. This conclusion emphasises the need to see religion and the material factors of culture in a complex interaction rather than seeing one as structure and the other as superstructure.

One of the most interesting aspects of Weber's work is his application of the theoretical approach to different religious traditions. A fundamental aspect of these analyses is the presentation of each religion as consistent and rational within its own specific context, and, as in his work on Protestantism, the interrelationship of religious ethos and the economic spirit of the specific society in question. His comparative work covers religion in China – Confucianism and Taoism, religion in India – Hinduism and Buddhism, and ancient Jewish religion. In each one of these cases Weber is concerned with demonstrating the relationship between the distinctive forms of religion and the equally distinctive forms of social and economic structure.

His analyses of Chinese society and religion are a good indication of his general comparative method. In his analysis of Chinese society and religion he presents an argument which both demonstrates why capitalism was unlikely to develop in Chinese society, and equally why Puritanism as a religious ethic was more suited to capitalist acquisition than was Confucianism. Weber suggests several reasons to explain why Chinese society militated against the development of capitalism: the extended family or kin group protected the individual against economic hardship and this was a disincentive to the 'work ethic'. Control of the alienation of land from the kin group prevented the easy accumulation of capital in the form of land, and there was a disincentive to technical innovation. Although he suggests that there were other elements, which could have led to the development of capitalism, the strength of these could not stand against the elements mentioned and even more importantly the ethos that was validated by Confucianism.

Confucianism was first and foremost the religion of a particular status group, the educated elite. As a religious ethos it validated their access to, and control of, power and the maintenance of their status within Chinese society. One of the fundamental themes of Confucianism was harmony and maintenance of societal order, which was seen as mirroring the cosmic order. In regard to its evaluation of work it considered economic affairs to be morally problematic. Equally in its emphasis on harmony it rejected both extravagance and thrift. The elite view the pursuit of wealth as a challenge to internal harmony. This emphasis on harmony and preservation of order were elements of an ethos that were clear obstacles to the development of capitalist forms of acquisition. Many of these points are specifically highlighted in the conclusion of Weber's discussion in which he compares the significant aspects of the Protestant and Confucian ethos. Through discussion of the salient similarities and differences in the two, Weber brings out the essential nature, as he sees it, of each.

Reinhard Bendix in his analysis of Weber's sociology of religion draws together some of the themes that are developed in Weber's comparative studies. For his detailed discussion of these themes see Reinhard Bendix (1992), *Max Weber: An intellectual portrait*, Anchor Books: New York, pp. 269–72. These themes amount to an existential philosophy that is characteristic of all human societies. Two of these themes highlight aspects of Weber's approach that have not been developed to this point. One of the most significant of these relates to the nature of the divine developed as a response to specific social conditions. He suggests that the god idea will be formulated in a way which 'fits in' to the political structure of the ruling or religious elite. He also suggests that use of prophecy, a system of religious power that can challenge authority structures, will be directly related to the level of control in the political structure. Thus, in China, where there was a highly centralised bureaucratic system, prophecy was tightly controlled, whereas in ancient Israel, in which there was little central control, prophecy was highly developed. This final element is closely related to Weber's depictions of Chinese and Israelite society – Chinese society was depicted as static and Israelite society as dynamic.

One of the influential aspects of his comparative work is the concept of 'ideal type'. An ideal type is an analytical construct created by the observer. It presents associations among related elements and organises them into a coherent structure. Although the ideal type is an abstraction and thus does not represent directly any specific ethnographic situation, where the elements, which it includes, are found it allows the specific relationships to be clarified and facilitates the comparison of a set of empirical data with other similar sets of data.

For the purposes of our discussion, it is the final element, the comparative possibilities, which is most important. Despite the fact that Weber presented the different social systems, for example, Chinese and Indian as coherent and logical, the mutually exclusive systems, the concept of ideal type allows the comparison between these different systems. The systems as a whole were not essentially comparable, but aspects of the internal structures and the relationships among these structures were. Thus, Weber could compare and differentiate between religious attitudes to this world and their relationship to particular economic and familial structures or examine the relation of charisma and prophecy to aspects of centralisation and authority.

One of the most influential aspects of his analysis of ideal types and their role within religion is found in his discussion of authority and particularly charisma. Weber outlines three forms of authority: traditional authority, rational-legal authority and charismatic authority. Only charisma will be discussed here. Charismatic authority is that which is found in specific individual qualities and their attraction to a particular group or society. Charismatic authority is based on direct personal appeal. A key aspect of his understanding of charismatic authority is that it arises in the relationship between the charismatic leader and the group. The presence of the qualities that are considered charismatic are not sufficient, a group in a particular condition with particular needs is also necessary for the creation of this type of authority. Weber suggests that charismatic leadership in part arises in response to social conditions of chaos and crisis. Perhaps one of the most important features of charismatic leadership is that it is revolutionary. It challenges existing order and structure, and replaces them with new forms and structures. To an extent charismatic leadership is the reverse swing of the pendulum of history with structured organisation and routine being the forward swing.

Weber also analyses the processes in groups when the charismatic leader dies. He suggests that in order to continue groups need to find ways to sustain the authority. He suggests that groups develop structures in which the charisma is 'routinised'. In some instances structures are developed in which the charisma is passed down to the successor, in other cases the authority is transformed into either traditional or rational-legal authority.

This ideal type is clearly very significant regarding the processes within religious groups. It allows the analysis of different types of leadership and particularly the revolutionary quality of charismatic leadership. Unlike the functionalist approach, which is essentially static, Weber's model allows a much more dynamic analysis of processes within religious groups and society as a whole.

In addition to his discussion of different forms of authority Weber also examined the ideal types relating salvation to asceticism and mysticism. He developed a schema with four possible types. The first, 'inner-worldly' asceticism emphasises activity in this world as a means to achieving salvation. The ascetic aspect is developed through hard work and self-denial. 'Other-worldly' mysticism emphasises that salvation can only be achieved by rejection of this world. The mystical aspect is found in the contemplation of eternity and the rejection of this world as an illusion. 'Inner-worldly' mysticism accepts the importance of this world, but views it as a means for the supporting of a mystical life; some aspects of Jewish mysticism fit into this category. The final type is 'other-worldly' asceticism.

This form of asceticism seeks to overcome the earthly desires, and salvation is gained through this process. These ideal types are helpful in comparing the ethics developed by different religious systems and relating those ethics to the economic sphere. Clearly each one of these religious positions will affect the economic structure of the society.

One of the problems which has been raised regarding Weber's approach is its implicit and explicit use of evolutionary theory. Weber's analysis suggests that societies progress based on increasing rationalism. Religion is portrayed in this context as a sacrifice of intellect, and thus something that will wither away with the increased use of rationality. In spite of this concept of progress, Weber does not accept the commonly held view of unilinear evolution, the concept that all societies develop along a single path. His view, illustrated in his discussions of the different religions and societies is closer to that found in the twentieth-century theories of multi-lineal evolution. This multilineal model suggests that different societies develop along their own paths of development, though there might be a common underlying process, as seen in Weber's concept of increasing rationalism.

A second and perhaps more significant problem is found in Weber's use of empirical data. Although questions have been raised regarding his description of Protestantism, particularly that of the early Reformation, more serious problems are found in the depiction of the different religions and societies upon which he bases his specific and more general con-clusions. His analysis highlights, for example, that Chinese religion and society is essentially static. This ethos of continuity and stability is mirrored in his depiction of Chinese culture, which is essentially ahistorical. Thus, to an extent he can be accused of presenting an incomplete set of empirical data that either shapes or is shaped by his conclusions.

– JOACHIM WACH –

Joachim Wach (1898–1955) develops aspects of Weber's approach, par-ticularly respecting the comparative analyses. He also provides a link to the phenomenological analyses examined below. His work also links into the work of Bryan Wilson and other sociologists who have attempted to develop classifications of different forms of religious organisation. This element is particularly seen in his detailed typology of religious systems and religious authority. In several respects it is closely related to Weber's discussion and use of ideal types.

In his theoretical introduction to *Sociology of Religion* (1944), Wach suggests that Weber's most important work is his comparative analyses of different religious systems. Although he is appreciative of Weber's attempt to construct a 'systematic sociology of religion', he suggests that the emphasis on the relationship between economics and religion might be overstated. He argues that this relationship forms only one of a myriad of different relationships within a social system; one could equally study the relationship between religion and art or religion and politics. Wach states:

> Like the study of 'religion and art' or 'religion and legal institutions', the examination of the complicated interrelations of economics and religion is of great significance in the general investigation of the relationships between religion and the whole gamut of social activities. But the study of 'economics and religion' is by no means identical with a sociology of religion. (1944: 3)

Economics is an essential motivating feature of structural interrelationships but it is not the only one.

Wach also points out that Weber's comparative analysis is incomplete. Weber did not, for example, study Islamic religion and society or that of 'primitive' religions. He also suggests that Weber's analysis was problematic because Weber was critical of religion. As noted below, Wach, in his use of Otto's view of religion (discussed in depth in the final chapter of Part I), moves in a very different direction. Wach emphasises that in order to understand religion properly the sociologist must feel some positive connection to his subject and must analyse it sympathetically.

These points are specifically illustrated in Wach's brief discussion of definitions of religion. He suggests that, following Otto, the best definition of religion is: 'Religion is the experience of the Holy' (1944: 13). He argues that, unlike those definitions used by anthropologists and psychologists that see religion as a purely subjective phenomenon, this definition allows religion to be analysed and understood in an objective way. Religion is the actual experience of something, it is not purely the subjective creation of individuals or groups. This definition underlies Wach's emphasis on religious experience as the basic, indefinable, dynamic yet objective heart of religion.

Wach differs from Otto in two significant respects. Whereas Otto saw the holy as being an additional faculty of the mind alongside the rational, the moral and the aesthetic, Wach sees it as being a more fundamental faculty than are the other three. Religion is in effect the structure with the other three faculties being the superstructure. He employs an analogy of a tree – religion is the trunk of the tree and the other faculties are the branches (1944: 16). Wach also sees the experience of the holy in a much more dynamic way than does Otto. He suggests that, when looked at from the macro level it appears to be singular, but from the micro level it is manifold and diverse.

Wach's discussion of the sociological consequences of the study of religion brings out some additional aspects of his approach. Like Durkheim and Weber, Wach sees religion as serving an integrative function. Although he mentions that it might also have a 'disintegrating function' his discussion exclusively stresses the integrating aspect. He highlights the fact that this process is reciprocal. Religion is both created by a group and at the same time creates that group. He also discusses briefly the roles of doctrine and worship as means of creating or strengthening group cohesiveness.

His second sociological consequence relates to the role of attitude or relationship with the world that characterises specific religions. Following the work of Weber, he suggests that different religions are characterised by different ways of relating to the world. These attitudes, he suggests, arise from the religious experience that underlies the particular religion. As these experiences are translated into material or concrete form, they lead to both a way of relating to the world and a way of acting within it. This attitude is the fundamental object of comparative sociological study. The attitude that arises from the particular religious experience will shape the way that individuals and groups understand and act within society as a whole.

CHAPTER 4

Sigmund Freud and the Psychological Tradition

Sigmund Freud (1856–1939) has been one of the most influential thinkers on religion of the twentieth century. Although those following him have rejected many of the specific details of his analysis, the role of the unconscious and the critical evaluation of religion as a form of illusion have persisted. Freud developed his theory in two related texts, *Totem and Taboo* (1950), published in 1913, and *The Future of an Illusion* (1961), first published in 1927. *Totem and Taboo* examines the origin of religion and ritual, and *The Future of an Illusion* gives critiques on the nature and role of religion in society and examines the future of religion in modern society.

Totem and Taboo closely examines two related phenomena – the nature of totemism, considered by many at the time to be among the earliest form of religion, and taboo, the system of prohibitions and dangerous object. Although the four chapters were originally published separately, together they develop an extended argument in which Freud demonstrates the relationship between totemism, and therefore religion and Oedipus complex, and taboo, and by extension all religious ritual and neurotic acts or rituals.

Freud opens the argument by introducing the analogy between 'primitive peoples' and 'neurotics'. This analogy is particularly important because it underlies the entire argument developed in the book. The analogy rests on two interrelated concepts – the explicitly stated concept of cultural evolution and the implied concept of recapitulation.

Freud accepts the concept of unilineal evolution. One of the primary themes of the evolutionary model was the equation between modern hunters and gatherers, in Freud's terms 'savages', and the earliest stages of our own development. Thus practices associated with societies existing today could be used to indicate practices and ways of thinking that were characteristic of our ancestors living thousands of years ago.

Freud's argument, through its introduction of the analogy between 'savages' and neurotics implicitly alludes to the theory of recapitulation. The theory of recapitulation argues that the development of the individual mirrors the evolutionary development of the species. This theory was originally developed regarding biological evolution, encapsulated in the statement 'ontogeny recapitulates phylogeny', and subsequently applied, as in the case of Freud, to the evolution of culture. In biology it was argued that the fetus goes through the same stages of development, albeit in shortened form, as had the species in its evolutionary history. The supposed fishlike characteristics of one stage of fetal development were seen as a recapitulation of a fishlike stage in our evolutionary history. Similarly, childhood development was seen as mirroring the stages in cultural evolution. The neurotic was seen as being stuck in a 'childlike' stage and thus equivalent to both the child and the 'primitive'. As Freud further develops his argument the recapitulation model becomes increasingly clear. Thus, as discussed below, the child's and indeed the neurotic's experience of the Oedipus complex can be understood as the recapitulation of a stage in the cultural evolution of society.

The first chapter introduces two interrelated themes: totemism and incest. Freud argues that these elements are closely interrelated. As suggested above, totemism was understood to be a very early form of social organisation in which a specific group, a clan, identified itself with a particular object, often an animal and occasionally other aspects from the natural world. Freud emphasises two aspects of totemism; first, the prohibitions related to the totemic object, which he develops more fully later in the book, and second, the role of clan exogamy, that is, the prohibition on sexual relations between members of the same clan.

Freud explains the practice of clan exogamy as being a means of preventing incest. It prevents any form of sexual relations not only between a man and his mother or sisters, but also between the man and any female members of his clan. All of these women are classificatory sisters or mothers (that is, defined as sisters and mothers without actually being so) and thus equally forbidden. The article suggests that far from being an incidental aspect of totemism, exogamy and incest are integral reasons behind the practice as a whole. Although Freud also uses the discussion to explain the unconscious motivations behind the prohibition on social relations between a man and his mother-in-law, the significant role of the discussion in the argument as a whole is the placement of incest at the heart of totemism and ultimately at the heart of religion. The argument concludes with a restatement of the equation between the child, the neurotic and the 'savage'.

In the second chapter Freud moves on to the seemingly unrelated issue of taboo. In part he justifies this association by suggesting that like totemism, taboo is seen as the earliest form of law, emerging in the dawn of human society. Freud presents a survey of the descriptions of taboo, highlighting that taboos can be associated with a wide range of objects and actions, and that they often include a strange element of contagion, with prohibition and danger moving from one object or action to another. Freud suggests that psychoanalysis of neurotic rituals and prohibitions reveal a set of very similar processes to those found in taboo. He argues that four key aspects of taboo are also found in obsessional or neurotic patients: no obvious reason for the specific prohibitions; they are supported by internal motivations and processes; they move easily from one object to another; and they lead to ritual performances.

His discussion of the common basis of the two sets of practices returns to the assumption of recapitulation. It focuses on the development of the psyche in childhood, the desire to touch the sexual organ or other sexual object and the prohibition against touching as the basis of the neurosis and the taboo system. At all three levels of recapitulation the desire and the processes which arise from its prohibition are unconscious and thus beyond the conscious knowledge of the actors.

In attempting to determine specifically the unconscious basis of the taboo system, Freud reintroduces totemism, focusing again on its two main features: prohibition on killing the totemic animal and clan exogamy, that is, the prohibition against incest. He suggests that underlying these two prohibitions are the most basic of human desires and thus taboo is the unconscious response to the prohibition against them. Although Freud's discussion continues with a detailed examination of forms of taboo, the association made here is the next stage in his overall argument. It establishes that totemism and the taboo complex, and by implication religion, rest on the prohibition against these two fundamental desires – killing the totemic beast, and incest. The chapter also establishes that rituals, from totemic ritual to religious ritual, are directly akin to the obsessional rituals created by children and especially neurotics.

The third chapter moves in a seemingly divergent direction. It picks up the theme of animism, the belief that the world is populated by spiritual agents, which was presented by some scholars as an alternative model for the origin of human religion. The chapter also examines the nature of magic, demonstrating that the two phenomena are closely interrelated, and are stages in the evolutionary development of religion.

Although the chapter does not directly develop the arguments deployed thus far, it introduces two new elements. One of the significant features of the discussion of animism and magic is the concept of the 'omnipotence of thought'. Freud argues that animism arises not so much as a means of speculating about the nature of the world, but as a means of controlling it. Thus, while animism in a traditional sense is a description of the nature of the world, magic is its necessary concomitant – magic is the technique of animism in controlling the world. The nature of magic is particularly important in Freud's argument: magic arises from our need or desire to control the world around us, it however, is based on an overestimation of the power of ideas; it assumes that we can shape material reality with our minds. Because magic arises from our desires and is a faulty depiction of the world it could be characterised as an illusion in the sense used by Freud in *The Future of an Illusion*. Thus this chapter lays both the groundwork for the general argument that Freud will employ in that volume, seeing religion as an illusion, and opens an additional role for religion as a psychological construct; religion also serves as an attempt, albeit mistaken, to control or influence the world around us.

The second important aspect of the argument is the clear presentation of an evolutionary sequence. On a broad scale Freud outlines three stages of cultural development: the animistic stage, the religious stage and the scientific stage. Each stage is characterised by a different valuation of the 'omnipotence of thoughts'. He suggests that in the animistic stage there is an overvaluation of self, reflected in the overvaluation of ideas in relation to the objective world. The religious stage is characterised by a weakening or indirect overvaluation of ideas. Gods are seen as the source of power, but human centrality is maintained through the ability to influence how gods act. In the scientific stage Freud suggests that most of this faulty worldview has vanished, with people realising that they are but a small and insignificant part of reality.

Freud links this argument to his analogy with human development and neurosis, and thus the concept of recapitulation. He suggests that the three stages in human development are directly mirrored in three stages of psychological development. The three stages, as in the discussion of totemism and taboo, are stages of psycho-sexual development. The stage of animism is associated with that of auto-eroticism, in which sexual instincts are directed solely at the self. The second stage, associated with religion, is an extension of the auto-erotic, the self is still the sexual object, but it is now focused in a somewhat indirect way to the ego. The final stage, analogous to the scientific stage, is when the sexual object is no longer the self but rather the/an other. The chapter on animism thus strengthens Freud's overall analogy between religion and the development of religion with childhood development and most significantly with neurosis.

The final chapter brings together the themes introduced and synthesises them through the Oedipus Complex. Freud returns to a description of totemism and draws together what he considers to be the four key elements of the totemic system: totems were originally animal; totemism was originally matrilineal; killing or eating the totem was prohibited; incest and sexual relations within the clan were prohibited. After discussing other theories that seek to explain the origin of totemism, Freud introduces his own theory, which is presented as a myth of the origin of religion and culture.

Freud initially examines the prohibition on eating the totemic animal; based on the work of William Robertson Smith he suggests that this prohibition was ritually broken in a totemic feast in which all of the men, dressed as the animal, would consume its flesh. The ritual was full of guilt at the act and fear, and only supportable because all of the men were required to perform it together. Interestingly this act becomes the basis of all sacrificial cults and thus demonstrates that Freud's arguments should be understood as relating to all religions. He interprets this totemic feast, via psychoanalysis, as symbolically killing the father – hence the emotional ambiguity which accompanies the act.

The act and the association of totemism with the father is contextualised by Freud's 'myth' of the origin of religion and culture. He suggests that originally people lived in primal hordes. These hordes centred on a father, his wives, daughters and sons. Only the father had sexual access to the women. The brothers, desiring the women and hating their father, band together, kill and eat him, following which the brothers are filled with guilt and remorse. As a result, they prohibit what he has forbidden, that is sexual relations with the mothers and sisters, and transfer their feelings towards the father to the totemic animal. The totemic feast is thus a re-enactment of the original crime and filled with the same ambivalence as had characterised the original event.

The guilt and ambivalence arising from this primal murder also lead to the creation of the norms of religion and society. The image of the father is projected into the totemic animal and becomes even stronger. It becomes the unconscious basis for the prohibitions; for example, those against incest and murder. All religions are seen as a development from this original act of violence and the resulting guilt and ambivalence.

The events described in this myth are substantially identical to those presented by Freud in the Oedipus Complex. This complex is presented in the myth of Oedipus, a man who kills his father, marries his mother and in guilt and remorse tears out his eyes. It is also understood to be a complex that is part of childhood development, in which children have these desires and need to repress them or redirect them into rituals and fantasies.

Elements of the complex are also present in neurotics who have remained at that stage of development. Thus the analysis of totemism and its relationship to the Oedipus Complex return to the concept of recapitulation that allows Freud to bring all three elements of the equation together.

In the conclusion of the chapter Freud picks up the connection between the totemic, Oedipal feast and other religious practices and beliefs. He addresses specifically the question of how god is introduced into the equation. Freud suggests that psychoanalytical evidence demonstrates that god is a projection of the father, hence the religious language which specifically calls god 'father'. This association, and the observation that gods are often associated with animals, leads Freud to posit that the god concept is derived from the original totemic animal, and thus goes back to the original primal father. The remaining discussion in the chapter traces how the psychological forces, which led to the origin of religion, are progressively transformed and culminate with the sacrifice of Jesus on the cross. Although Freud does mention the possible existence of mother goddesses, his theory does not specifically address how and why they came to exist. It does, however, attempt to expand from religion to a theory of culture. Thus, the primal murder is seen as leading not only to religion and god, but also to the various forms of patrilineality in culture.

The Future of an Illusion, although a somewhat less ambitious volume than Totem and Taboo, develops Freud's argument in several significant directions. In The Future of an Illusion Freud develops a more abstract discussion of the origins of religious beliefs. His analysis suggests that religious beliefs ultimately arise as a response to the precariousness of human existence. Because we have a psychological need to make our existence tolerable, we create gods who give order and meaning both to the chaotic natural world and the vagaries of life in society. Ultimately these gods, as in Totem and Taboo, are a projection of the father – in this case as a protector and a lawgiver (associated with the superego) rather than the more ambiguous figure created by guilt and Oedipal desires.

This discussion of the origin of religion in helplessness also relies on recapitulation and specifically on the analogy between children and our ancestors. Freud argues that the process seen in the origin of religion mirrors a process in childhood development. The child, almost intrinsically helpless, views the father as a source of power and order. The father as a stern authority figure is somewhat ambiguous, hence the ambiguity discussed in Totem and Taboo. Religion develops from this source as the child grows and realises that his helplessness is not solved; he then projects his feelings and relationship with his father to beings who give order but are also feared.

Religion, and the association between god and father play an important role in relation to law. Religion views god as the lawgiver. From a psychological perspective this concept is both true and false. It is true, that god as the projection of the father plays an important role in the development of the superego, that aspect of our personality which sets limits on our exercise of instinctual desires. It is false in that it attributes this to a supernatural or divine source.

Although Freud has laid the groundwork for study of religion and has given it an important social and psychological role, his work is essentially a critique of religion. This critique rests on the epistemological character of religion. Religion is not based on reality. It arises as a solution to our fears, but ultimately it is a false solution. Religion is based on wish fulfilment and thus is viewed by Freud as an illusion. It is thus analogous on the individual psychological level to the fantasies created by neurotics to resolve their individual psychological crises.

Given that Freud has an underlying evolutionary basis to his analysis, the question arises as to the future of this illusion, that is religion. Is religion a necessary illusion for civilisation or can it be replaced by a more true understanding of reality? Freud clearly indicates that it would be better for human beings not to be bound by the prohibitions established through illusion, but instead to act on the basis of intelligence. He couples inhibitions connected with sexuality, support of the monarchy and religion as all obstacles to the full development of human intelligence. The volume concludes with a clear statement that society can and must do without religion, and that science can provide for everything currently on offer by religion.

Freud's theories underlying psychoanalysis were increasingly challenged as the last century drew to a close. Many of his arguments relating specifically to religion, although suggesting interesting avenues of research and discussion, are also problematic. Underlying much of his discussion is the theory of unilinear cultural evolution and interrelated with it the theory of cultural recapitulation. Both of these lines of argument have been challenged, and in many respects have been considered untenable since the early part of the twentieth century.

Freud applies the unilineal theories of cultural evolution developed by Lewis Henry Morgan and Edward Burnett Tylor. Both of these theorists assumed that cultures developed in an almost deterministic way through a single line of development concluding with the modern industrialised West (in both of their cases Victorian Britain or the United States). Anthropologists from the time of Franz Boas have demonstrated that this view of cultural evolution is challenged by ethnographic evidence. It is demonstrable that each culture has its own specific historical trajectory and that there is no one line of development. This specific historical development is shaped by both the contingent inventiveness and choices made through time; the shape of a culture is as much shaped by the diffusion of ideas as those developed internally. The arguments against unilinear cultural evolution undermine the use of modern hunting and gathering societies as directly analogous to our own past – these modern societies have in any case had as much time as our own society to develop and change, even if such changes are not found in relation to technology. Freud's model of cultural evolution is also highly problematic because of its inbuilt ethno-centricity – it purports to argue from an 'objective' scientific position from which all other societies and indeed people within our own society can be judged, assessed and ranked.

The theory of cultural and/or psychological recapitulation has also been challenged. If, as we have suggested, the concept of unilinear evolution is untenable, then a view that all children's psychological developments necessarily recapitulate exactly the same stages as cultural development clearly cannot be defended. If recapitulation were to occur it could only reflect the development of the specific culture. The concept of recapitu-lation, even culturally specific recapitulation, is also highly problematic. In the case of fetal development, if recapitulation actually were found (most biologists do not agree that it is) then at least the genes provide a deterministic mechanism to explain how and why it happens. In the case of culture and its reflection in psychology no such mechanism exists that could lead to recapitulation as described and employed in Freud's arguments.

The historical reconstruction proposed in *Totem and Taboo* is also highly flawed. Freud based his discussion of the 'primal horde' on some specu-lations in Darwin, which have no support in ethnographic or archae-ological evidence. The theory has a number of assumptions about all early human societies, for example that they were matrilineal and based on a senior or dominant male with adult females and juvenile males, that do not seem to be supportable. The first of these assumptions is based on Freud's need to see all the women in the group as mothers or sisters and is thus based on circular logic; the second is based on a purely hypothetical analogy between early human societies and the behaviour of some primates. Given the significant differences between humans and even our most closely related primate cousins, this analogy seems particularly weak. The theory also requires that the primal murder has been either repeated in all human communities or that we are all descended from one such community; neither one is convincing. Evidence from archaeology and palaeontology of the very early spread of modern forms of humanity undermines the credibility of either of these possibilities. Even if such an event had occurred, the theory requires that it be transmitted to both the individual and society. As already argued regarding recapitulation, there is no such mechanism. Genetic transmission can only account for inherited traits, it cannot account for transmission of acquired traits.

A similar range of ethnographic problems is found regarding other arguments deployed in *Totem and Taboo*. Following the work of Durkheim and more significantly Robertson Smith, Freud assumes that totemism is the earliest form of religion and, basic to the development of religion in all societies, he also assumes that the covenantal form of sacrifice is equally ubiquitous. Neither of these assumptions has proven to be the case. As A. L. Kroeber suggests in an early critique of *Totem and Taboo*, the form of sacrifice described by Robertson Smith is both geographically and temporally limited, and is not as early or widespread as required by Freud's argument (1979: 21).

Based on his use of recapitulation, Freud's analysis employs a sleight of hand which suggests the equivalence between individual experience, related psychological states and social constructs; this use of smoke and mirrors allows him to make the analogy between religion and neurosis, and between religious ritual and obsessive rituals. If the concept of recapitulation is removed, there remains no compelling evidence that would link up these phenomena, which work on such significantly different levels. Freud's theory almost requires the existence of a societal mind and unconscious mirroring that of the individual. Short of mystical or Cartesian thought, returning him to the realm of religion and thereby illusion, speculations on the location and nature of a societal mind and collective unconscious pose insurmountable theoretical problems.

The discussion in *Totem and Taboo* and to a lesser extent in *The Future of an Illusion* centre on the Oedipus Complex as the motor for both society and religion on one level, and the individual psyche and its development on the other. Freud's analysis suggests that all individuals and societies share this particular psychological complex. Freud thus assumes the psychic unity of all humanity. If we were to accept this premise, we would need to see these psychological states as being biologically rather than culturally determined. Freud's own argument, however, challenges the genetic status of these complexes, as it introduces a hypothetical historical event to explain their presence and prevalence.

Even if we accept the premise that the Oedipus Complex is real in a Western European context, we could not assume that it was necessarily present in other societal contexts. Freud's assertion that it is universal is only a hypothesis; he does not demonstrate it using good empirical data. We would also be correct in challenging its almost biological basis, and asking whether it is a culturally constructed psychological complex, perhaps limited to Freud's time and place. Ethnographic data from societies with different forms of social organisation than our own, for example, with the father having little or no role in the raising of the child, suggest that the Oedipus Complex is not universal. Rather, it is limited to those societies, if indeed present at all, which have a similar social organisation to our own. It is not unlikely that in different societies, with different family structures, a range of complexes will exist, which are intrinsically related to the culture in which they are found. It is thus unlikely that religion owes its origin to a single event or psychological state.

This aspect of Freud's model forms part of an essentialist definition of religion; that is, seeing religion as having its roots in an essential aspect of human nature. If his model is made more abstract, that is, referring to cognitive or unconscious processes that enable us to shape or deal with our experience as human beings without presupposing particular ways of doing this, then the hypothesis becomes a useful analytical tool, reflecting the psychological unity of humanity but also allowing for the particularity created by human beings in different cultural contexts. Thus psychological elements may play a significant role in shaping religion, but their analysis must be much more subtle and empirically grounded than that offered by Freud.

– CARL GUSTAV JUNG –

Although in many respects Jungian analytical psychology has been less influential than Freud's psychoanalytic theory, Jung (1875–1961) has had a profound effect on some modern trends within religion. This is particularly true of the New Age movement in which many individuals and writers draw heavily on Jung's discussion of the psyche, myth and religion. Two aspects of Jung's work facilitate this repackaging of his theories. First, unlike Freud, who was highly critical of religion and saw society as moving progressively away from religion, Jung views religion as essentially positive and nurturing. Second, Jung's concept of the collective unconscious and some of the mystical language used in relation to it, fit very well into the Eastern mystical traditions that have been appropriated by many within the New Age movement. Elements of Jung's discussion seem very similar to the theological, experiential approach found in the work of Otto (see below). His discussions at times suggest an experience of absolute unity, which has significance to both the individual and society. This element comes to the fore in the work of many of Jung's followers, particularly Joseph Campbell (see below).

In order to discuss Jung's understanding of the role of religion it is necessary to touch on some aspects of his analysis of the human psyche. Like Freud, Jung saw the psyche as essentially dynamic, with different elements relating to each other in different ways. Like Freud, Jung distinguishes between the individual conscious and unconscious; he also, however, adds in an additional level that transcends the individual – the collective unconscious.

The conscious is composed of two main elements, the ego and the persona. The ego develops through life in relation to the unconscious, it is the source of our way of relating to and understanding of the world. The persona, or multiple personae, is the mask with which we interrelate with others. These personae can be highly specific and contextual. Jung describes the next level, the unconscious, as being the repository for all those aspects of self, which we want to ignore or forget. It is the shadow side of our personality.

The collective unconscious is the significant level in relation to religion. It is the repository of rather abstract entities called archetypes. These archetypes are understood to be the common inheritance of all human societies, and are essential to the individual in their development towards maturity. The archetypes are personified embodiments of different elements of personal psychological development. The collective unconscious includes the non-rational aspects of psyche that are essential to healthy maturity. This aspect of growth is, for Jung, the primary role of both religion and his form of analytical psychology. The common possession of the collective unconscious by humanity as a whole is the source of the commonalities of religious inspiration and the essential common basis of all religions.

The archetypes are the stuff that religion, dreams and myth are made of. Each archetype relates to an aspect of psychological development, and thus, the individual's relation to them and the collective unconscious as a whole is depicted as a journey. Both Jung and Campbell take up this analogy as the basis of their interpretation of myth. Archetypes are embodied in various personified forms, for example as a wise old man or divine child, or in other cases, in specific acts, for example slaying a dragon. The most significant archetype, god, is seen as an image of the self – though an image with objective reality outside of the self.

Because the archetypes reside in the collective unconscious, they are in some sense outside of the individual. Thus they are simultaneously psychological realities of personal development and collective realities.

This dual level of functioning allows Jung to explain the similarity (or he might say identity) between individual and collective artifacts. Thus his analysis brings together myths, which are collective phenomena, with dreams and fantasies, which are individual phenomena. His argument that the collective unconscious and the archetypes are universal also allows him to analyse together myths, fantasies and dreams of societies widely divergent in time and space.

Although it is possible to make a strong distinction between Freud and Jung on religion in relation to its status, both share certain common features. The most significant of these is the basis of religion in the unconscious. Freud saw religion as emerging from the individual unconscious, and viewed it as essentially negative, giving way to a scientific outlook that was essentially rational. Jung saw religion as emerging from the collective unconscious, and as part of the essential maturation of the psyche it was a positive feature of society. Freud and Jung also shared an important concept of the psychic unity of humanity – this concept is essential to all non-judgemental approaches to religion and society.

For Jung, religion, therefore, is closely related to processes within the collective unconscious, and their role in individual development. The myths, gods and heroes out of which religion creates a narrative are all reflections of archetypes and serve to guide individuals through their journey to maturity. Given this analysis, Jung seems to be arguing that religion is part of, or a reflection of, an internal psychodynamic process; the way that different internal faculties interact with each other.

Although some of Jung's discussions, especially his appropriation of the work of Rudolf Otto and Eastern mysticism, suggest a transcendental object, there is some ambiguity in his analysis. For the most part he attempts to have the experience of otherness while still placing the location of that otherness in the unconscious. Following Otto, Jung viewed the essential nature of religion as being the experience of the numinous – an experience of an ineffable other which is beyond control. He differs from Otto, perhaps only in part, in seeing the numinous as internal rather than external.

Jung also shares a final theoretical similarity to Freud, that is, the concept of recapitulation. This concept underlies much of his discussion and is clearly developed in his discussion of myth and its role in 'primitive' society. Jung's description of the way that 'primitive' people experience their world is particularly telling and problematic. His characterisation follows the work of Lévy-Bruhl, who argues that the mentality of 'primitive' man is different from our own. Whereas modern thought is understood to be essentially rational, 'primitive' thought is pre-logical and essentially collective. 'Primitive' thought is understood to be highly emotional, with little or no sense of the difference between subject and object, all of nature is subjectivised and personalised.

Jung, in a similar vein, suggests that 'primitive' thought is essentially unconscious – all of experience is understood unconsciously rather than rationally via reflection. To an extent the psychodynamic model, which we have discussed thus far, is not present in his analysis of 'primitive' thought. His discussion suggests that there is no distinction between the conscious and unconscious minds. In a discussion of Eastern religion, which he suggests does not distinguish between mind and material, he states, 'the only known analogy to this fact is the mental condition of the primitive, who confuses dream and reality in the most bewildering way' (Jung, 1969: 499). This confusion of conscious and unconscious thinking is also specifically stated in 'The Psychology of the Child Archetype':

> Primitive mentality differs from the civilised chiefly in that the conscious mind is far less developed in scope and intensity. Functions such as thinking, willing, etc. are not yet differentiated; they are pre-conscious, and in the case of thinking, for instance, this shows itself in the circumstance that the primitive does not think *consciously*, but that thoughts *appear*. The primitive cannot assert that he thinks; it is rather 'something thinks in him'. The spontaneity of the act of thinking does not lie, causally, in his conscious mind, but in his unconscious. (Jung, 1969b: 153)

His discussion suggests that 'primitive' people live in a world in which there is no distinction between the products of dreams and visions, and that of sensory experience.

The analogy between myth and fantasy, specifically neurotic fantasy, is explicitly stated in the following quotation:

> We can see almost daily in our patients how mythical fantasies arise: they are not thought up, but present themselves as images or chains of ideas that force their way out of the unconscious, and when they are recounted they often have the character of connected episodes resembling mythical dramas. That is how myths arise, and that is the reason why fantasies from the unconscious have so much in common with primitive myth. (Jung 1969a: 38)

This quotation with its equation of 'primitive myth' and modern neurotic fantasy emphasises Jung's use of recapitulation. It also emphasises Jung's ethnographically insupportable suggestion that in 'primitive' societies, human beings effectively have no conscious volition but live purely in the realm of the unconscious.

Jung's use of recapitulation is also demonstrated in his extension of this analysis to children in Western European societies. Jung suggests that childhood perceptions and experience is different from that of adults. Children, like 'primitive' people cannot distinguish between their conscious experiences and the unconscious. Thus, as part of their development children are analogous to the adults of supposed earlier forms of our society. The analogy, like that of Freud, is also extended to his discussion of neurosis.

As indicated by the discussion of Jung's thought there is a significant difference in his use of recapitulation and his valuation of religion in relation to modernity than is found in Freud. Although as noted Jung equates 'primitive', children, and neurotic experience, this equation is not negative. Jung, unlike Freud, does not see modernity as positive and 'primitive' as negative – 'primitive' is positive precisely because it is more fully related to the collective unconscious, hence, the conscious articulation of archetypes in myth. Modernity is partially negative due to its attempts to ignore the collective unconscious. It is precisely in this point that Jung presents a positive valuation of religion. Both religion and Jung's own analytical psychology are doors into the collective unconscious; they open up the possibility of healthy maturation, which is increasingly absent in modern life. Thus for Freud religion is negative because it is connected to the unconscious, while for Jung it is positive precisely because it is so connected.

As will be immediately apparent Jung's theory is problematic in many of the same ways as that of Freud. The theory of recapitulation and the associated theory of unilinear cultural evolution, both of which are central to Jung's discussion, have already been discussed above in relation to Freud. Jung's distinction between 'primitive' and modern thought is built on the same presuppositions, and has additional problems of its own. This distinction has been addressed and tested by anthropological studies. No study supports this distinction. The empirical evidence demonstrates that all societies have their own forms of rationality and ability to interact rationally with their environments. No evidence supports the existence of communities that function purely on the level of the unconscious; rather there seems to be a common mix of functioning via both the conscious and unconscious, rational and non-rational in all forms of human society.

The collective unconscious and the archetypes are also problematic on several levels. The collective unconscious is contestable both in respect of its logical status and its empirical or ethnographic status. Location is a fundamental logical problem relating to the collective unconscious: does it reside inside or outside of the individual human being? If the collective unconscious is rooted within the individual, yet shared in the same way by all individuals, it would need to be part of the genetic endowment that makes or defines us as human – all human beings would need to share the specific genetic structures from which the collective unconscious emerges.

This genetic or inherited aspect is specifically stated by Jung; see for example 'The Psychology of the Child Archetype' in which he states:

> We must assume that they correspond to certain collective (and not personal) structural elements of the human psyche in general, and … are inherited. Although tradition and transmission certainly play a part, there are, as we have said, very many cases that cannot be accounted for in this way. (1969b: 155)

This statement, while mentioning the role that enculturation and diffusion might play, clearly gives priority to an inherited foundation to many of the archetypes and the collective unconscious.

The genetic nature of the collective unconscious has problems on two levels. First, if it includes, as sometimes indicated by Jung, elements which are acquired traits, then as in the case of our discussion of Freud, there could be no genetic mechanism that would transmit them from one generation to the next; genes transmit inherited traits not acquired traits. Second, if the collective unconscious includes no acquired traits, there still is a problem in relation to content. Jung describes very specific symbols representing the archetypes that are shared by divergent cultures; it is unlikely that genetic inheritance would pass that level of specific cognitive material. It is much more likely that the content is culturally specific and acquired, rather than inherited.

If the collective unconscious has no basis in genetic inheritance, it must derive from a source external to the individual. If, as Jung suggests, it is a universal human phenomena then it could not reside in cultural formations, as cultures worldwide are highly divergent. As a universal phenomenon separate from culture, Jung seems to be proposing a somewhat mystical entity, which is separable from all individuals and communities and is found in the same way, regardless of time and space. Such a mystical entity moves outside of the province of social scientific or psychological study and into the realm of theology.

If we return to a scientific paradigm, the collective unconscious, if it exists, must be found in the interaction between a specific society and the individuals within that society. If this is the case, however, the collective unconscious is relativised to the specific culture or community at that particular time and place. Rather than a universal collective unconscious, the collective unconscious is culture specific and changing through time and space as the individuals and community change. It cannot be a mystical entity either inside or outside the individual, but must be something with which the individual interacts via the process of enculturation. Similarly, maturation is no longer a simple unitary phenomenon, but becomes equally relativised with each community having its own understanding of maturation.

The last part of this discussion introduces part of the ethnographic or empirical problem with the collective unconscious. The collective unconscious and its specific content, the archetypes, as universal phenomena do not seem to be demonstrable in the ethnographic data. If we only touch on their relation to wholeness and maturation, different societies have developed very different models of what it means to be human let alone what it means to be a mature human. There seems no compelling reason to accept Jung's concept of wholeness over those found in different societal contexts – wholeness and maturity are cultural constructs and cannot be properly understood as abstractions outside of that cultural context.

The archetypes are also problematic on several levels. Challenges to their use can be raised on two levels: theoretical and ethnographic. If the archetypes are examined in terms of their use as analytical descriptors, in many cases they seem much too simple or broad. They appear to have such wide application that they actually serve little or no analytical purpose. Although this broadness may be justified due to their theoretical universality or pervasiveness, in practice it reduces every myth and religious structure to saying exactly the same thing. It ignores the possibility that in different cultural contexts different issues or questions might be more significant. Some of the other archetypes, while being narrower in range, are so closely tied to specific aspects of human biological structure that they do not need any external explanation, that is, they can exist separately from the collective unconscious.

The second problem is ethnographic. Jung's analysis, like that of Freud, assumes that symbols have a relatively constant meaning. Thus if a symbol is found to have a specific meaning in one culture it is assumed that that meaning will be present wherever that symbol is found. Jung's theory of archetypes relies on this assumption, and indeed, in a circular form of argumentation the supposed presence of the same symbol in different cultures is seen as proof of the existence of archetypes. Ethnographic data demonstrates that symbols and their interpretation are highly culture specific and vary significantly even within cultures. Thus, the view that symbols can be seen as exemplifying universal archetypes has no empirical support (unless, of course, following the example of Freud, we assume that only we are privileged to properly understand what the symbols really mean).

It is not impossible that Jung is correct that archetypes and the collective unconscious exist. They can, however, only exist at the level of a specific culture or community. Communities do create complex symbolic entities, which may play the role of archetype, such that individuals in the community might use these entities to express different aspects of their psyche.

And, through the process of enculturation it is probable that individuals within a community might share a limited collective unconscious, which is the collective repository for the shared symbolic entities. The key points are that this process is culture specific and relies on cultural transmission for its existence.

– JOSEPH CAMPBELL –

Although Joseph Campbell (1904–87) did not consider himself to be a follower of Jung, many of his ideas concerning myth and religion reveal the clear stamp of Jung's influence. Campbell's works include a variety of different takes on Jung, at times recapitulating his ideas and at others being somewhat selective. Thus, in some cases he accepts Jung's view that the unconscious is inherited and in others he follows Freud in seeing it as acquired (Segal, 1999: 119). Nonetheless the tenor of his discussion is consistently shaped by Jung's concept of some form of collective unconscious and archetypes.

Campbell's work highlights some of the problems that are inherent in Jung. Eastern mysticism, particularly the emphasis on spiritual unity, is one of the themes that underlies much of Campbell's writing. Although like Jung, Campbell sees this as an internal process, at times the discussion moves towards the realm of theological mysticism rather than analytical study of myth or religion. Campbell's emphasis on this basic religious experience also leads him to interpret almost all myth and religion as expressing this single type of experience.

At times Campbell's work reads more like psychotherapy rather than academic analysis. This aspect is particularly seen in one of his most widely read works, *The Hero with a Thousand Faces* (1968 [1949]). The book seems to have two separate goals: first, the elucidation of the significant level of similarities between different mythological systems; and second, taking the reader through a journey of self discovery in which they, like the hero, become aware of the essential unity of the self and the universe.

The pilgrimage or journey is the primary metaphor with which Campbell examines myth (as a component of religion) and individual development. The archetypes that he examines cluster around the movement along the pilgrimage; they are seen, as in Jung, as the steps in the development of the psyche. They reflect the individual's journey to self-awareness, and are concomitant to that spiritual awareness. Unity of the psyche reflects unity of the cosmos.

Campbell's use of archetypes is even broader than that of Jung. In many cases they seem so broadly based that it would be impossible to tell a story without them. The archetypes include obstacles on the journey or super-natural aid, each of which is almost infinitely expandable to include almost any mythological element. The archetypes are so inclusive that they are effectively useless; all stories have them or they would not be stories. On the basis of these inclusive archetypes Campbell trawls over the mythologies of the world, nets those elements that fit his argument and brings them together, totally out of context with other similar elements.

Many of these aspects are found in his discussion of the 'world navel' (Campbell, 1968: 40–6). Rather than contextualising the material, Campbell suggests that the culmination of all myth is the 'release of the flow of life' into the world. This energy comes from the symbolic centre of the universe, the 'cosmic navel'. He then selects a range of sources from Buddhist to Native American to support this contention. A key part of his argument is that once a connection has been made anything that pertains to one myth pertains to all myths. The range and diversity of material, which is used to exemplify this theme is quite wide and could include the conclusion of almost any story. Campbell, following Jung, suggests that this ubiquitous element is not only a common narrative element, but is found in all myth because it reflects an aspect of the collective unconscious, that is, it is an archetype. As an archetype it relates to an aspect of development of the psyche – the movement from the self-centred ego to 'transpersonal centredness'. Unlike most of Jung's discussions, Campbell takes the argu-ment one stage further; he suggests that the narrative element and arche-type reflect part of a spiritual journey as well – the archetype represents the perception of the transcendent unity. Campbell's arguments, with their wide-ranging application and theological undertones, are recapitulated in a contemporary figure, Eliade, who takes the phenomenological study of religion in many similar directions.

CHAPTER 5

Rudolf Otto: The Idea of the Holy

Rudolf Otto (1869–1937) is in a certain sense the odd one out in this section; his work is strongly theological in character rather than being social scientific. His approach to religion, however, is significant to the understanding of modern theories of religion because theorists from the phenomenological approach take up many of his ideas, and, as discussed above, are also influential on a wide range of other theorists, particularly Jung and his followers. Otto's theories are also influential on many theologians of the twentieth century. His influence is particularly found in the work of Martin Buber. Otto is also different from the theorists discussed in that his approach is partially backward-looking; addressing issues raised by Kant and Schleiermacher rather than issues of central concern to modern approaches; for example, the relationship between religion and culture.

Otto follows the nineteenth-century neo-Kantian thinkers in seeking the essence of religion, particularly the *a priori* or irreducible faculties of the human mind that underlie religion and the religious experience. Otto's ideas are most fully developed in *The Idea of the Holy* (1958 [1917]). This work discusses the holy as the fundamental human faculty that is the foundation of all religion, and ultimately attempts to demonstrate that this faculty is most fully developed in Christianity.

Otto develops his approach to the holy from the work of Kant and Schleiermacher. Kant distinguished between three basic human faculties: the rational, the ethical and the aesthetic. Each of these faculties was irreducible, and thus *a priori*. Kant suggested that religion had its foundation in the ethical faculty, in the practical world of action. Schleiermacher accepted Kant's basic understanding of human nature, but argued that religion arose from the aesthetic faculty rather than the ethical. Both Schleiermacher and Kant's theories did not depend on the existence of a transcendental other; in each case religion arose from human needs or subjective experience. In the case of Schleiermacher religion arose from the subjective, internal feeling of being a creature and finitude – both subjective feelings without the need for an actual external object.

Directly addressing both the specific human faculty from which religion emerges and the question of the nature of the object of religious experience, Otto opens his argument with a discussion of the role of rationality in religion. As indicated above, both Kant and Schleiermacher associate religion with faculties other than the rational. Otto follows suit; his discussion of the relationship between the rational and non-rational aspects of religion is significant to his general discussion of religion. It is also the basis of comparison between religions and of his argument that Christianity is the highest form of religion. His opening argument suggests that although religion includes, and indeed should include, elements of the rational in beliefs and conception, the content of religion cannot be entirely based on rationality; religion must also include the non-rational. Given this, he is clearly indicating that religion cannot emerge solely or even essentially from the rational faculty of human nature. As his argument develops there is a clear emphasis on the non-rational aspect of religion; it forms the basis of his concept of the holy. However, Otto does not believe that religion, in its fullest sense, can solely emphasise the non-rational; this leads to mysticism. Religion must also have a balance of rational elements.

In spite of this acceptance of a role for the rational, Otto places the emphasis in his work and the basis of religion in the non-rational. It is in this part of his discussion that he moves away from the Kantian paradigm. Unlike Kant and Schleiermacher, Otto argues for a fourth faculty in human nature; a faculty which is solely related to religion, the faculty of the 'holy'. The faculty of the holy becomes the irreducible *a priori* basis for all religion. This element and the object that it perceives is ultimately non-rational because it is intangible; it has what Otto calls an 'over plus of meaning', and thus is beyond the possibility of description or analysis.

The holy as an additional category of mind, a category distinctive to religion, is part of a significant conceptual move. It is associated with an argument relating to the feelings that underlie the religious experience. Otto suggests that the feelings associated with religion are not the same as those found in other spheres. There may be some overlap, but ultimately the feelings associated with religion are unique and thus the experience of religion, like the faculty that underlies these feelings, is unique. Otto's argument is important because it takes religion out of the realm of social scientific analysis as a construct that is part of culture. Religion becomes something separate from other human constructs; it is based on its own faculty, and thus can only be understood in its own terms. This conceptual move becomes the basis of the phenomenological analysis of religion, which also sees religion as somehow separable from other cultural constructs and essential in nature.

The nature of the faculty of the holy and the distinction between Otto, on the one hand, and Kant and Schleiermacher, on the other, further essentialises religion and prevents the use of any form of humanist analysis. Otto, unlike Kant and Schleiermacher, sees religion as relating to and arising from a transcendental other. Thus religion, far from being a subjective human response to feelings of dependence or need for an ethical basis, emerges from the interrelationship between the faculty of the holy and an objective other, which Otto calls the *Mysterium Tremendum et Fascinans*.

The construct *Mysterium Tremendum et Fascinans* emphasises the different elements of Otto's conception of the transcendental other. In short, *mysterium* emphasises that god is wholly other, unknowable and ineffable; *tremendum* brings out the aspect of majesty and power that underlies authentic religious experience; *fascinans* develops the interrelated themes of awe and fascination. Otto examines each of these elements and illustrates in an evolutionary model how religious experience of god slowly developed and encompassed all three of the different aspects of the holy. Otto uses the three elements and the aspect of rationality and non-rationality to construct an evolutionary model of the development of religion. As a Christian theologian he was ultimately interested in demonstrating how these threads culminated in Christianity. He describes the nature of this process in *The Idea of the Holy*:

> By the continual living activity of its non-rational elements a religion is guarded from passing into 'rationalism'. By being steeped in and saturated with rational elements it is guarded from sinking into fanaticism or mere mysticality, or at least from persisting in these, and is qualified to become a religion for all civilised humanity. The degree in which both rational and non-rational elements are jointly present, united in healthy and lovely harmony, affords a criterion to measure the rank of religions – and one, too that is specifically religious. Applying this criterion, we find that Christianity, in this as in other respects, stands out in complete superiority over all its sister religions. (1958: 142)

This quotation illustrates Otto's conclusion that Christianity most fully develops the relationship with the holy, a relationship that must include both the non-rational 'personal assurance' and the rational 'principles', provided that both the non-rational and rational are *a priori*. In this section and in many others throughout the book, Otto has a preconceived notion of what is essential or best in religion, and perhaps not surprisingly when judged by his criterion Christianity, in this as in other respects, is always seen as superior to other religions.

The difference in approach and methodology between the theologian and the student of religion is clearly demonstrated in Otto's work. It is seen in the quotation just presented and in more developed form in the penultimate section of the book in which he discusses the basis of comparative religion and the reasons for such a study:

> This is what must be borne in mind in the comparison of religions, when we seek to decide which of them is the most perfect. The criterion of the value of a religion cannot ultimately be found in what it has done for culture, nor in its relation to the 'limits of reason' or the 'limits of humanity' (which, forsooth, are presumed capable of being drawn in advance apart from reference to religion itself!), nor in any of its external features. It can only be found in what is the innermost essence of religion, the idea of holiness as such, and in this perfection with which any given religion realises this. (1958: 173)

Aside from the fact that this perfection is clearly presumed to be found only in Christianity – viz., 'Christian religious feeling has given birth to a religious intuition profounder and more vital than any to be found in the whole history of religion' (1958, 173) – there are several differences in approach from the work of prior and concurrent scholars. The most significant of these is the search for the most perfect exemplar. Although nineteenth- and early twentieth-century scholars may have had similar evolutionary and ethnocentric perspectives, as discussed above, most approaches to religion, particularly comparative approaches, are not qualitatively comparing the phenomena under analysis. Rather the comparative method is meant to highlight the similarities and differences, and attempt to explain the basis of those differences.

A second key area of difference with most perspectives, other than phenomenology, is the essentialist nature of his argument. He contends that religion cannot be analysed in terms of rationality, ethics or any other societal function, because these can be analysed in relation to non-religious aspects of culture as well. According to Otto, religion can only be analysed in terms of its unique non-rational element. Most modern approaches to religion do not essentialise it to this degree; anthropology, for example, examines all elements of religion in relation to their cultural context. If religion is to be analysed, it can not be defined as unique – its uniqueness must arise from the analysis and cannot be motivated by a presupposed non-rational transcendental other.

As a work of theology, Otto's work, from the perspective of religious studies, is a source of data. It is not an analysis of religion, it is a particular insider's view of religion, based on his own religious experience and beliefs. As a set of data it could be placed in its context and analysed historically or sociologically in that context. If, however, it is examined as a work within the academic framework of the study of religion it highlights several problems. It bases its analysis on the necessary existence of an unobservable transcendental other. While such a transcendental other may or may not exist, it cannot serve as an explanatory basis because it is unobservable and therefore not amenable to social scientific analysis. Its existence and the conceptions relating to it arise solely from individual experiences and faith. Belief that it exists and experience of it form part of the data rather than part of the analysis. Otto compounds this problem by suggesting that only someone who has had this experience would be able to understand his work. A good analysis of any subject must at some level be understandable even by someone who has not shared the experience.

Otto's work is also intrinsically evolutionary and ethnocentric. Based on his own theological presuppositions and beliefs, which are untestable, he establishes a comparative analysis in which his understanding of Christianity is the basis upon which all other religions are tested. Not surprisingly, as we have seen, Christianity always is superior.

Otto's work, however, has served as the basis for many of the thinkers in the phenomenological school. They have taken up his concept of the holy, the ineffable religious experience, as the unifying feature of religion. This unifying feature has allowed them to see religion as something separable from its societal context, needing unique methods of study and analysis. It also underlies a theme, set in motion before Otto by Max Müller, which sees the role of the study of religion as working towards the development of a new unified and essential form of religion. This theme is expressed in a less theological way in the concept of history of religion, that is religion in the abstract, as opposed to history of religions, which traces the individual trajectory of different religions.

– INTERIM CONCLUSIONS –

In this section we have introduced many of the significant themes that underlie the modern scholarly discussion of religion and distinguish it from theological discussions of religion. In a sense, a number of dichotomies can be distinguished in relation to the theories discussed thus far: insider/outsider, essentialist/reductionist, individual/society, evolutionist/relativist. Each of these dichotomies has been developed in different ways in the theories of religion developed throughout the twentieth century.

The insider/outsider dichotomy has been the basis for the distinction between theology and the study of religion/s. Theologians are seen or see themselves as insiders speaking about their own experiences or understandings, from the perspective of their own faith and beliefs. The study of religion is seen as an outsider's perspective, with religion examined as an objective phenomenon, with which the student has no subjective relationship. Within the study of religion this dichotomy has also been specifically emphasised in the phenomenological approach's attempt to distinguish itself from the other social scientific approaches. Many phenomenologists have argued that the only way to understand religion is from its (the religion's) own perspective and that any external model of analysis is by definition reductionist and automatically denies the possibility that there might be truth in the insider position. Despite the fact that many sociological, psychological, and anthropological approaches denied any value to the insider approach and were perceived as imposing an external model on the data, many more recent discussions have sought to validate the insider view, while also maintaining an analytical framework in relation to it. If the insider view is the only view presented we move from analysis to description and religious studies to theology.

The essentialist/reductionist like the insider/outsider dichotomy also separates theology from the study of religion. Theologians, who see religion as arising from some type of relation with the transcendent, almost by definition, see it as distinct from other societal phenomena. Although they might accept that religion serves other social functions, these are secondary. This dichotomy, however, is also found within the study of religion, primarily, though not exclusively, between phenomenology and the other sub-disciplines. As suggested above, many phenomenologists see religion as a unique phenomenon, separable from other cultural constructs. They may distinguish religion in this way because it relates to a unique faculty of the mind, a unique area of human experience, or following Otto, accept that underlying religion is a fundamental and unique experience of a transcendental other. On the basis of this type of essentialist characterisation, they argue that religion has a history separable from the history of particular religions and particular cultures. Due to this essentialist approach they argue that methods developed for the study of other cultural constructs are not appropriate for the study of religion – it must have its own unique methodologies. The other sub-disciplines have historically tended to view religion as culturally or psychologically contextualised and have thus tended to be reductionist, viewing religion, for example, as a product of psychological needs or specific societal needs. In some cases, however, non-phenomenological approaches have been critiqued as reductionist for arguing that religion is, or the study of religion relates to, a human construct rather than accepting or analysing the possibility of an actual supernatural or transcendental basis.

In challenging the form of essentialism found in Otto and other similar approaches we are not by definition challenging essentialism. As suggested above, another variation on essentialism is found in the psychological theories, which see religion and other social institutions, indeed all of culture, as arising from psychological structures of mind that are the common biological inheritance of all humanity. This form of essentialism seems to be more defendable, provided that it does not attempt to introduce content as well as structure.

The dichotomy of individual/society is found both within theology and the study of religion rather than distinguishing between them. The essential element of the argument rests on whether religion emerges from some type of individual experience or that it emerges in response to some aspect of society. The psychological approaches are good examples of the individual side of the dichotomy. In both Freud and Jung, religion centres on elements of the psyche, the unconscious in Freud and the interaction of the individual with the collective unconscious in Jung. The individual element is also found in Otto, with true religion ultimately being based on an individual experience of the holy. The societal side of the dichotomy is illustrated by Durkheim's concept that religion arises as a response to the beginnings of society, with god being an embodiment of society. Although many modern theories continue to emphasise one or other side, theorists are increasingly interested in seeing how the two levels relate to each other rather than seeing them as almost mutually exclusive.

The dichotomy of evolution/relativism is best exemplified regarding the evolutionary perspective by the theorists discussed thus far. Almost all of the thinkers were influenced by nineteenth-century ideas of unilinear evolution. Weber is the only thinker to move in a significantly different direction; he begins to intrude on the model of multilinear evolution, an approach also found in some of the more sophisticated materialist approaches. We have already highlighted some of the problems associated with the unilinear model. Most twentieth-century theories have tended to move more towards a limited relativist position, seeing each religion or culture as having its own trajectory of development. The major exception is those theories that attempt to discover an overall pattern in the development of religion. There is, however, one additional exception, that is, those theorists who argue for the progressive movement towards secularisation. Although many of these theorists are not explicitly evolutionary, the view that cultures increasingly move towards secularisation as they modernise is intrinsically evolutionary.

PART II

Continuing the Discussion

Introduction

Part II takes up the major issues addressed by the volume, that is, modern theories of religion. Each of the chapters focuses on one of the major theoretical approaches to the subject. We make no attempt to cover all theories or thinkers. Rather, we have selected some of the most significant, particularly those that exemplify the aspects of the approach in general. While we are interested in the specific aspects of the theories, we are also and perhaps more importantly interested in examining the underlying argumentative basis for the theories. The analysis of the varying argumentative bases for an essential element is one of the significant themes of the volume as a whole, that is, the problematisation of the term religion and of definitions of religion.

Many of the dichotomies highlighted in the conclusion of Part I highlight the debates that underlie debates developed in this part: insider/outsider, essentialist/reductionist, individual/society, and evolutionist/relativist. The inside aspect of the insider/outsider dichotomy is perhaps the most fundamental aspect of the phenomenological approach. Although the approach does not claim to be written by insiders or to be a recapitulation of a theological statement, it does claim to be the most accurate and direct representation of the insider point of view. As will be discussed, this self-characterisation seems to be an inaccurate representation of the material produced by the forms of analysis associated with phenomenology. The womanist aspect of the Feminist approach also claims to represent an insider point of view. In doing so, however, it eschews the possibility of critically interacting with the culture of institutions it discusses. Most of the other approaches emphasise the outsider aspect of the dichotomy. Interestingly, many ethnographic descriptions of religion, although based on an external theoretical framework, seem to take more account of insider understanding than do phenomenologists.

The essentialist/reductionist dichotomy also characterises a clear distinction between the phenomenological approaches and many of the other approaches discussed here. The phenomenological approaches claim that religion is some thing essentially different than other cultural objects and must be understood holistically and using theories that are defined in relation to it. The other approaches discussed, though occasionally having essentialist aspects to their definitions (as for example do most of the psychological approaches), tend to see religion as part of a broader social context and analysable using the tools developed to discuss other cultural constructs – these other approaches are seen by phenomenologists as reducing religion to having a function in relation to the individual or society, or reducible to some aspect of our psychological experience.

The debate respecting the individual and society is most clearly found between the psychological and most of the other theoretical approaches. The issues underlying this debate relate in part to the perceived functions and origins of religion. The psychological approaches often see religion as emerging from either a biological aspect or psychological complex of the individual – and argue for its universality on the basis of the physic unity of humanity. Other approaches emphasise the institutional aspects of religion and thereby function, origin or persistence in relation to different categories of groups.

The final dichotomy of evolutionist/relativist is largely redundant in the twentieth century. Most approaches have largely done away with the more problematic aspects of the evolutionary side of the debate. As indicated in the discussion, however, some theories do retain evolutionist undertones – as for example does the secularisation theory in sociology. The relativist side of the debate, however, has not fully won the day. Many approaches retain aspects of ethnocentrism. Perhaps the very exercise of defining religion or anything is intrinsically ethnocentric. The persistent theme in this volume of challenging and problematising definitions is an attempt to argue for a more relativistic approach.

CHAPTER 6

Sociology, Methodological Atheism and Secularisation

Sociological approaches to religion derive from a wide range of theoretical precursors: these include Marx, Weber and Durkheim, as well as other figures from the anthropological, economic and psychological traditions. Although due to their different presuppositions these approaches develop very different analyses, at least until recently most sociological approaches shared certain basic presuppositions. The discussion presented here attempts to highlight some of these presuppositions by examining three different areas of sociological discussion of religion.

The first and most important part of the chapter develops some of the significant theories of religion. These theories, while all sharing some aspects of the functionalist tradition, inherited from Durkheim and Weber, focus on different aspects of human social behaviour. The first group of theories is specifically functionalist, seeing religion as a social institution that exists to fill either individual or social needs.

The second type of theory focuses specifically on religion's role in relation to meaning and the validation of cognitive systems. The final approach, rational choice, while including these elements of functionality, focuses on the social process of exchange of rewards and costs as the basis for religion and other forms of social action. The last two sections of the chapter develop two areas of sociological theorising. The discussion of secularisation draws its inspiration from the Enlightenment and positivist ideas of human knowledge. Depending on the significance of the functions attributed to religion, different thinkers argue either for or against the rise in secularisation. The final section takes up some aspects of the Weberian methodology of categorisation and ideal types, examining theories concerning the roles of sects within religious structures.

Perhaps the most fundamental of these presuppositions underlying the sociological approaches is the relationship between religion and society. Most sociologists and anthropologists see religion as a social institution that develops in relation to its societal setting. Thus, religion like any form of knowledge is socially constructed and can only be properly understood in relation to its social context. This implies that religion should not be seen as something that is *sui generis*, that is, which is essential, universal, and separable from its particular social context. In this sense, most sociologists of religion can be theoretically distinguished from religious phenomenologists and psychologists who have generally argued from a more essentialist understanding. The constructivist approach suggests that religion must be understood using theories applicable to other social institutions, beliefs and practices, as well as being analysed in relation to those other institutions, beliefs and practices.

A second methodological approach that is shared by most sociologists is 'methodological atheism' or 'agnosticism'. This approach argues that for the purposes of sociological analysis any claims for the divine or supernatural status of a religion or religious object should be put on one side and human, social origin should be assumed. The claims made by the believers themselves about the status of their religion or religious objects should be seen as data to be studied rather than as an authoritative statement about the nature of the object under study. The analyst must assume that the object being studied is a social rather than divine product. As such, religion can be analysed and understood in terms of approaches used to study any human institution. Some have argued that 'methodological atheism' has given way in many sociologists to 'substantive atheism'. Indeed, many sociologists do seem hostile to religion and use different evolutionary models to suggest that religion is a stage of human understanding that will not withstand the challenges of science and modernisation.

Although an approach based on 'methodological atheism' may be used as a means of denying validity to any internal models of explanation, this is not a necessary implication. While this approach clearly brackets off supernatural origin or status, there is no necessary reason why other forms of internal explanation cannot be examined. An internal explanation can be tested for validity in the same way as sociological explanations can be tested.

Methodological atheism should also specifically not be a statement about the truth claims of a particular religion. It merely states that for the purposes of study such truth claims are not relevant, primarily because they are not testable using the methodologies of social scientific analysis. The search for humanistic explanations of religious beliefs and practices is not necessarily a denial of supernatural explanations. The human social explanations are the province of sociologists; the supernatural or transcendental explanations are that of theologians or religious practitioners.

As suggested above, sociologists have followed many different theoretical paths in analysing the role of religion in society and its relation to that society. One of the most influential theoretical approaches during much of the twentieth century was that of functionalism. This approach to culture in general and religion in particular is associated with the work of Durkheim (see above) and is further developed by Parsons and Merton. The functionalist method of explanation, which seeks to determine the functional roles which particular beliefs or practices play for the individual or society have been developed in a number of ways; some have carried on the societal emphasis found in Durkheim and Radcliffe-Brown, for example Kingsley Davis, and others the more individual, psychological approach of Malinowski, as in the work of Milton Yinger and to some extent Bryan Wilson. Robert Bellah, discussed between these two types of functionalist approaches, to some extent links them, suggesting that the societal and individual arguments relate, at least in part, to different levels of societal evolution.

Kingsley Davis, in a text book attempting to cover all aspects of human society, *Human Society* (1948), presents a structural-functionalist definition of religion that has much in common with the anthropological structural-functionalists, particularly Radcliffe-Brown (discussed above in the chapter on Durkheim and Functionalism). His approach emphasises that society must be examined from an holistic perspective – with each part functioning in relation to and for the whole of society. Specific institutions must be explained in terms of the role they play in 'satisfying societal needs' (Davis, 1948: 519).

Like Radcliffe-Brown and his other structural-functional predecessors, Davis argues that cohesion is the primary societal need. The best way of fulfilling this function is sentiment and that such sentiments work better if they are not understood than if they are. Religion is the means by which such sentiments are validated. One of the areas of societal cohesion in which religion plays a significant role is the rejection of private individual ends (goals or desires) in favour of societal ends. The belief in the super-natural realm, religion, inculcates the value of these group ends through its collective rituals, concepts of values, and supernatural consequences and rewards. This discussion reveals the major thread of the model of functionalism employed by Davis; it is a model in which societal functions and needs are of primary interest and value. This does not mean that Davis is unaware of the role or functions that religion plays for the individual, as for example how it helps integrate the personality; these functions are, however, clearly of secondary importance.

Robert Bellah in 'Religious Evolution' (1964) brings together both a functionalist definition and an evolutionary model, which owes much to debates at the conclusion of the nineteenth century. He opens his discussion with a relatively simple definition of religion, that is, that religion is a symbolic means of allowing individuals to understand or relate to 'ultimate conditions'.

His system of evolution specifically focuses at the development of this symbolic system rather than the ability of people to be religious or the nature of the ultimate conditions. Although he believes that it is possible to make qualitative judgments about these systems, he does not believe that more evolved systems are necessarily better than the less evolved. His evolutionary model, however, against the trend of contemporary evolutionary theories is unilinear, tracing one line of development rather than multilinear, tracing many possible lines of development. The model traces five stages in the development of religion from 'primitive religion' to 'modern religion'. A key feature of his evolutionary model, in a similar vein to Durkheim, is that of increasing complexity and specialisation. These themes are taken up by many of the other sociological models discussed below; this is particularly true in models of secularisation, which are intrinsically evolutionary models.

'World rejection' is one of the key themes in Bellah's argument. This refers to those aspects of religion or the religions themselves that reject this world in favour of some type of spiritual world. This concept becomes significant with Plato and the rise of the 'world religions' and plays a major role in the history of religion as a whole. He suggests, however, that it is not present in 'primitive religions'. His discussion of this level is similar to that proposed by the theory of 'primal religions' discussed at the conclusion of the chapter on the phenomenological approaches. Bellah argues that 'primitive religions' are not world rejecting, in fact they do not distinguish between the natural and the supernatural. They are specifically goal-oriented, for example fertility or rain. Religion for them is particularly focused on these ends and functions to assure them of the successful achievement of these ends. Based on his view of complexity, he suggests that neither, myth, ritual nor religious organisation are differentiated from other aspects of social behaviour. Following Durkheim, Bellah views religion as ultimately serving as a mechanism for social solidarity.

As Bellah moves through his evolutionary model, each level becomes progressively more complex, with religion increasingly differentiated from other spheres of social action. Thus, in 'archaic systems' mythical beings are no longer identified with, but rather are objectified and distanced from ordinary human action. Priestly roles are increasingly distinguished and formalised. The progresses through 'historic religion' and 'early modern religion', culminating in 'modern religion'. 'Modern religion' is characterised by a complex symbolic system, with the removal of religious monopolies and an increasing personalisation of religious symbolism. Unlike the secularisation theorists, Bellah sees this process as one in which individuals become increasingly responsible for making their own religious decisions in response to ultimate issues. At each level of development, Bellah argues that there is an increase in freedom, and that in part the function of religion is related to the maintenance and enhancement of that freedom.

Milton Yinger in *The Scientific Study of Religion* (1970) also argues for the use of a functional definition of religion. He argues that rather than defining religion in terms of essence, a better form of definition would focus on process (1970: 5). He justifies this by suggesting that a functionalist approach is useful both in respect to comparative analysis, and to the analysis of the role that religion plays within society. He also suggests, somewhat differently from his predecessors, that such an analysis should work on three levels: culture – norms that shape behaviour, character – the individual level, and society – the patterned interaction of relationships. If these three elements are kept in mind it is clear why a functionalist definition is necessary, a statement of essence would not address any of these issues. He also adds a caveat to the definition, 'religion is an effort (not always successful) to perform certain functions' (Yinger, 1970: 6). This caveat prevents us from automatically defining out religious traditions that do not seem to fulfill the assumed functions.

Yinger draws his definition of the specific functions of religion from both theologians, for example, Paul Tillich, and sociologists, for example, Robert Bellah. Both thinkers, as indicated above regarding Robert Bellah, point to the issues of ultimate concern to humanity as the basis of religion. Yinger, in attempting to define what the ultimate concerns are, focuses on the individual's response to existential issues. These issues include a need to understand the fact of death, suffering, understanding itself, and the need to control our own passions. Of these issues, only the last serves an instrumental purpose in relation to society. Yinger suggests that ultimately religion is rooted not in intellectual questioning and the rationalising process, but rather in the emotional need to respond to these fundamental issues.

Yinger's formal definition of religion adds the social dimension much more firmly into this mix:

> Religion, then, can be defined as a system of beliefs and practices by means of which a group of people struggles with these ultimate problems of human life. It expresses their refusal to capitulate to death, to give up in the face of frustration, to allow hostility to tear apart their human associations. The quality of being

religious, seen from the individual point of view, implies two things: first, a belief that evil, pain, bewilderment and injustice are fundamental facts of existence; and, second, a set of practices and related sanctified beliefs that express a conviction than man can ultimately be saved from those facts. (Yinger, 1970: 7).

Yinger's definition emphasises that the individual existential experiences are ultimately responded to at the level of society, and that salvation or a model of it is the functional response to these existential problems. Yinger, rejecting the secularisation thesis espoused by many other sociologists (discussed below), argues that this essential function is a necessary part of any society because the existential issues are universal. Thus, although religion will of necessity change over time, as its functions will always persist so too will it be found in all societies no matter how modern or rational.

Yinger picks up several issues that arise from a functionalist definition that are more generally applicable. Raising one of the fundamental problems associated with this type of definition, that is, of where the boundaries of the phenomena can be drawn given that many institutions or practices may share the same or similar functions, he asks whether private practices or beliefs could be considered to be religion? He responds to this question in the negative. Like other sociologists and anthropologists, he argues that religion is a phenomena associated with society or a group within society. He follows Parsons in suggesting that the feelings that are addressed by religion, although individual (in the sense of character) arise only in a social context and thus religion arises solely in a social context. He also addresses the question of whether non-theistic systems are religions? Based on his functionalist approach, these systems do not pose a significant problem; they are only defined out if the definition focuses on specific beliefs rather than the issue of believing.

Bryan Wilson in *Religion in Sociological Perspective* (1962) explores the function of religion in similar terms to those deployed by Yinger. Wilson, however, also reintroduces into the argument the distinction between manifest and latent functions. As indicated above, in the discussion of Merton, manifest functions are those that are the conscious intent of the belief or ritual, or the conscious explanation of the religious object by those within the believing community. The latent function is that which is attributed to the religious object by the external observer.

Wilson suggests that the 'explicit and manifest function of religion is to offer men (sic) the prospect of salvation' (1962: 27). Thus salvation, in whatever form it is constituted in different cultures, is the primary, manifest function of religion. Salvation can resolve the problems of death through some form of eternal life or reincarnation, or in societies in which death is not problematic it can resolve problems of evil and suffering in this life. Wilson does include in this concept an evolutionary underpinning; he suggests that 'higher religions' utilise spiritual forms of salvation, that is, forms which remove salvation from the testable, empirical realm of experience; while 'lower' religions utilise 'articularistic' forms of salvation, that is salvation from specific ills, the success or failure of which is observable (Wilson, 1962: 29). The significant feature of salvation for the sociologist, he suggests, is that it provides assurance against anxiety. His discussion focuses on the individual psychological needs for assurance and resolution of suffering.

At the latent level of function Wilson moves closer to the societal role of religion. He highlights a number of different latent functions that have been identified by sociologists in relation to traditional societies. First, religion has the role of validating society and societal structures. His use of this argument is closer to that of Malinowski than Durkheim. He is not suggesting that religion is a reflection of society; rather that religion is a charter for society. Second, Wilson suggests that religion helps groups define or set boundaries for themselves. Religions are particularly important in this regard as placing the group or individual within an eternal and divinely sanctioned framework. Third, religion serves to regulate emotion. It provides a strong means of social control and thereby allows society or groups to function. Wilson also addresses the question of whether these latent functions continue to be present in 'advanced societies'. He concludes that although these latent functions may have been significant in other forms of society, they are no longer significant for contemporary societies. In these societies all of these roles are either absent or filled by other forms of social institution. We shall return to this aspect of Wilson's argument and his concept of rationalisation in the discussion of secularisation theories towards the end of this chapter.

The explicit functionalists examined here are only a small subset of a significant trend in the sociological analysis of religion. Although their analyses are generally geared towards very different forms of society than examined by the functionalist within the anthropological tradition, they share many of the same presuppositions and problems (see the discussion in the chapter on Durkheim and Functionalism). The problems are even more clearly highlighted in the work of some sociologists who demonstrate both functions and dysfunctions of religion, leaving the reader to ask if the two effectively balance; can function really be an explanation for the existence and persistence of religious practices? As discussed above, the functionalism ultimately can only serve as a partial analysis; its form of circular reasoning (an institution has a specific function, and that function is then used to explain the existence of the institution) undermines its utility as a comprehensive explanation of social action.

There is, however, a significant difference between most anthropological functionalists and the sociological functionalists, that is, the sociological approaches' strong evolutionary bias, which is particularly evident in Wilson's analysis. This evolutionary presupposition, as suggested below, is a primary feature of the secularisation model, which clearly assumes that as society gets more rational, religion will cease to have a place; and, that this process of rationalisation is a normative part of societal development. It is perhaps significant that sociology has not strongly articulated the concept of cultural relativism, a concept which until recently was a significant foundation stone of anthropology. This allows sociologists to build their general bias against religion, moving towards substantive rather than methodological atheism, into their analytical models.

Peter Berger represents a much more creative and innovative approach to religion. His work develops an aspect of Weber's analysis, that is, the social construction of religion, and the ideological interrelationship between religion and society. It takes as its starting point the problem of meaning, and uses it as the basis for the interrelated construction of both society and the individual. Berger's approach develops the distinction between two aspects of religion in relation to meaning, 'religion and world-construction', that is, the extension of meaning into the world and cosmos, and 'religion and world-maintenance', the legitimisation and preservation of those systems of meaning, particularly society and its institutions.

The first of these concepts develops the significant role that religion plays as part of in society in constructing the world in which we live. The key aspect of this concept is that humans, perhaps by definition, give or impose order, which Berger refers to as *nomos*, onto the world. This order, or an aspect of it in society, is at one and the same time created by people, and equally it shapes people's very perception of their existence.

The relationship between these two elements is dialectical – with a three-stage process, 'externalisation, objectivation, and internalisation' (Berger, 1967: 4). The externalisation process is one through which we impose order upon the world. This order derives from the human brain or human action and is not intrinsic to the world. Through the second process, objectivation, the ordered objects are given objective reality, that is their order is perceived to be a given, rather than something subjectively created by people. The third process, internalisation, is one in which the external objectified order is internalised, that is, taken into our consciousness and in effect shapes that consciousness on the basis of the ordering principle. An essential aspect of all three of these processes is that they are essentially social, and function through a process of socialisation.

Berger argues that society is both an expression of order and a creator of order on the individual level – this order is necessary for the existence of society and ultimately the existence of the individual. As part of the objectivation process, society and the order it represents needs to be seen as a given, that is, it must be taken for granted. This is achieved to some extent through the process of socialisation, through which we make natural aspects of our socially constructed universe; race, for example, is a cultural construct that is assumed to be a biological given. These are limited and do not provide a fundamental basis for the *nomos*. Religion is the extension of this process to the very nature of existence and the cosmos, and thus an even more significant means of objectivation. Religion, in its world-building role, is the extension of order onto the very cosmos itself. The 'sacred cosmos' established by this process is then objectified and re-internalised as the objective, sacred order of reality.

Religion thus serves to create an ordered cosmos, and thereby extends the order that underpins society into the 'totality of being' (Berger, 1967: 32). It also serves to maintain and legitimise the social order. Social order, or society, is inherently precarious, owing to individual needs, motivations, and desires. In order to maintain itself, society develops different means of legitimising its institutions and the social order they represent. Religion is a particularly effective tool for legitimisation as by definition it presents a relationship between the social order and the cosmic order – suggesting that the limited human order has its basis in ultimate reality. He states:

> Religion legitimates social institutions by bestowing upon them an ultimately valid ontological status, that is, by locating them within a sacred and cosmic frame of reference. The historical creations of human activity are viewed from a vantage point that, in its own self-definition, transcends both history and man. (Berger, 1967: 34)

Religion, therefore, through its externalisation of societal order unto the cosmos, legitimises society because society reflects that same order.

Berger's discussion also suggests an important relationship between this legitimisation process and religious activity. Unlike the idealists, Berger is not arguing for the primacy of ideas, and therefore theologies, rather he places the emphasis on religious practice. He suggests that religion is rooted in everyday life (Berger, 1967: 41). Therefore most of the issues that it legitimises are related to everyday activity rather than the theological constructs of the experts. His argument suggests that there is an inter-relationship between legitimisation and activity; legitimisation arises, at least for the most part, from living and acting rather than thinking.

Berger's arguments present a very sophisticated variant on aspects of Weber and Durkheim. The significant points of relationship are found in the view that humans are driven by the need to find or impose meaning on experience, the connection between societal order and cosmic or religious order, that is, that religion is an externalisation of society and its order, and, in the dialectical relationship between the individual and society. The arguments also develop some aspects of Marxist analysis in the discussion of the legitimising role of religion. The arguments also contain an aspect of functionalism, in suggesting that religion arises to fill a basic human need, that is, to order or perceive order. Many similar aspects are found in the work of Clifford Geertz; his work is discussed in the chapter on anthropological approaches to religion. Berger and Geertz, as well as Luckmann, can be challenged for over emphasising the role of cognition in religion and society.

Thomas Luckmann's work is closely associated with that of Berger and shares many of the same presuppositions. Luckmann's work, however, even more strongly emphasises the role of religion. This emphasis is foreshadowed in the introduction to *The Invisible Religion* in which Luckmann, referring to both Weber and Durkheim suggests: 'the problem of the individual existence in society is a religious problem (Luckmann, 1967: 12). He argues that there is a convergence in the sociological thought of Weber and Durkheim, which sees the understanding the individual in society as emerging from the study of religion.

One of the significant argumentative moves, which Luckmann makes, is the deconstruction of the association between religion and church or religious institution. He suggests that this association, and the empirical decline of attendance at these public institutions, has led sociologists to assume a progressive decline in religion and the advance of secularisation. Sociologists, he suggests, see churches as 'islands of religion (or irrationality)' in an increasingly secularised world (Luckmann, 1967: 23). Luckmann, however, argues that religion is not coextensive with its institutional form, but has a much wider basis in society – he suggests that religion is rather 'the conditions under which "transcendent", superordinated and "integrating" structures are socially objectivated' (Luckmann, 1967: 26). In other words religion is a broad category of phenomena that locate the individual in society.

Luckmann, in deconstructing this association, is suggesting that while institutions are an example of religious behaviour, they do not constitute the whole of religion, and in fact, an important question which needs to be addressed is that of the nature of religion prior to becoming institutionalised and how and why it became institutionalised? These questions become significant in relation to Luckmann's understanding of religion. Religion is directly associated with 'symbolic universes' of meaning that join together 'everyday life' and the transcendent or religious cosmos (Luckmann, 1967: 43). Luckmann's arguments suggest that religion and social life are in many senses identical.

Luckmann's discussion of the nature of symbolic universes shares many features with Berger's arguments. Luckmann suggests that they are 'objectified meaning systems', that is, they are human models, which are externalised and considered to have objective reality. The difference between religion and other 'systems of meaning' is that it is associated with the transcendent. The process through which all meaning systems are created is that of self-awareness, the consciousness of the self – which is understood to be a uniquely human process, through which human beings transcend their biological nature. For Luckmann this consciousness can only arise in society, consciousness of the self depends on awareness of others. Thus, religion as a system of meaning, is necessarily social, though not institutional in origin (Luckmann, 1967: 44).

Luckmann's discussion places religion at the heart of this process of social and individual consciousness. He suggests that the processes out of which the self emerges are religious in nature (Luckmann, 1967: 49). This process is the source of religion; it is the basis upon which, based on historical circumstances, the institutions of religion are constructed.

Luckmann is not suggesting that this process occurs on an individual basis. He recognises that individuals are born into societies that have constructed sacred universes and worldviews. These worldviews are passed on to children through socialisation, and become the basis through which the individual becomes a person both on a social and individual basis. Luckmann's discussion of this process mirrors Berger's analysis of internalisation – the worldview, which is perceived as objective, becomes the basis for individual subjective action in the world.

Luckmann's analysis, while sharing certain problems with Berger's approach, most notably the over emphasis on meaning and the latent functionalism, also has certain problems of its own. The most significant of these is the association of religion with the development of self-awareness, and perhaps all social existence. At one level, it is problematic because the various terms lose any analytical value. If all social life is religious, then religion is no longer a category that can be discussed or meaningfully compared. This association is also problematic because it does not seem to have any argumentative basis. There is no clear reason why this process should be considered religious except for the possibility that it underlies the development of religious meaning systems (or meaning systems which he defines as religious); it also underlies meaning systems that would not be identified as religious.

Rational choice theory moves in a very different direction than that proposed by the sociological theories discussed thus far. It does, however, address many of the same questions, particularly the issue of secularisation that has interested sociologists since the beginning of the twentieth century. The major proponents of the approach, Stark and Bainbridge, developed the rudiments of the theory in several works including *The Future of Religion* published in 1985. Stark and Bainbridge's theory attempts to link a comprehensive theory of religious action or choices with a general theory of human action and choices. They state:

> We are launched on the immodest task of constructing a general theory of religion. We propose to deduce from a small set of axioms about what humans are like and how they behave, and from a larger number of definitions, a series of propositions explaining why religions exist, how they originate, how religious movements are transformed – indeed, answers to the whole list of classic questions. (Stark and Bainbridge, 1980: 114)

Religion as a category of human action can thus be understood in the same terms as other forms of behaviour. Their claim is that they are deploying a deductive theory, which based on a few axioms can derive through logical deduction more complex propositions.

Due to the limitations of space we will touch only on some of the more indicative of the axioms upon which their theory is based. The most significant of these is that human behaviour is shaped by rewards and costs – a basic principle of exchange theory; humans seek rewards and avoid costs. People will, however, accept a cost if they perceive it as leading to a reward of greater value. They also suggest that human behaviour is shaped by weighing of costs and rewards, for example, if there are two rewards people will choose the most valuable. These rewards can be understood in capitalist terms; rewards can be exchanged and people will seek to get the best rate of exchange. When rewards are unavailable people will accept compensators, which explain or promise future reward. The most significant of the compensators, general compensators, are beliefs or promises that compensate for a 'cluster of rewards' (Stark and Bainbridge, 1980: 121). Compensators are means of explaining why a reward is unavailable, giving some non-verifiable assurance of future reward, or explaining how a future reward might be attained. Compensators cover a wide range; they include resolutions of the problem of death, the hereafter is a promise of future reward, the truth of which cannot be determined and hence it is a compensator rather than a reward. Promises or models of salvation are also good examples of religious compensators.

Religion arises from the last of these propositions. The most 'general of compensators' need to be supported by the supernatural. Only a supernatural compensator could explain the problem of death or the purpose of life. Thus, they argue, since these compensators are a necessary feature of human behaviour, based on the exchange model, and since there will always be rewards that are unattainable, religion will exist in every form of society. The defining characteristic of religion, they suggest, is that it is a system of compensators that relies on the supernatural. This aspect of their argument specifically addresses those definitions that are wide enough to include political ideologies or science. They suggest that such definitions blur the significant differences and conflicts between these very different social constructs. The use of general compensators as opposed to more limited areas of compensation also allows them to maintain the theoretical distinction between religion and magic.

Thus far they have demonstrated the necessity of religion, as a system of general compensation in society – a system that provides explanations and replacements for significant rewards that are unavailable. Following their economic paradigm, they argue that where a product exists, enterprises will develop to sell that product. Religions and religious institutions are the producers and merchandisers of this social product. Their argument also introduces the aspect of power, which as they suggest has some Marxist overtones. Those with social power will have greater access to real rewards, and thus will be less interested in religious compensation, while those with little or no power, and thus little access to real rewards, will be more accepting of compensators. In spite of this power principle, they also suggest that since some rewards are beyond the reach of even the most powerful, all members of society will have an interest in these compensators – this has a clear relationship with the functionalist argument about the role of religion in resolving existential problems.

If these principles are taken together we can draw a number of conclusions. First, religion, as compensation for things that are outside our reach or understanding, will exist in all societies. Second, religion as a system of supernatural and general compensators is distinct from non-supernatural ideologies on the one hand and magic on the other (magic has specific limited ends and thus is not a form of general compensation). Third, individuals without power will develop specific forms of religion which will compensate for their inability to gain access to the goods of society. Fourth, all members of society, even the most powerful, will require some form of religion. These are only a simplified and summarised exemplification of their approach; they argue that this exchange model can explain every aspect of religious behaviour. We will address certain applications of the theory in the discussion of secularisation below.

The rational choice has a number of logical inconsistencies. Many of these have been addressed in an article, 'The Stark-Bainbridge Theory of Religion: A Critical Analysis and Counter Proposals' by Roy Wallis and Steve Bruce (1984). The first logical problem is in relation to the status of compensators and rewards. Wallis and Bruce suggest that the distinction between the two is problematic. If the internal distinction between rewards and compensations is understood to be based on reality, then it assumes that the people accepting the compensation are aware that it is not a reality. If they accepted it as a reality, it would be a reward rather than compensation. Equally they argue, if compensators are explanations of how to gain a reward, how can this be seen as compensation? Compensation and explanation are not the same. An explanation for how to gain salvation might not be perceived as a reward, but it might be perceived as the sole way of gaining the reward. The concept of rewards is also problematic – the thesis seems to suggest that rewards must be material and tangible. Neither of these elements seems a necessary component. They also challenge a basic feature of compensators, that they are unverifiable whereas rewards are understood to be verifiable. They suggest that the issue of verification as explanation is far from clear cut even in the case of obtainable rewards, and has been challenged in recent scientific models (Wallis and Bruce, 1984: 13–15).

An additional question that can be addressed to rational choice theory is its basis in a capitalistic mode of discourse. The primary feature of the theory and its basic understanding of human behaviour rests in a model of exchange that is closely related to the capitalist model of exchange. It assumes that this model is intrinsic to human behaviour. It is possible to challenge this assumption on two levels. First, it is possible that the behaviour described is not intrinsic but arises from socialisation in capitalist, market societies. Behaviour in other social settings might have other modes of exchange or valuing rewards and costs. Second, it is possible that the Stark-Bainbridge hypothesis is an example of how economic structure shapes ideological constructs in order to validate those economic structures.

The theory is also more generally challengeable as a model of human behaviour. It assumes that human action is essentially rational. All of the choices they describe involve the balancing of different options and the attempt to choose the options that will lead to the highest reward either here or in the hereafter. Although they recognise that some of these choices might be made on the basis of false or unverifiable information, nonetheless the process is intrinsically rational (and based on a unitary model of human rationality). While much of human behaviour is rationally governed it is likely, as suggested by Freud and other psychological theorists, that aspects of our behaviour are not governed by conscious rationality, but are shaped by potentially non-rational aspects of personality. Thus, to focus solely on the rational aspects seems to be a rather incomplete picture of either human social behaviour or religion.

Danièle Hervieu-Léger takes up aspects of the debate about definition and secularisation in 'Religion as Memory' (1999). She suggests that definitions that set religion in opposition to modernity or rationality cannot be maintained, indeed with the proliferation of new forms of religion a definition or understanding of religion needs to be developed that shows that these modern manifestations, far from being incompatible with modernity, are directly related to processes within modernity: modernity both undermines religion while also creating the need for it.

In relation to these various forms of religion and religiosity that have proliferated in the modern world, Hervieu-Léger suggests the need for a new definition of religion that escapes the limitations of previous models. Her definition has two main elements. First, rather than focusing on substantive elements or functions, she focuses on an action, that of believing. She suggests, 'Religious believing can be usefully defined – in an ideal-typical manner – *as a particular modality of the organisation and function of the act of believing*' (Hervieu-Léger, 1999: 87). By focusing on the practice of believing, her model allows for transformation in the content and structure of religion and religious institution. She does, however, specifically differentiate belief from other modes of knowing, beliefs are those aspects of knowledge that we accept without the possibility or desire for verification. The second aspect of her argument is the proposition that such beliefs are grounded in a concept of tradition, what she calls a 'heritage of belief' (Hervieu-Léger, 1999: 89). This heritage of belief is understood and socially constituted through shared memory – she suggests that religious groups define themselves by means of a 'chain of memory' linking them to the past and projecting into the future. It is the process of transmission of these memories, creating and recreating them, that constitutes the basis for religion. Hervieu-Léger's model has some very significant points in its favour. It provides a basis for discussion that does not impose a specific content or qualitative judgment and it is applicable in any cultural setting. The aspects of belief and heritage, however, are somewhat troubling. By focusing on belief she makes an implicit distinction between scientific and religious practice and the concept of heritage or chain of memory may be too restrictive in relation to patterns of belief or modelling that do not look to tradition as the basis of their identity either in terms of belief or continuity.

– SECULARISATION –

Rational choice theory and other theoretical models can be examined in practice through their application to the question of secularisation. Secularisation, or the decline of religion in favour of secular models of explanation and social control, has been a significant concern for all sociological theorists and remains a subject of considerable debate. The process of secularisation was implicit in Marx's analysis, which saw religion as a reflection of alienation; with the eventual end of alienation so too would religion give way. Freud's analysis also emphasised the progressive move towards secularisation. It provides the main argument developed in *The Future of an Illusion*; he suggests that the move to progressively greater rationality provides the basis for the end of the psychological need for religion. Secularisation and the possibility of some form of civil religion is suggested by Durkheim.

Larry Shiner in 'The Concept of Secularisation in Empirical Research' (1967) outlines the history of the term 'religion', and more importantly presents six different definitions that underlie different sociological analyses. The first usage of the concept is the 'decline of religion'. This usage suggests that the different aspects of religion are progressively losing their significance and eventually religion will disappear. Examples of this type of definition include the increasing use of rational explanations in place of mythological explanations or the decreasing prestige of clergy (Shiner, 1967: 209). The second definition, 'conformity with this world', examines the focus of particular religious traditions. It suggests that as religions move their focus to worldly issues, the distinction between religion and other social institutions becomes progressively weaker (Shiner, 1967: 211). The third definition, 'disengagement of society from religion', assumes that at one time religion set the agenda for social action; religion was seen as providing the worldview or basis of both understanding and action. This view suggests that society is progressively taking over these roles, and becoming 'an autonomous reality'. Religion is relegated to the sphere of private spirituality and has little or no influence on institutions or society (Shiner, 1967: 212). The fourth definition, 'transposition of religious beliefs and institutions', focuses on the progressive transformation of institutions or beliefs that were once grounded in the divine to the social or secular sphere. One example suggested is the transformation of the religious messianic idea to the Marxist understanding of revolution (Shiner, 1967: 215). The fifth definition, 'the desacralisation of the world', refers to the advance of scientific modes of explanation; it points to the progressive use of scientific or rational models to explain things that were once the province of religion. This form of secularisation culminates in a world without room for mystery or the spiritual (Shiner, 1967: 216). The final usage, 'movement from a sacred to a secular society', focuses on the openness of society to change, suggesting that this openness will culminate in progressive reduction of the religious end of the polarity (Shiner, 1967: 216). Although Shiner concludes that the term religion is too variable to be useful, his analysis of the different meanings of the term is very useful for the discussion of some of the theories of secularisation.

Bryan Wilson's analysis of secularisation owes much to the Durkheimian and functionalist traditions. It focuses on the functional roles which religion played for society, and argues that these roles have either been weakened to such a degree that religion is no longer an effective means for providing them, or that other social institutions have taken over the roles once played by religion. A significant feature of his argument relies on Durkheim's analysis of differentiation. Durkheim had argued that as society develops religion is relegated to a progressively smaller field of play. Ultimately, with the rise of other specialised institutions taking over its functions, religion as such is effectively socially marginalised.

Wilson's argument works on three levels: the first in relation to rationalisation, the second, legitimisation and the third, social control. All of these levels relate to aspects of function. The first level is associated with the explanatory function. Religion once provided explanations for the world and the way the world works. With the rise of the scientific method, religion's explanatory role becomes increasingly marginalised. He states:

> The decline of western religion has been associated with the emergence of new and more powerful influences on the shape of western culture, in particular the two agencies that we have already mentioned: the growth of science and the development of the state. (Wilson, 1982: 80)

The growth of the state challenges an additional area of function, self-definition and legitimisation. Whereas once religion played these roles, in an increasingly rationalised society, this function can no longer be fulfilled by recourse to the transcendent, but instead has been transferred to the will of the people themselves.

The final area of functionality that has been reduced or removed is that of social control. In his discussion of the latent function of religions, social control played a prominent role. This function, however, depended on religious unity and authority. Religious unity, in order that the morals inculcated be shared, and authority, the ability to impose those values. With the rise of Protestantism and the fragmentation of religions in society neither of these elements was retained. Thus, religion no longer served to adequately underpin the moral order. In modern societies, Wilson suggests, this has led to a moral breakdown, or at the very least a much more individualised morality. In spite of his analysis, however, Wilson is troubled by this move towards secularisation – he suggests that the gains of rationalisation will not outweigh the losses to cultural diversity and richness. The functions once served by religion, particularly in relation to morality, may not be filled by any other institution (Wilson, 1982: 88).

Roy Wallis and Steve Bruce suggest a similar, though more developed, approach in 'Secularisation: the Orthodox Model' (1992). They suggest that modernisation can be subdivided into three main areas: 'social differentiation', 'societalisation' and 'rationalisation' (Wallis and Bruce, 1992: 9). They define secularisation as the 'diminishing social significance of religion' (Wallis and Bruce, 1992: 11). Interestingly, in spite of the fact that they offer a substantive definition of religion, what religion is rather than what religion does, their definition of secularisation is essentially functionalist: it is based on what religion does in relation to society. They define religion as:

> Actions, beliefs and institutions predicated upon the assumption of the exist-ence of either supernatural entities with powers of agency, or impersonal powers or processes possessed of moral purpose, which have the capacity to set the conditions of, or to intervene in, human affairs. Further, the central claims to the operation of such entities or impersonal powers are either not suscept-ible to, or are systematically protected from, refutation. (Wallis and Bruce, 1992: 11)

This definition argues that religion can be defined by specific content, that is, the supernatural and particular aspects of morality. The only argu-mentative basis for this inclusion is broad, contemporary common sense. Given that common sense is a cultural construct, belonging to a specific culture or subculture, and reflects specific ideological presuppositions, the use of this definition more broadly than the specific culture out of which it emerged is highly questionable. Its lack of analytical use, as suggested, is indicated by the fact that their analysis makes no use of it; rather, their definition focuses on the roles that religion played, for example, welfare, identity and explanation; that is, the basic elements of traditional func-tionalist explanations.

The concept of social differentiation develops Durkheim's thesis of the progressive differentiation of roles and institutions. Whereas religion once played a wide range of roles in society, for example, welfare, education, specialist institutions, relegating religion to a smaller realm of social significance eventually took up these roles (Wallis and Bruce, 1992: 12).

Societalisation refers to the progressive movement of society from processes of local control and organisation to central control and organisation. Since, they suggest, religion draws its power from the community, as the community loses significance so too does religion. This is specifically significant in respect to legitimisation and communal definition, significant features of religion, which are directly related to a local community (Wallis and Bruce, 1992: 13). The concept of rationalisation relates to the way people think. Citing the work of Weber and Berger, they suggest that this is a process through which there is an increasing use of rational patterns of thinking, as in the development of the scientific method. As rationalisation develops it increasingly encroaches on the sphere of religion, and provides better answers to the questions that were once the preserve of religious argumentation (Wallis and Bruce, 1992: 14). Each one of these elements develops aspects of Wilson's approach and ultimately rests on a functionalist interpretation of religion. Steve Bruce has repackaged many of these aspects with some additional theoretical elaboration in *God is Dead: Secularisation in the West* (2002).

Peter Berger stands on both sides of the secularisation debate. His original work presented a strong and influential argument in favour of the secularisation thesis, while in his more recent work he has moved in the opposite direction. We discuss Berger's arguments for the secularisation theory here, and those challenging it below. Berger's definition of secularisation is similar to Shiner's fourth type of definition (Berger, 1967: 107). Many of Berger's arguments are closely related to the work of Weber, particularly his association of tendencies inherent to Christianity and their relation to the rise of secularisation. It is significant in respect to his general theoretical approach that pluralism is a significant component in the rise of secularisation. If religion provides a connection between structure and cosmos, then religion needs to be monolithic to maintain and objectify this order. If religion is divided into competing units, all of which are in some sense equal, it can no longer provide either the world-building or world-maintaining aspect that is essential to it. Religions in effect become subjectivised and lose the ability to objectify (Berger and Luckmann, 1966: 81).

Berger suggests that although secularisation is not a necessary component in the historical development of religion, it is an inherent feature of Christianity and thus of Western culture in general. He suggests that the elements which led to secularisation were present in the origins of Christianity (that is, the features of the Judaism out of which Christianity emerged: the radical monotheism, the rationalisation of ethics, transcendence of the Jewish God and the Jewish rejection of mysticism) and reached their culmination in the Reformation and the rise of the various forms of Protestantism. The significant development facilitated by the Reformation is a contraction in the role and significance of the sacred. He states:

> Protestantism divested itself as much as possible from the three most ancient and most powerful concomitants of the sacred – mystery, miracle, and magic. (Berger, 1967: 111)

The sacred becomes increasingly narrow and separated from everyday life, and even within the realm of religion, the role of rationality is progressively more important. If secularisation is the progressive removal of the significance of religious symbols and institutions for everyday life, it is clear why the transformations in religion heralded by the Reformation also heralded the development of secularisation.

Berger also suggests that the institutional structure of Christianity, the church, is a significant feature in the process of secularisation. The church is unique in the monopolisation and control of all aspects of religion, removing them from other social realms. This concentration of the sacred in one institution means that the rest of the world is seen as secular. This allowed more and more elements to be moved from the realm of the sacred to that of the secular, making the sacred and the church progressively less important (Berger, 1967: 123).

Pluralism, Berger suggests, is also an important feature in secularisation. He argues that the plurality of denominations and competing religious institutions is both brought about by the secularisation process and actually contributes to that process. Berger suggests that the historical monopoly of religion by a state church, and the necessary association between the state and the church that this implies, maintained the strength and significance of religion. Once this monopoly was broken in the Reformation (though some state churches attempted to continue) it led to increasing religious pluralism. With religious pluralism came competition with non-religious rivals as well; individuals could either choose how to be religious or how not to be religious. With religion becoming a matter of choice, it also became increasingly individual and private rather than public.

Rational choice theory, as suggested by the discussion above, argues against the secularisation model. From the initial presentations of the model, Stark and Bainbridge argued for religion being a necessary concomitant of the system of exchange. They suggest that there will always be significant rewards that are beyond human grasp and thus there will always be compensators that need to be supported by the supernatural. The theory does suggest a weakening of religious commitment among those who have access to power and resources, but in spite of this weakening, even those with such access will still share certain fundamental compensators.

Rational choice theory, however, goes beyond this simple argument for the continued existence of religion; it also presents arguments for the differences in religious commitment in Europe and the United States. Many scholars have observed that the process of secularisation has worked differently in these two parts of the western world. While in Europe there has been a general decline in religious commitment, apparently in opposition to the level of modernisation, commitment to public religious structures has been maintained in the United States. Rational choice theory, with a continued strong emphasis on its capitalist metaphor, suggests that this has to do with the nature of religious markets within the two areas. The theorists observe that European religion was historically structured in a different way to that of America. Broadly speaking, the European system was characterised by monopolies that were backed up by state power. Since these monopolies had no competitors they saw no need to be flexible in relation to the needs of their markets. As long as their constituencies had no choice this was not a problem. With the liberalisation of religious membership, these religions did not provide sufficient rewards or compensation for their adherents and thus there is a progressive falling away. The American system on the other hand has always been characterised by pluralism. With the existence of many competing traditions, each religion had to be flexible enough to keep in line with its markets. Thus, pluralism, far from weakening religious commitment, as suggested by Berger and others, is necessary for continued religious commitment. It is perhaps unsurprising that the systems, which are considered to fail in this model, are similar in description to the supposed structures of communist regimes, while the successful systems are identical to the structures of American capitalism.

As suggested above, Peter Berger has moved from being an exponent of the secularisation thesis to being a critic of it. In the opening chapter of *The Desecularisation of the World* (1999) he highlights some of his arguments which challenge the thesis. He suggests that far from being an increasingly secular world, empirical data suggests that the world may be moving in the opposite direction. The easy association of modernisation and secularisation does not seem to hold true. Modernisation and its effects are seen to be more complex, in some situations leading to decrease in religious commitment and in others to increasing it. He suggests that one of the significant falsifications of the thesis is found in relation to adaptation. The theory suggests that religion will only survive to the degree that it adapts to the secular world. In fact, religions that attempted such adaption have failed while religions that have rejected adaptation have succeeded (Berger, 1999: 4).

What then is the intellectual basis for the secularisation thesis? Berger suggests that part of it is the enlightenment bias against religion. He takes this argument a step further in suggesting that thesis has focused on a subculture and therefore missed what is happening on a wider societal level. He argues that among the international educated elite there has indeed been a process of secularisation. This subculture, which shares enlightenment values, is similar in most parts of the world. It is, however, a subculture and does not represent society as a whole. Berger suggests that the religious upsurge is a populist movement, which in part is a reaction against the elite subculture. Sociologists have misunderstood this phenomenon because they have tended to speak to other educated people, that is, other members of the secularised elite.

In order to respond to the apparent rise in religious commitment Berger sets forth a number of questions and responses. First, what are the origins of this phenomenon? He suggests two possible answers and a related question. On the one hand, one of the effects of modernity is to undermine long held assumptions; this creates a crisis of meaning to which the rise in religion is a response. On the other hand, secularisation and modernisation belong to an elite culture; the rise in religion is related to the resentment felt by the masses against this elite. He, however, adds to this an additional question; he asks, given the historical ubiquity of religion what needs to be explained is the presence of secularisation rather than that of religion? Second, does the rise in religion have a future? He suggests that although, given the complexity of the world, predictions are difficult, it is likely that the twenty-first century will have a similar level of religious commitment to that of the twentieth century. Berger argues that he is not persuaded by those approaches that see modern fundamentalism as a last gasp of religion in the face of secularisation (Berger, 1999: 12). His final question deals with the relationship between different 'resurgent religions' and society. Although they do have clear differences based on context, they share a common critique of the attempt by modern societies to do without some type of transcendent reference.

It is perhaps impossible to judge between these two models on the basis of the empirical data. As the theorists suggest, the data can be read to support either theoretical approach. There are some specific methodological issues that can be addressed. The first issue relates to the use of a substantive definition in Bruce and Wallis' argument. As suggested above, the definition is at odds with the remainder of the analysis, which seems to work with a functionalist model rather than a substantialist one. Putting this conflict aside for the moment, there seems to be little logical support for using a substantialist model. The only ground for including the supernatural within the definition of religion seems to be that it is considered to be essential from a common sense perspective. Since such a perspective is shaped by our own cultural norms and expectations, this usage is somewhat problematic, particularly if it is precisely this element that becomes the basis for the arguments about increasing secularisation.

The move from the substantialist to functionalist argument is a necessary one for the secularisation thesis. It is not enough to describe a change in beliefs, which would be the outcome of a substantivist argument, one must also explain the sociological context that led to that change, and this moves to the functionalist realm. It is here, however, that secularisation theories, particularly those which see secularisation as a necessary development, are particularly problematic. They suggest that through the process of modernisation other institutions will fill the functions, which were once filled by religion, and religion will necessarily wither away. These models tend to have as an underlying logical basis a concept of unilinear cultural evolution. This kind of logical basis has been significantly challenged both by the empirical data and through an examination of its essential ethnocentric basis.

– STRUCTURES OF RELIGIOUS INSTITUTIONS –

One of the most fruitful areas of the sociological discussion of religion has been the nature and relationship between different forms of religious organisations, particularly that between churches and sects, and more recently cults. This discussion has historical significance, in relation to the diversification of religious institutions, particularly in the United States and in terms of recent developments; specifically new religious movements (NRMs).

The initial creative impetus is found in Weber's distinction between church and sect, and is specifically developed and elaborated by Ernst Troeltsch. Both Weber and Troeltsch defined a church as a political institution that is able to maintain social control through control over religious symbols or sacraments. It is a highly formal structure into which someone is born, and which seeks to hold universal sway over a particular society. Membership is in principle obligatory. Within a church, charisma is associated with office rather than an individual. It is an ideal type that is roughly exemplified in the European established churches. The sect is a very different form of religious organisation. Membership in the sect is voluntary, based on evidence or a test of spiritual or ethical qualities.

Charisma in a sect is associated with the individual rather than the office. Weber suggests that a sect has only a limited existence, and unless it develops into a church it will only last for the generation in which it was founded. Troeltsch added a further dimension to this definition. He suggests that there is a different ethos in churches and sects. The church is by definition a conservative movement that seeks to control its adherents and is associated with state power. The sect is a small grouping that is inwardly focused, emphasising individual relationships and perfection. Sects tend to be protest movements on the periphery of society.

In addition to these two institutions Richard Niebuhr introduced that of the denomination. The denomination was understood to be a development from the sect, coming in its second generation; that is, at the beginnings of the routinisation proposed by Weber. Sects were originally characterised by Niebuhr as protest or rejectionist movements that tend to challenge different aspects of the establishment. They are also, and perhaps most significantly, often ascetic – and thus have the potential (as already discussed by Weber in relation to the Protestant ethic) to build up economic resources. The denomination stage is characterised by compromise and an attempt to gain social respectability. The theology of a denomination as opposed to a sect tends to be less exclusive. A significant aspect of Niebuhr's analysis of this process is the association of theological processes with economic and social processes. He states:

> The religious life is so interwoven with social circumstances that the formulation of theology is necessarily conditioned by these. (Niebuhr, 1929: 16)

As the individuals composing a sect become more socially established, economically secure, and interested in the status and education of their children, the theology of the sect transforms from antiestablishment to one which is increasingly willing to accommodate with the norms of society. The denomination, however, remains distinct from a church in that it does not seek to be universal.

Although there are other sociological theorists who have taken up this question, the most significant developments are found in the theories of Bryan Wilson. Wilson focuses specifically on the nature of sects. He highlights eight elements that characterise the ideal type: exclusivity, monopoly on truth, lay rather than professional organisations, all members religiously equal, voluntary, concern for maintenance of spiritual standards by members, total allegiance and protest. The last element is either against established churches or more commonly against society (Wilson, 1982: 91–2). As an ideal type, it should not be expected that every empirical example of a sect would have all of these elements. Different combinations are found in each sect depending on its socio-cultural context.

Wilson's main contribution, however, is in his analysis of the different types of sects. He proposes a seven-fold classification: conversionist, revolutionary, introversionist, manipulationist, thaumaturgical, reformist and utopian. The defining feature of each one of these subgroups is the nature of their 'response to the world' (Wilson, 1969: 363). This aspect is closely associated with Wilson's view of the manifest function of religion discussed above. The conversionist sect considers the world to be corrupt. Its focus is on the saving of souls, and it believes that only through such a process can the world be changed. The theology of conversionist sects is direct and personal, emphasising the relationship with god in direct and emotional terms. It focuses on preaching and other means of evangelising. The revolutionary sect also rejects the outside world, but rather than attempting to convert it, is willing to transform it, through force if necessary. It views events in the world as pre-determined and emphasises eschatological or millenarian texts. Membership is controlled with a strong emphasis on purity and internal conformity, and the sect views itself as a vanguard for transformative events. The introversionist sect rejects the world in a very different way. It neither seeks to convert or transform the world; rather it seeks to remove itself from the world. These groups emphasis deep spiritual experience and have no interest in bringing in new members.

Manipulationist sects tend to accept the goals and values of the outside world, but reinterpret them into a more spiritualised form. They often claim to possess special knowledge allowing them to successfully pursue these ends and claim that this knowledge is the only true way of reaching these goals. These groups include Christian groups like Christian Science, and non-Christian groups like Scientology. The thaumaturgical sects share certain similar features with the manipulationist sects, for example, a positive attitude towards the outside world and its goals. They, however, are less universalistic and they focus on personal experience. They also place a strong emphasis on the possibility of supernatural events and miracles rather than knowledge. The reformist sects were once revolutionary but over time have changed their stance to the world. They seek to reform the world rather than transform the world. By holding themselves apart, these sects seek to act in the world while not being of the world. The final category, the utopian sects, stand between the reformist and the revolutionary in their attitude to the world. They simultaneously withdraw from the world while seeking to remake it in a communitarian image. They can be characterised as seeking social reorganisation as opposed to the social reform of the reformist sects and transformation of the revolutionary sects. Although many of the elements, particularly of the first four types, relate specifically to Christian sects, the model proposed provides an interesting and fruitful avenue into the analysis of a wide range of modern religious phenomena.

Wilson also provides a brief discussion of the social context into which different types of sects can emerge. Thus, for example, manipulationist sects, because of their universality will appeal, he suggests, to a more educated class rather than being a working-class phenomena. Because they emphasise the achievement of worldly aims, they will appeal to that class which shares those aims. From a functionalist perspective, these sects respond to the highly competitive nature of modern society (particularly in relation to these goals) and serve as a means of relieving the tensions associated with this competition. The other types of sects can be similarly contextualised to specific cultural contexts and societal functions. One of the most interesting and significant aspects of the arguments relating to church, denomination and sect, as well as the subcategories of sect is that of transformations. Wilson addresses the interrelationships between these different social structures and the ways in which one type of structure can transform into an other.

This chapter on the sociological approaches to religion has examined three aspects of the approach: the definitions of religion, secularisation and structures of religious organisation. All of the definitions and examples given share a common emphasis on the interrelationship between religion and society. Each discussion was predicated on the need to explain and contextualise religious phenomena to their societal contexts. This inter-relationship argues against the types of essentialist models of religion proposed by psychological and phenomenological approaches.

Although the definitions of religion presented are diverse and in some cases consider themselves to be mutually exclusive, they are all essentially functionalist. Almost all of the discussions focus at some level on the role that religion plays for the individual or society. The only definition, which directly claims to move in a different direction, that is, Bruce and Wallis' use of a substantive definition, is belied by their actual analysis, which is consistently functionalist. However, it is true that these definitions, like all functionalist definitions, are ultimately substantive – with a function rather than a particular belief serving as that basic element. The problem associated with this type of substantive argument is perhaps best indicated by the rational action model, which uses a form of capitalist market relations as its universal or substantial basis. The problems inherent in that model suggest the need for a more dialectical form of functionalism, which moves beyond an imposed ideological understanding of society, by both challenging and responding to the object being analysed. The definition used must also recognise, as do some of the more sophisticated sociological analyses, that human beings in different class or social contexts may have different needs or ways of interacting, thus necessitating models that develop different possibilities of function and different possibilities of describing how human beings interact.

CHAPTER 7

Psychological Approaches

Although Freud and Jung have probably been of greater significance to the development of psychology, the work of William James has set much of the agenda for the psychological analysis of religion. Although we do not discuss his ideas in any detail, it might be useful to highlight some aspects of his analysis as a way of opening up the discussion of some of the more recent trends in the psychological analysis of religion.

Two aspects of James' approach are relevant to the issues discussed in this chapter, that is, his definition of religion and its implication, and his discussions of religious experience. Like most of the psychologists discussed here, James based his definition of religion on individual experience. Thus he states:

> Religion ... shall mean for us the feelings, acts and experiences of individual men in their solitude, so far as they apprehend themselves to stand in relation to whatever they consider to be divine. (James, 1982 [1902]: 31)

This definition provides a substantialist basis for identifying particular phenomenon as religious; they are religious if they include the aspect of 'standing in relation to ... the divine'. The definition, however, does not specify that the divine or transcendent actually exists or indeed specify any particular kind of transcendent. Thus, although James' definition is limited, excluding any sociological or psychological phenomena that lack this aspect, it is highly inclusive in the range of material that it can encompass. The elements in James' definition are highly influential and reoccur throughout psychological discussions; see below, for example, a functionalist formulation of this definition developed by Batson and Ventis.

James' definition of religion is also significant in that it moves away from seeing religion as arising from an essentialist basis. Unlike Freud or Jung in psychology or Otto in theology, James suggests that religion does not have a single source in the human psyche. There is no specific religious emotion or faculty. Religion is thus not *sui generis*, unique and foundational, as it was understood to be by many philosophers and theologians. This view that religion can arise from many different parts of the psyche is further developed in the work of Gordon Allport.

In spite of the substantialist basis of the definition, James' argument also has a functionalist aspect. James suggests that religion has the positive function of making those aspects of our lives that are intolerable, tolerable. It allows us to do those things that we need to do to function both as individuals and individuals in society. Although the different psychological theories examined below develop different areas of functionality, a functionalist aspect does seem to be consistently found. The form of functionalism, however, as we see in James' work tends to be highly focused on psychological function with little or no attention to the functions that religion might play in relation to society.

James also discusses in some detail the nature of religious experiences; indeed it is one of the major foci of *The Variety of Religious Experiences*. His discussion of religious experience and its role in religion moves to a more essentialist form of argumentation than found in his general discussion of religion. This essentialist aspect is illustrated in a generalised model of mystical or religious experience. He suggests that all religious experiences include four elements: they are ineffable, authoritative, limited in duration and the mystic is passive. This discussion take a specific model of mystical experience and extends it, in a prescriptive way, to all religious experience. It is important to note, that the experience that he describes is grounded in the self, and the externalisation of the self, and does not rely on a transcendent other. The move to an essentialist argument is not uncommon in the psychological argumentation presented below. It probably derives from the nature of the discipline. If human psychology is unified, that is, all humans have the same psyche, then a significant degree of human ways of experiencing must also be unitary. It is clearly granted that human beings all have the same biological basis for their psyches, what is not accepted is the degree to which that biological basis determines our psychology.

Abraham Maslow is associated with an approach to human psychology and the psychology of religion in the tradition of James. This is not to say that his model is significantly similar to his, rather it suggests that his work fits into a tradition of more speculative psychology, developing a comprehensive understand of human minds and motivations. His approach was initially labeled Humanistic Psychology and latterly Transpersonal Psychology.

One of the clearest explorations of his understanding of psychology and specifically psychology in relation to religion is found in *Religions, Values, and Peak-Experiences* (1964). In this book he defines the nature of religion, its relationship with science and, ultimately, its basis in the peak-experience.

He opens his discussion by suggesting that both science and religion have been understood in too narrow a way. This narrow form of definition has suggested that religion and science belong to two separate areas of understanding. The division between the two had negative effects on each. Science, so conceived, became too 'mechanistic', it considered values or spirituality to be outside of its purview. This narrow focus suggested that values could never be empirically tested or verified (Maslow, 1964: 11). A similar, though opposite trend is found respecting religion. Religions gave up the realm of empirical fact, often opposing scientific method and results. Neither of these approaches to existence is sustainable, Maslow refers to the separation as a 'dichotomising pathology', both must be redefined and brought back together.

Religion, in its dichotomised form is seen as particularly problematic. With the removal of the empirical, natural aspect of human experience, religion was doomed to stagnate and become increasingly irrational. Dichotomised religion could not discover, test itself or improve. Rather, it claimed to be 'complete, perfect, final, and eternal' (Maslow, 1964: 13). This type of religion defines all of its aspects in a similarly partial way; thus, faith becomes 'blind faith'. Dichotomised religion is thus conservative and authoritarian.

He suggests that the issues dealt with by religion can not be left with religion, but science as it is presently constituted does not wish to take them. He suggests that the solution is an 'expanded science, with larger powers and methods, a science which is able to study values and teach mankind about them' (Maslow, 1964: 17). Although scientists will disagree with the theologies of organised religions, they should not avoid trying to answer the questions addressed by those theologies. Unlike those scientists who view people attempting to address spiritual questions as abnormal, Maslow considers people who are not concerned with them to be abnormal (1964: 18).

Maslow's argument depends on this return of the spiritual and values to science, because he is also attempting to ground the basis of these things, spiritual experience, within a model of the human psychology. Maslow connects traditional concepts of religious experience, the basis of the revealed religions, with his concept of 'peak-experiences' (1964: 19).

Peak-experiences, or experiences of the transcendent, are not supernatural phenomena, rather they are 'perfectly natural' and thus are open to analysis by the psychologist or scientist. The argument developed by

Maslow, which sees all religious experiences as this unitary human phenomenon, has strong essentialist basis. He states:

> To the extent that all mystical or peak-experiences are the same in their essence and always have been the same, all religions are the same in their essence and always have been the same. (Maslow, 1964: 20)

Not only do they share a common underlying experiential basis, but ultimately, since that basis leads to the development of values, they should share a common set of values as well. Anything that is specific or particular about a religious experience, based on the emphasis on identity of these experiences, arises from the local context and is not relevant or significant. Thus, the experience can be embodied in a wide range of forms, theistic or non-theistic; the form is not significant.

Maslow also presents a developmental model of religions that also touches on different types of people and moves us a step closer to the location of 'peakers' in a developmental model of human psychology. The basis of religion is found in the prophet, a person who has had a transcendental experience that allows him to understand god, the world, and particularly the self. Religions, however, are organised and carried on by a very different type of person. This person, 'the legalist', has no awareness beyond the material, he is conservative and organisational; under this form of leadership the original revelation is increasingly lost; religions become a form of idolatry and lose the essential experimental basis (Maslow, 1964: 23). Maslow's discussion has many similarities to Weber's analysis of the development of religious structures, moving from the charismatic form of leadership to the bureaucratised.

This discussion of leadership suggests that specific personality types will have peak experiences. He suggests that while all people can have peak-experiences, some people are afraid of them and deny having them. These 'non-peakers' tend to be overly rationalistic and materialist; seeing peak-experiences as a form of insanity.

Maslow's model of personality development focuses on the healthy personality as distinct from other theorists who had focused on the pathological. Maslow suggests that the process, which ultimately leads to the peaker, is a process of self-actualisation. It is the function of the societal institutions, for example the family or education, to assist in normal development – to reduce any areas of discomfort. With the removal of discomfort, the individual has space to grow and self-actualise. Ultimately the process of self-actualisation is one of being true to one's self. Self-actualisation ultimately leads to peak-experiences.

The features of peak-experiences include a number of elements that might be understood in a religious way. Malsow lists twenty-five of these elements; we shall touch on a few to exemplify his arguments. A significant feature of many experiences is the sense of unity – the perception that every aspect of the world is linked together in an intrinsic way. This experience is also accompanied by a sense of meaningfulness and value that is similar to the religious integrative functions. The second feature of these experiences is the feeling that the experience is uniquely real. The experience moves from a sense of categorising and judging to one in which each object is uniquely real and significant. Peak-experiences also often include a sense of detachment from the human; the world takes its place in its own terms outside of human needs. It is perceived 'in its own Being (as an end in itself)' (Maslow, 1964: 61). A final example is the perception of value. It creates a feeling in which the world is seen as intrinsically worthwhile, even evil is brought into a holistic sense of value.

The elements that are listed by Maslow have similarities to many discussions of mystical experiences; the significant feature of his argument is that it is a naturalistic process, which although it can be understood as religious, does not depend on anything outside relationship between the individual psychology and the world. In spite of this naturalistic element, as suggested above, Maslow's argument presents an essentialist understanding of peak-experiences and religion. His analysis selects those elements that he values and excludes as irrelevant those elements that fall outside of that category. Maslow's analysis of true religion as emerging from a specific type of individual experience seems specific to a particular cultural location; it fits into a privatised view of religion specific to the late nineteenth century to the mid-twentieth century, mirroring the discussions of religion in a wide range of disciplines from theology as exemplified in Buber and Otto, and phenomenology in Eliade. It reflects the particular values of Maslow, his own understanding and perhaps experience of religion, and may not usefully be extended beyond that cultural time and place.

Gordon Allport's work moves in a very different direction to that of Maslow. His most influential work focuses on the distinction between extrinsic and intrinsic religion, discussed below, and the psychometric scale, which was designed to examine correlations with these two forms of religion. Much of the groundwork for this distinction is developed in *The Individual and His Religion* (1951). This book presents a developmental model of religion, focusing on a comparison between mature and immature forms of religion.

The initial sections of the book lay the foundation for a definition of religion that rejects the essentialist position that is found in Freud, Jung and Maslow. His work, like their analyses, focuses on individual subjective religion as opposed to the institutional forms that are studied by the other social sciences. He suggests that this form of religion has always existed and will continue to exist even if institutional religion withers away. In spite of this placement of the significant elements of religion firmly within the individual psychology, however, Allport argues that it does not arise from an essential experience or psychological faculty.

After reviewing some of the arguments in favour of a single religious sentiment or experience, Allport suggests, following James, that religion does not arise from a single emotional or subjective experience. A variety of different emotions can be harnessed to focus on a religious object; it is the focus and intention of the focus that makes the particular emotion religious rather than the specific emotion used. In addition to the rejection of a specific or unique religious emotion, Allport also rejects the possibility of a specifically religious content. In spite of this lack of specific emotion or content on the wider level, Allport concludes that the individual does create his or her own structured form.

> He is likely to have a well-organised personal sentiment that can presumably, with intensive psychological study, be accurately construed and understood. Even though in their religious lives people are not consistent with one another, they are as a rule markedly consistent with themselves. (Allport, 1951: 7)

Religion, as a structured and significant phenomenon, is essentially individual and the psychology of religion, as per the emphasis of psychological analysis, must focus its attention on the subjective individual rather than the institutional forms of religion.

Allport also rejects the possibility that religion has a common source or origin within the psyche. He suggests that theories that place religion within the unconscious, as in Freud, are difficult to test, and even if correct are too narrowly focused. He argues that personal, subjective religion is a mixture of both conscious and unconscious elements. He is, however, willing to make a general statement about the nature of 'well-formed' subjective religion:

> Perhaps the most striking fact about subjective religion is the contrast between its essential simplicity when, well-formed, it is playing its part in the economy of the personal life, and its extreme complexity in the process of forming. (Allport, 1951: 9)

This essential simplicity forms one of the key elements of his view of mature religion and is a significant feature of his later discussions of types of religion.

If religion cannot be identified with its institutional forms and includes no essential content or emotion, what then is it? Individual religion seems to be closely associated with maturity and is shaped by five main elements: 'bodily needs', 'temperament', psychogenic interests', 'pursuit of rational explanation' and the 'surrounding culture' (Allport, 1951: 10). The first of these, 'bodily needs', could better be described as needs and desires. These desires include the need to resolve the problems of fear and death. On the positive side, religion responds to the desire for love. Any desire or need can be the basis for religious acts or feelings. The different desires are reflected in different ideas about the nature of the divine. Thus, for example, god's omnipotence responds to the need for order and security. 'Temperament' is clearly a significant factor in shaping the individual's expression of personal religion. People with different temperaments will be drawn to different expressions of the divine. 'Psychogenic interests' or desires are different from the bodily desires in the sense that they are externalised and objectified. Thus, if, for example, we desire knowledge, we objectify knowledge outside ourselves and call it truth. As we mature, these objects become more abstract; thus truth may initially include a small body of facts, and through maturity it becomes a category through which particular facts can be judged and evaluated. The concept of god may be an example of the objectivation of the self – which in part 'conserve(s) all other values of selfhood' (Allport, 1951: 17). The next aspect of the argument is the 'pursuit of meaning'. Allport suggests that the elements discussed thus far are essentially emotional, but religion also has a rational side. After all other desires are filled, one essential question remains: 'What is it all about anyhow?' (Allport, 1951: 19). Religion is a response to this question; it is both a search and the answer. 'Culture and conformity' are elements that conclude this part of his argument. Allport does not agree with a strong conception of cultural conformity. His argument at this point discounts the sociological arguments for latent functions. Thus he suggests that if people thought that religion was a means of legitimising society they would abandon religion. People are religious he suggests for their own personal reasons, rather than for reasons of conformity. In spite of this caveat, he does agree that culture is a significant tool in shaping how people express their private, internal, religious motivations. If the underlying bases of the first four of these areas are examined together, Allport's model seems to share many elements with the functionalist model proposed by Malinowski (see above).

Alongside these functional aspects of his analysis, there is also a substantive element, albeit on the individual level and given the aspects of individual variation. He states:

> Shall we then define the mature religious sentiment as a disposition, built up through experience, to respond favourably and in certain habitual ways, to conceptual objects and principles that the individual regards as of ultimate importance in his own life, and as having to do with what he regards as permanent or central in the nature of things. (Allport, 1951: 63)

The definition includes two substantive features, the undefined aspect of ultimate importance, and the elements of permanence. Unlike many other substantive definitions, however, the nature and content of these categories is left to the individual.

The final elements of Allport's discussion of mature religion move him closer to an essentialist model. His discussion sets out universal criteria for mature religion, losing any of the individualistic or relativist aspects of his previous discussions. He suggests that the mature religious approach includes six elements: differentiation, dynamic, leading to a 'consistent morality', 'comprehensive', 'integral', and 'heuristic' (Allport, 1951: 63).

'Differentiation' is used by Allport to suggest the complexity of mature religion. Immature religion focuses on one aspect or experience, mature religion uses a number of different complexly related and structured elements. Differentiation also includes within it the ability to be critical and reflexive. The 'dynamic' element refers to the fact that mature religion is not the servant of our desires but the master of them. It is not directed by self-interest. Fanaticism in religion is a feature of immature religion; it is shaped by desires, conscious and unconscious and reflects the inability to be reflexive or critical. Allport suggests that 'consistency' is another significant feature. This consistency arises from a mature, 'seasoned religious outlook' (Allport, 1951: 73). Mature religion is also comprehensive in scope. It provides a basis from which the complexities and chaos of life can be comprehensively ordered. As part of this comprehensive model, religion gives life both meaning and value. Allport uses this aspect of comprehensiveness as a means of arguing against the inclusion of many secular ideologies, for example Communism, as religions. He argues that although they include many of the elements of religion they usually fail in respect of this aspect: although such ideologies may encompass much of our experience, there are always areas they leave out; religion would provide meaning for all areas with no residue. The 'integral' aspect has been touched upon in several of the others; it refers to need for a pattern or structure. All of the complex elements must be made to fit together in a consistent and patterned way. The final element, 'the heuristic character', suggests that in mature religion all beliefs are held tentatively. The individual is willing to test his beliefs and if necessary change them. Faith is understood to be 'a working hypothesis' (Allport, 1951: 80).

Allport's analysis of religion is interesting from two perspectives. First, in attempting to utilise three different types of definition – functionalist, substantive and essentialist – it demonstrates the difficulty in defining religion, particularly if one is examining something as ephemeral as personal religion. It also illustrates the role of cultural context in shaping the definitions that are used. The final elements of his discussion, for example, as with most essentialist models, are highly specific to a particular sub-culture's (academic America) understanding of religion and provides an essentially ethnocentric basis for the evaluation of religions. Second, the discussions of religion that arise from a somewhat speculative basis, become the basis for psychometric scales of religiosity and form the basis of a wide range of discussions both within and outside psychology.

The extension of the elements discussed above into the distinction between intrinsic and extrinsic religion is the most important and in-fluential aspect of Allport's work. Essentially, mature religion is equivalent to intrinsic religion. He describes intrinsic religion:

> Religious sentiment may be of such an order that it does provide an inclusive solution to life's puzzles in the light of an intelligible theory. It can do so if the religious quest is regarded as an end in itself, as the value underlying all things and desirable for its own sake. By surrendering himself to this purpose (not by 'using' it), religion becomes 'intrinsic' value for the individual, and as such is compre-hensive and integrative and motivational. (Allport, 1963: 301)

Intrinsic religion is clearly viewed as the psychologically positive ex-pression of religious values. Extrinsic religion is associated with immature religion, and is the religious sentiment expressed by most people (and by implication most forms of organised religion). This form of personal religion is self-centred, with a concept of the divine that favours individual interests. This form of religion is a validator of self or group and is a form of 'self esteem'. Religion in this sense serves individual ends rather than being an end in itself. Allport associates this form of religion with prejudice (and fanaticism and fundamentalism). The basic issue is that unlike intrinsic, mature religion in which the self is extended, in extrinsic religion the focus is on the self as self (Allport, 1963: 300). This distinction between different types of religion and other aspects of social behaviour, for example, prejudice, became a significant area of psychometric analysis, that is, a statistical method of analysis that seeks correlations between different sets of data. Aside from the validity of these two forms of religion, their use in psychometric analysis is questionable, as is their correlation with other forms of behaviour; the distinction is, as suggested above, inherently ethno-centric. It takes a particular model of religion that is considered to be valuable in a particular social context and presents that model as being real religion, while at the same time rejecting other models as immature or unreal.

Batson and Ventis in *The Religious Experience* (1982) trace the development of Allport's model and some of the issues related to its methodological application. They suggest that the original formulation, given above, was not empirically testable as the distinction itself was highly subjective. In order to give the theory a more empirical basis Allport and his colleagues developed questionnaires to identify the two categories of religiosity. The correlations found in many of these studies have not supported the distinctions suggested by Allport. Many of the more complex scales developed subsequently have maintained Allport's distinction between intrinsic and extrinsic religion while adding other distinctions or variables. Thus, Batson and Ventis suggest that the intrinsic, mature model suggested by Allport contains two models, one an ends orientation and the other a quest orientation; and the immature model is redefined as a separate means orientation (1982: 158–61). This provides them with a 'three dimensional frame work', which provides a basis for further empirical analysis. They conclude their discussion with a very important observation. Many of the analyses based on Allport's model have assumed that intrinsic religion is equivalent to 'true religion' and extrinsic religion to 'false religion'. They caution against using this kind of evaluative approach as 'it might suggest some rigidity and simplicity on our part'; unfortunately they weaken this point by both suggesting that the quest model might ultimately prove to be true religion and that such an evaluation might ultimately be possible (Batson and Ventis, 1982: 169–70).

Several recent psychological theories have been fruitfully applied to the study of religion. Daniel McIntosh outlines the application of one of the most interesting of these, schema theory, in 'Religion-as-Schema, with Implications for the Relation Between Religion and Coping' (1997). McIntosh suggests that religion can best be viewed as a 'cognitive schema', a model which explains both what religion is (psychologically) and how religion functions (1997: 171).

A cognitive schema is a mental model of some area of knowledge. It is an organised representation of that area, including clearly defined relations between the different elements included in that domain of knowledge. A significant aspect of the schema is that it is developed experientially. It is constructed by individuals in relation to their environment, using encounters and other experiences to modify and develop its specificity. We all use a variety of different schema for different areas of knowledge, for example, the self, other people or objects. McIntosh presents the following illustration of what the God schema might look like:

A God schema might include, for example, assumptions about the physical nature of God, God's will or purposes, God's methods of influence, and the interrelations among those beliefs. (McIntosh, 1997: 172)

The God schema, like all others, can change or develop in responses to new experience or knowledge.

Although the schemas touched on thus far are specific to objects or areas of knowledge, McIntosh suggests that there are also higher-level abstract schemas that will include a selection of these more specific schemas. Such a schema might be religion. It might include the God schema as well as others; for example, death, sin, or good and evil. In spite of this higher level of inclusively and abstraction, abstract schema are understood to work in much the same way as the specific schema.

Although schema are subject to change, and constantly do change, they change in a specific way. The basic structure of the schema is relatively stable. In spite of new information and experience it tends to remain the same, the information or experiences are 'adapted' to the schema rather than the other way around. The contents of the schemas change through 'modification' but the schema or theory remains the same, and often persists in spite of the new information (McIntosh, 1997: 172).

The schema model shares some theoretical interests with the work of Peter Berger, discussed above in the chapter on Sociology. Both approaches are concerned with how we perceive and construct the world around us. The schema theory argues that the schema that we bring to a situation or particular experience shapes our perceptions. Psychologists suggest that schemas shape both what we perceive and how we perceive; we only perceive something for which we have a schema, and since the schema is essentially organisational, it shapes how we relate the object of perception to other cognitive objects (McIntosh, 1997: 173). One of the essential roles of a schema is that it allows the mind to go beyond perception or experience. Based on the model, the individual can fill in the gaps. These elements are particularly relevant to the religious schema. It allows religious people both to perceive the world in such a way that it fits into that schema, and more importantly it allows them to organise and interpret the data of experience in a religiously meaningful way – a way which would be very different from someone without that religious schema. It also allows them to make assumptions about experience that are not backed up directly by perception.

One of the significant points of McIntosh's application of the schema model to religion is found both in what it implies that religion is and religion isn't. As discussed in the chapter on phenomenology, many scholars have argued that religion is a unique form of knowledge and experience, needing methodologies and theories specifically designed for its study. McIntosh's analysis suggests that religion is a cognitive system like any other cognitive system, for example physics, and can be understood using models that can be more broadly applied. It also suggests, clearly, that religion is not unique, and it also suggests that at least in terms of content and structure, religion can be defined in an essentialist way. There is no logical reason why there cannot be culturally specific religious schema, the content of which is constantly modified by individuals based on their own life experiences.

The second part of McIntosh's discussions moves into a more specifically functionalist analysis of religion as a schema for coping with the traumatic experience. The range of issues touched on are directly related to the many areas specifically dealt with by religion and the ritual process. They include points of life transformation – birth, marriage and death – as well as other forms of traumatic experience. The religious schema is understood to be not only a way of signalling these events but more importantly to be a structure for coping with them.

McIntosh develops two areas through which the religious schema can help in the coping process: 'cognitive processing' and 'finding meaning' (1997: 178–80). The aspect of 'cognitive processing' refers to the ability of schema to simplify the process of dealing with information or experience. If we have a pre-existing schema, we can quickly fit the data into it and process it. Thus the coping with the experience can occur more quickly as cognitive integration is quicker. The need for explanation or meaning as a mechanism for coping is highly significant. The concept of the religious schema clearly relates to this process as it allows the events to be fitted into a pre-existing explanatory system and thus gives those events meaning and perhaps value.

McIntosh closes his discussion by suggesting the value of this model in understanding conversion and evangelism. The model is built on a concept of change through modification and thus is helpful in evaluating the effect of events on religious systems. It also can examine the role that traumatic events might play in transforming schema more significantly as part of a conversion process. Finally, it also facilitates the analysis of evangelical discourse as method or attempts at creating or transforming religious schemas.

Peter Hill, in 'Toward an Attitude Process Model of Religious Experience', applies psychological cognitive theory to the area of religious experience. A key aspect of his approach is the role of 'attitude'. The focus on attitude is not seen as conflicting with other models, but rather as complementary. It could, for example, be one element of the religious schema. The significant feature of an attitude is its role in categorisation, particularly 'some sort of good-bad evaluative dimension'. Thus, an attitude is essentially an evaluation associated with a particular object. The strength of association between the two elements is directly related to the 'accessibility' of the value (Hill, 1997: 185). Controlled and automatic processes are, in addition, relevant features of attitudes. This highlights the fact that some cognitive processes require conscious attention or control while others are automatic and occur without attention or control (Hill, 1997: 186).

One aspect of the automatic and controlled dichotomy is its possible association with different strengths of religiosity. Thus, an individual with a high degree of religious connection may have an automatic attitudinal response to a particular religious stimuli, while an individual with a weaker degree of religious connection may only have a controlled response, requiring a greater degree of conscious thought or effort. Hill cautions against a premature characterisation of the automatic process as a less thought out, than mature form of religious belief. He suggests that this characterisation is based on confusion between the process, automatic or controlled, and the content of that process (Hill, 1997: 189).

Hill argues that the three main features of attitude theory, that is, 'attitude importance, attitude accessibility, and the automatic/controlled attitude distinction' provide a useful process model for the study of religious experience (Hill, 1997: 190). Each of these elements can be used in relation to other theoretical models for examining the nature and role of religious experience. A particular area of significant application is found in regard to religious commitment. The three areas can be used both to conceptualise the commitment, and can provide a cognitive explanation for that commitment by examining the role of automatic or controlled processes.

The approach is also useful in understanding the resiliency of belief systems. Hill suggests that automatic attitudes are less prone to change or be challenged than controlled attitudes. Thus the dichotomy could be very useful in understanding conversion narratives and other forms of evangelism. It is also suggested that automatic attitudes correlate with behaviour more consistently than do controlled attitudes. This again raises interesting questions of the nature of belief, attitude and action. In some cases the actions might not reflect the attitudes of the actor – challenging the common assumption of the significance of action in relation to thought.

The nature and source of religious experience has been an ongoing question in the study of religion. Thus far we have examined it in the context of several theoretical approaches, that is, Jung and Maslow; it has also been examined using more empirical approaches. One such approach is found in the work of Daniel Batson and Larry Ventis, which presents both a theoretical argument and empirical backup for it. They emphasise that religious experiences and choices are socially influenced or conditioned. Although religious choices might appear to be free, they are determined by social context (Batson and Ventis, 1982: 27).

Before moving to a more detailed discussion of their understanding of religious experience it might be useful to touch briefly on their definition of religion. Their definition moves strongly in a functionalist direction. They state:

> We shall define religion as whatever we as individuals do to come to grips personally with the questions that confront us because we are aware that we and others like us are alive and that we will die. Such questions we shall call existential questions. (Batson and Ventis, 1982: 7)

This functionalist definition shares elements with that of Malinowski and Peter Berger. It is perhaps unsurprising that Batson and Ventis should move in this direction as their analysis of religious experience shares many presuppositions with sociological analyses. The significant difference between this psychological formulation of functionalism and other forms of functionalism is the absolute emphasis on the individual. Although Malinowski, for example, also emphasised the individual he was also clearly aware of the social aspects of religious experience, both in terms of construction and function.

Batson and Ventis suggest that our actions and choices are shaped by social interactions analogous to elements of drama. The individual has a predetermined script that shapes his or her actions. They highlight three related areas that play a part in shaping behaviour, thinking and feeling: social roles, social norms and reference groups. The first of these highlights the effect of position or status on behaviour, the second, norms, are the often unstated rules, and the third, reference groups, provide the pressure to conform. Both religious and non-religious questions are equally determined by the pre-existing scripts (Batson and Ventis, 1982: 31–2).

These elements help us to understand religious experiences on a number of related levels. Experiences perceived of as religious are often highly emotional events that fall outside normal experience. The type of experience we have, the emotions we feel, will be shaped by the script. In part, these events become meaningful through a process of interpretation; very often these interpretations will arise from the reference group. The elements also suggest that a range of sociological factors will shape the kinds of experiences we have and the way they are interpreted. These factors include race, gender and class. They do, however, caution against seeing social influence as the sole determining factor. Individual aspects, for example the individual psyche, can appropriately be cited alongside the social factors that their study emphasises.

Batson and Ventis' discussion of how and why individuals have religious experiences moves into a more functionalist form of argumentation, though as indicated above, their definition of religion is functionalist. They outline a psychological sequence, harking back to a suggestion made by William James, for dealing with personal problems that is the basis of religious experience. The fundamental basis of this sequence is existential crisis. The crisis leads to a sense of despair and ultimately self-surrender, which is a necessary element of giving up the old way of being or thinking. The final two stages are 'new vision' and 'new life' (Batson and Ventis, 1982: 82–6). The new vision involves some form of illumination that culminates in a new way of living based on that vision. In their summary of the argument they define the outcome of this process as follows:

> Religious experience involves cognitive restructuring in an attempt to deal with one or more existential questions. (Batson and Ventis, 1982: 86)

Religious experience thus serves an individual functional need, resolving existential crisis through the restructuring of ways of thinking and living, but as per the first part of their discussion, both the ways of thinking, the crises, and their resolutions are culturally constructed.

Other psychologists have attempted to develop arguments suggesting that religious experience has a strong physiological or chemical basis. This approach is associated with attempts to explain aspects of culture and personality using evolutionary or biological models as opposed to cultural or experiential models. One of the strongest advocates of this type of model is found in the work of Michael Persinger (1987). Persinger's work suggests that religious experiences can be directly associated with particular chemical states and their affects on the temporal lobe. These biological states, which can be artificially stimulated and simulated in the lobe, cause individuals to have the feelings, convictions and experiences associated with mystical states. These experiences, because of their religious content, are interpreted as experiences of the divine and are understood or explained using available religious symbols. Although Persinger's arguments convincingly demonstrate the processes that occur in the brain, leading to a religious experience, they are only a partial explanation. What is interesting about religious experiences goes far beyond the fact of having an experience. We are also interested in why particular people in particular social settings have the experiences, why they take different forms in different social setting, how they are given the culturally specific content that they have, and how they are used both by the individual and society. Persinger begins to address the biological question; other psychological analyses, for example, Batson and Ventis, address many of the other issues; and anthropological and sociological models take the personal aspects of the experience and place them into a societal context.

In this discussion we have touched on a wide range of psychological theories relating to religion and religious experience. The particular theories examined were chosen for two reasons, because they presented a developed and comprehensive view of religion, and in order to exemplify the different approaches in modern psychology, particularly the theoretical and empirical. The approaches discussed, as in the other social scientific disciplines, have a wide range of variation in the types of definitions used, thus we have seen functionalist, substantialist and essentialist forms of argumentation. Nonetheless, most of the psychological analyses have an underlying impetus in the direction of an essentialist understanding of religion; this underlying approach is probably based in the consensus that human psychology is the common inheritance of all human beings. It also emphasises the down-playing of cultural elements in the construction of the human psyche. Perhaps the most significant limitation in psychological models is the emphasis on the individual as opposed to society. Most of the models discussed focus on personal religion and consider the institutional aspects of religion to be at the most secondary and, more commonly, insignificant. This overemphasis ignores the fact that religion is as much, or more, a social phenomena as an individual one – many people's experience of religion rests on the institutional aspects rather than on any type of personal experience. It also ignores the possibility that even where religious experience is present, it may be a highly structured social experience, with both individual and social functions.

CHAPTER 8

Phenomenology and the History of Religion

This section brings together a number of related disciplines, which although arguably distinct, have a wide range of convergences, and the advocates of the different disciplines have often shared common presuppositions and moved between the different approaches. The two main approaches covered here are phenomenology of religion and history of religion/s. In addition we will also touch on some scholars who fall more neatly into comparative religion. Perhaps the most important commonality found between these approaches is the use of cross cultural, comparative typologies. The different disciplines, however, use these typologies in different ways. The history of religion/s approach has, as indicated by the name, emphasised the aspect of historical development, and to some extent historical particularity. In some thinkers the emphasis has been on an argumentative move from the history of particular elements of religions to the history of religion in a more abstract and humanly universal sense. Phenomenologists have tended to be less historically oriented; focusing on the nature of the religious objects being studied, and using typological (comparison of specific objects) or morphological (comparison of structures) analyses to discover the underlying meaning or essence of those objects. The area of comparative religions is much more diverse, tending to include a wider range of analytical models often borrowed from other disciplines, particularly anthropology and psychology, and also phenomenology and history of religions.

Phenomenology has its origin in the nineteenth century; the term phenomenology was coined by P. D. Cantepie de la Saussaye in 1887. In its original conception it was understood to be a descriptive approach to religion – moving away from the search for either essences or origins (see the discussion about Kristensen for a defence of this position). The phenomenological method, however, works on two levels; it both describes and categorises the elements of religion, but perhaps even more importantly, it claims to describe the consciousness of those people, the believers, who practice a certain religion. A key feature of both the early works in the discipline and continuing throughout the twentieth century is this emphasis on typological analysis.

This leads us to the three of the predominant methodological themes in the phenomenological study of religion: *epochē*, *einfühlung* and the eidetic vision. These three elements come from the work of Husserl in relation to the reconstruction of philosophy and were adapted by the phenomenologists of religion to their field of study. While the typological aspect is the essential basis of the comparative phase in phenomenological studies, the concepts of *epochē* and *einfühlung* are underlying methodological approaches to the material that is being studied and underlie the distinctiveness of phenomenology as a discipline.

Epochē is defined by Ninian Smart as: 'the bracketing out or suspension of one's own beliefs' (Smart, 1986: ix). It also refers, in a sense closer to the use of the concept by Husserl, to the bracketing of the beliefs of the people being studied. This concept of bracketing out one's own perspective whether it be theological or theoretical is fundamental. Phenomenologists argue that in order to understand the beliefs and perspectives of a particular group of believers one must take a neutral stance. If one applies a theoretical perspective, usually interpreted as a reductionist perspective that explains religion in humanist terms, denying the existence of a transcendental other, then it is impossible to take seriously the internal perspective of the believers. Similarly, if one takes a theological perspective then one either automatically accepts the internal perspective, or evaluates that perspective in line with one's own theology. Thus in order to avoid both of these problems the concept of *epochē* demanded a position of neutrality. As the discussion below indicates this led to two interrelated problems. Given the atheoretical bias of the concept, many phenomenological studies are overly descriptive, and, due to the dearth of analysis, many phenomenologists who were also believers were able to introduce their own beliefs into their analyses (see for example the case of Otto, discussed in the first chapter). The bracketing in of the people's beliefs also leads to argumentative pitfalls; if the bracketed beliefs are the only ones presented then phenomenology moves almost imperceptibly into a form of theology – as the bracketed beliefs are privileged by being the only forms of explanation presented.

The element of *epochē* leads some phenomenologists and theorists of religion to eschew clearly defining religion. In most cases this is not due to a lack of definition, but rather a definition that is taken for granted. The phenomenologists assume that their common sense definition of religion can serve as a foundation for analysis. This aspect of their discussions emphasises the problems with its naïve approach to academic analysis. The theory or definition is present but unstated, as such it also remains untested or challenged.

The concept of *einfühlung* is closely associated with that of *epochē*. It can be translated as empathy. In a sense it is a statement of how phenomenology differs from other disciplines; most other approaches to religion ignored the indigenous perspective or explanation. The concept of *einfühlung* suggests a position of empathy from which the analyst should take the viewpoint of the believer as a serious explanation for the phenomena. Like *epochē* it is essential to the descriptive basis of the approach.

The eidetic vision refers to the typological aspect of phenomenology and the search for the essences of the group of related phenomena. The typological aspect of phenomenology builds on the descriptive analyses. Rather than comparing religions as a whole, the phenomenological perspective divides religion into a number of distinct components. These components are categorised and grouped with components from other religions, and the group is analysed as a whole to determine its common basis – sometimes in searches for essences and sometimes for higher-level commonalities as in meanings.

The Meaning of Religion (1971) by W. Brede Kristensen presents one of the clearest expositions of the phenomenological method. In his general introduction, Kristensen clarifies the distinction between his approach and that taken by the History of Religion. Unlike History of Religion, which he suggests focuses on the particular historic development of the specific religion being studied, the phenomenological approach is essentially comparative. It develops a systematic and classificatory approach to the data in order to develop an overview that can be used to compare data from a wide range of religious sources.

He also suggests that phenomenology is distinct from the discipline of Comparative Religion as it was practiced in his time. He suggests Comparative Religion was essentially a means of determining relative value. It was part of the generally accepted evolutionary model, and religions were compared in order to assess their developmental position. Phenomenology, as understood by Kristensen, does not aim, at least primarily, to compare whole religions from the perspective of value, but rather, to decontextualise various elements of religion, associate them with similar elements from other religions and analyses those elements as a unit. He suggests that the goal of this analysis is 'to become acquainted with the religious thought, idea or need which underlies the group of corresponding data' (Kristensen, 1971: 2). The assumption underlying this model is that elements that are typologically similar have the same or similar religious value wherever they are found and thus historical or cultural context is not relevant to the analysis.

Kristensen does, however, make a valuable point respecting the value of different religious forms. He suggests that although phenomenologists are concerned with value, they understand this in a different way than had Comparative Religion. The value that is significant is not comparative, but rather is that of the 'believers themselves' (Kristensen, 1971: 2). This argument illustrates one of the consistent themes in the phenomenological study of religion, that is, a concern with the internal view and valuation of the religious practice.

He develops this attempt to penetrate the internal understanding further in a discussion of how the historian should approach the material. He suggests that it is impossible (and perhaps undesirable) for the historian to lose their objectivity and take a purely internal view. Such a view would be the end of any form of analysis; it would be purely descriptive based on our experience of, and acceptance of, the internal way of being and thinking. Thus, the historian must retain some degree of objective distance from the material. He should, however, on an imaginative or empathetic level try to 'approximate' the internal understanding (Kristensen, 1971: 7). This approximation must always be recognised as limited; it is not the same as an internal point of view, but nonetheless it allows the historian to approach the existential aspect of the material, however imperfectly.

Kristensen takes this argument a step further as part of a general critique of evolutionary models of religious development. He argues that the evolutionary view always sees a particular form of religion as a 'link in a chain'. This understanding, however, has no relation to the way that the believers see themselves. If, Kristensen suggests, we view a particular religion as 'primitive,' then we lose any possibility of empathising or understanding the elements of that religion – because we are ethnocentrically caught up in our religious presuppositions. He states:

> The historian and the student of phenomenology must therefore be able to forget themselves, to be able to surrender themselves to others. Only after that will they discover that others surrender themselves to them. If they bring their own idea with them, others shut themselves off from them. No justice is then done to the values which are alien to us, because they are not allowed to speak their own language. If the historian tries to understand the religion from a different viewpoint than that of the believers, he negates the religious reality. For there is no religious reality other than the faith of the believers. (Kristensen, 1971: 13)

This argument, although raising some very important points about the need for relativism and validation of internal understandings, is both internally illogical and academically untenable. If the phenomenological method is essentially typological and decontextualising as suggested above, then it is clearly inconsistent with the stated goals of validating only the believer's perspective. If, however, it only serves to describe the believer's perspective, then it is not an analytical methodology and is indistinguishable from theology.

In spite of these arguments about the internal point of view, Kristensen also emphasises the value of external analysis. He suggests that his comparative method, by bringing together a range of similar material, allows a deeper understanding than would the study of the specific individual phenomena. He states:

> Phenomenology tries to gain an overall view of the ideas and motives which are of decisive importance in all of History of Religion. (Kristensen, 1971: 2)

For Kristensen the typological and comparative aspects are the starting point of the analysis – its conclusion is an overall understanding of the history of religion rather than the history of religions.

Kristensen presents an indicative outline of his methodology as it applies to sacrifice. He observes that sacrifice is a very common phenomenon, and that this ubiquity cannot be due to chance. Thus, the commonality suggests that sacrifice, or at the very least the needs that it represents, must be in some sense (humanly) universal. The only way to determine this universal basis, he suggests, is through the comparative method. Those aspects that are common to all forms of sacrifice must be specifically analysed; this process will culminate in the underlying basis for the practice wherever it is found. In some specific cases the elements will be clearly found, in other cases less clearly; by bringing these and others together, Kristensen argues that the commonalities can be distilled. He is not, however, interested specifically in common practices, but rather in common meanings. Kristensen assumes that religious elements that are typologically similar will by definition also share the same underlying value or meaning. This example highlights the essential nature of the approach; it is not particularly interested in specific details or context but rather in the classification of phenomena, and the analysis of the categories so created.

The outline suggests that despite Kristensen's claim that phenomenology is particularly interested in how believers perceive, understand, and feel, by moving away from a contextualised and particularised analysis the approach has actually very little to say about an insider's point of view. The discussion of specific topics, which make up the majority of material covered in the book, is almost entirely comparative, with only brief discussion of each particular case. In the section on 'The Worship of Earth

God' the discussion covers at least eight religions in twelve pages, hardly enough space to outline the internal beliefs of a single religious perspective let alone to compare them in their own terms. The discussion, although bringing in a wide range of data, focuses on abstracted 'religious ideas' that seem to come from the phenomenologist rather than the people whose voices he is claiming to present.

After presenting the fundamentals of the phenomenological approach to religion, Kristensen takes up the question of how religion is to be defined (the method of definition rather than a definition itself). He argues that although many scholars have attempted to define religion on the basis of common characteristics, this approach has failed because none of the phenomena selected are present in all forms of religion. Thus he rejects a simple form of substantialist definition that defines religion as the basis of specific substance, for example the presence of a god or gods.

Kristensen also rejects (at least on the surface) essentialist definitions of religion as the basis of phenomenological study. He implies that the use of such models is inherently circular. The essence is determined in advance and is also the 'goal of the endeavour' (Kristensen, 1971: 8). Nonetheless he does not deny that religion has an essence, rather that the search for the essence is the province of philosophy rather than phenomenology; phenomenology, as a comparative approach, stands between history and philosophy. History's role is to trace specific developments in particular cultures: phenomenology compares the phenomenon between cultures while remaining tied to the specific empirical data; philosophy moves beyond the specific to determine the universal essence underlying the empirical data collected and compared by the other two approaches.

The essence of religion, however, is understood to be unique, moving beyond the normal confines of human knowledge. Kristensen suggests that in order to understand the essence of religion we must have some degree of religious experience ourselves. In making this argument Kristensen is in part attempting to deal with the underlying contradiction in his approach, that is, the conflict between the insider and outsider point of view. If the analyst must be an insider (and the specific religion of the analyst is not significant as all religion ultimately shares a common essence) then he mediates between the two points of view and, at least in part, obviates the contradiction. He takes the theological aspect one step further, suggesting that the study of religion is itself part of a personal religious developmental process; 'when religion is the subject of our work, we grow religiously' (Kristensen, 1971: 10).

Gerardus van der Leeuw's *Religion in Essence and Manifestation* (first published in 1933) is a classic and influential text in the phenomenology of religion. Van der Leeuw was a student of Kristensen and his work shares many elements with Kristensen's approach, while also moving in several distinctive directions. It develops the three main aspects of phenomenology developed in the work of earlier phenomenologists: *epochē*, *einfühlung* and typology. His work like many other phenomenologists, as illustrated in the work of Kristensen, also seems to move into a more theological vein. This theological aspect is particularly highlighted in Ninian Smart's foreword to van der Leeuw's magnum opus. Smart suggests that van der Leeuw stands on the threshold between phenomenology and Christian theology (see also a detailed discussion of van der Leeuw's commitment to Christian theology in Waardenburg, 1978: 187–247). He also suggests that this basis in a faith position strengthened van der Leeuw's application of the *epochē* and *einfühlung* aspects of his phenomenological analysis of religions; as a believer he was sympathetic to the beliefs of others or, at the least, the transcendental basis of those beliefs. Van der Leeuw also develops the aspect of *einfühlung* in his view of understanding – specifically the understanding of religion. Religion is understood to be a subject that can only be understood subjectively, thus the scholar can not approach it from a purely objective perspective, rather, as suggested by Waardenburg, van der Leeuw argues that the student has to 're-experience' the object, that is, make the object part of his own subjective experience (Waardenburg, 1978: 227).

It is also likely that this Christian theological basis to his approach also gives the work its underlying evolutionary basis; one of its differences from the work of Kristensen. As in the work of Otto, van der Leeuw seems to be presenting an evolutionary model that culminates in Christianity. The evolutionary aspect of his discussion is supported by an uncritical appropriation of the work of Lévy-Bruhl. Lévy-Bruhl has argued for a distinction between 'primitive' thought and 'modern' thought. While modern ways of thinking were understood to be essentially rational and individual, 'primitive' ways of thinking were pre-logical and essentially communal. This distinction, also developed in the work of Jung, has been strongly challenged by the evidence from a wide range of ethnographic contexts, which demonstrates that there is no essential difference in ways of thinking between different forms of human society. Interestingly, in spite of the lack of any ethnographic or empirical support this distinction has recently resurfaced in the concept of 'primal religions' discussed in the concluding section of this part of the volume. Although the evolutionary aspect of van der Leeuw is therefore problematic, it emphasises the strong focus on history in his approach to religion, an emphasis that distinguishes him from some other phenomenologists, most notably Eliade (see below) whose work is distinctly ahistorical.

In spite of his emphasis on history, the element of classification is also an essential element in van der Leeuw's approach. Van der Leeuw suggests that classification is the process of identifying a phenomenon and placing it into the context of other similar phenomena. Once elements have been categorised, then ideal types of the phenomenon can be abstracted from the category. Van der Leeuw's typology is somewhat different to that of Kristensen; rather than being specifically interested in objects, van der Leeuw is concerned with structures or relations, thus his work should be seen as morphological rather than typological. This emphasis on relations is seen in the structure of the book as a whole; each section focuses on a specific type of relation, for example the relations between god and man and between man and god.

Van der Leeuw develops a unique spin on the concept of ideal type; this is clearly indicated in a brief example using the soul:

> 'Type' in itself, however, has no reality; nor is it a photograph of reality. Like structure, it is timeless and need not actually occur in history. But it possesses life, its own significance, its own law. The 'soul', again, as such, never and nowhere 'appears'; there is always and only some definite kind of soul which is believed in, and is in this its definiteness unique. It may be said that the ideas of the soul formed by two persons, it may be in the same cultural and religious circle, are never wholly the same. Still there is a type of soul, a structural relation of distinctive soul-structures. The type itself (to repeat) is timeless; nor is it real. Nevertheless it is alive and appears to us. (van der Leeuw, 1986 [1933]: 675–6)

Thus, the ideal type is in part an artificial construction that is distinct from a particular example, but it is also real and ahistorical, revealing some essential features of the structure of relations being studied.

Van der Leeuw suggests that there are two ways of understanding religion: starting with the human perspective or starting from god (whom he believes to exist). If religion is examined from the human perspective, it relates to the study of 'intelligible experience' – the direct study of observable phenomena, or from the divine perspective, 'incomprehensible revelation' (van der Leeuw, 1986 [1933]: 679). The aspect of experience is a phenomenon, that is, an object that exists and appears to us, and thus can be studied. Revelation is not a phenomenon and therefore cannot be studied directly. It can, however, be studied indirectly because the human response to revelation is a phenomenon and thus is amenable to analysis.

On the basis of these phenomena van der Leeuw suggests that 'religion implies that man does not simply accept the life that is given to him' (1986 [1933]: 679). He suggests that religion is essentially the search for power. This power is variously described in his analysis; it includes value, meaning and power in a much more direct sense. The search for power, or perhaps following the second of his two ways of understanding, the experience of power, leads human beings to look for that which is greater than themselves, something from which they gain power or something which expresses power.

Part of this process, this search, is the structuring of reality. Taking a line that is further developed by Berger (see the section on sociological analyses of religion), van der Leeuw suggests that the world itself has no meaning. In the process of finding meaning, humans construct a meaningful world. In this sense, he suggests that religion and culture are identical.

Religious meaning, however, moves beyond the limited meanings of everyday experience. It is the form of meaning 'that on which no wider nor deeper meaning what ever can follow' (van der Leeuw, 1986 [1933]: 680). It is the culmination of the search for meaning, but it is always beyond reach. It is the edge of incomprehension.

Van der Leeuw's discussion clearly illustrates the presuppositions of the phenomenological approach. Its preliminary aspects, presented in a detailed analysis of power (the first 21 chapters of the work), are built from a typological analysis of power, bringing together many threads from different societies. This analysis leads to the development of the ideal type, of incomprehensible meaning', which is distinct from any particular instance of it. His discussions, as a whole, rely on the principles of *epochē* and *einfühlung*. They bracket out the reductionist aspects of analysis while through bracketing in retain empathy for the subject's perspective. This empathy is particularly clear in van der Leeuw's characterisation of 'religious meaning', which seems to be more descriptive theology than scientific or historical analysis.

Although van der Leeuw does not directly define religion in *Religion in Essence and Manifestation*, his analysis suggests a definition that has both a substantialist and essentialist basis. The substantialist aspect is clearly suggested by the role of power and its development in religion meaning. Although power, in certain of its manifestations, is relatively undefined, as the discussion progresses it seems clear that what van der Leeuw is developing is a definition based on a concept or experience of god/s. This focus on god/s is perhaps directly connected to van der Leeuw's theological presupposition that there is a god, and therefore religion is both man's response to god (the objects of phenomenology) and god's relation to man (revelation). As part of this substantialist argument, power can be subsumed under the concept of the sacred – as awesome and dangerous – and the dichotomy between the sacred and the profane. This dichotomy, which is similar to that of Durkheim, is taken up specifically by Eliade and becomes the basis of his version of phenomenological theology.

Van der Leeuw's discussion also has a clear underlying essentialist basis. Although this essentialist aspect is somewhat different from that of the Kantians and neo-Kantians who located religion within a specific *a priori*, van der Leeuw's arguments suggest a basis for religion that is no less fundamental or universal – perhaps the difference is that its origin lies outside the human consciousness in god rather than in a specific faculty of consciousness. The methodology outlined above culminates in ideal types; athough these are, as suggested above, partially artificial constructs they also have a reality that transcends both temporality and particularity. They are, for want of a better term, the universal essence of religion. As such, they must arise from some universal aspect, which is the experience of the transcendent, and provide an essentialist basis for the existence of religion.

C. J. Bleeker continues in the tradition of van der Leeuw, bringing together aspects of the phenomenological emphasis on the internal voice and the emphasis on the evolutionary and historical. His work suggests a three-tiered methodology that has been summarised by Biezais. The first level of analysis is 'the *theoria* of the phenomena', the second the '*logos*', and the third the '*entelecheia*' (Biezais, 1979: 145). The *theoria* refers to the analysis of the essence of the particular typological group, the *logos* the inner logic or structure of the elements, and the *entelecheia* refers to the inner dynamic, the developmental aspect that relates the phenomena to the development of the 'religious life of mankind' (Biezais, 1979: 145). This last level of analysis emphasises Bleeker's view that the enterprise of phenomenological analysis is ultimately about the history of religion rather than the particular history of religions.

Bleeker's position, while having the benefit of clearly articulating the different levels of analysis, is built on presuppositions that may undermine its analytical status. The most significant problematic presupposition is the concept of history of religion. This concept assumes that underlying all the particularities of culture and context all religions have an underlying impetus that is moving them in some direction; a direction that is clearly understood to be progressive and evolutionary. Given the huge diversity of human religions and the diversity in religious choices and meanings there seems to be little evidence to suggest this common historical basis. The only argumentative basis for this thesis is the typological system and the essentialist arguments that underlie it and arise from it. One may well ask, 'is it the typological system which creates the chosen similarities, and by selective analysis creates the means of these religious objects?' If there is no basis for a necessary common analysis of these only apparently similar elements, then there is no logical reason why religions share a common essence or a common trajectory; particularly since the empirical data suggests that religions are diverse and not singular.

It is possible that Bleeker's arguments for a historical trajectory for religion lies in a more fundamental theological presupposition, that is, the existence of a transcendental other. This view is supported by Bleeker's arguments about the nature of phenomenology as a discipline. He argues that unlike other disciplines, for example, anthropology and sociology, phenomenology and history of religions have a different goal – they seek to describe the 'different dimension' that characterises religion as opposed to other human constructs. He suggests that the role of the study of religions is to understand the relationship of human beings to the 'divine reality' (Bleeker, 1979: 175). If one accepts that the object of religion is distinct from an object and is the same for all religions then it is possible to posit a single trajectory for religion and a common essence for religious objects.

Bleeker also uses the transcendental other to establish a second feature that is common to many phenomenological arguments. If phenomenology of religion is ultimately aimed at understanding the relationship between god and humans, then the relationship between individual human beings and society is not directly relevant to the study. Therefore those approaches to religion that focus on the sociological factors in religion, that is, the disciplines that Bleeker considers to be reductionist, are not relevant to phenomenology, except perhaps in a very secondary way. This argument is also applicable to psychological approaches that see religion as emerging from the individual psyche. The theological argument deployed here provides an additional basis for the phenomenological methodology of *epochē*. The advantage of Bleeker's argument is that it, at least, provides a coherent basis for the rejection of other methodological approaches, that is, that it is based on the unique experience of the divine; arguably this aspect of his argument moves him out of verifiable academic analysis into the realm of theology and undefended and unarguable presuppositions.

Mircea Eliade is one of the most influential figures to emerge from the phenomenological tradition. He takes up many of the themes discussed thus far and transforms them into his own distinctive approach. One of the most significant features of his work as a whole is the distinction between the sacred and the profane, and his emphasis on the perception of the sacred as the basis of religion. He uses the term 'hierophanies' to describe the structures that allow humans to perceive the sacred; he states that the term literally means 'that something sacred shows itself to us' (Eliade, 1959 [1957]: 11). It is significant that he also uses the term archetype to refer to these structures, linking his thought back to the work of both Jung and Otto – Otto's theories of the sacred are the first to be positively examined in his *The Sacred and the Profane* (1959 [1957]). Hierophanies can be found in objects, in their simple forms, and in the 'supreme hierophany' Jesus Christ. All hierophanies, the basis of Eliade's definition of religion, simple or complex, are essentially the same, 'manifestations of something of a wholly different order' (1959 [1957]: 11). Thus, like many other phenomenologists, Eliade's discussion of religion relies on the experience of a transcendental other.

Eliade's methodology draws on the typological tradition of phenomenology. In *Patterns in Comparative Religion* (1958 [1949]) he draws together a wide range of religious material into a number of categories, for example hierophanies related to the sun or the moon. His use of this method, which in his case focuses on the structures of religion rather than specific elements, is much narrower than that of many other phenomenologists; he uses the typological method to discover the meaning and essence of the sacred. As in other phenomenological studies, his work is essentially ahistorical. Although he pays lip service to the historical context of the hierophanies that he analyses, his primary focus is on the universal qualities of these structures. The elements that are brought together include material from the Neolithic to Native American cultures. The assumption underlying his argument is that the underlying hierophany, or in some cases even the limited symbolic meaning of all of the elements brought together, is identical rregardless of temporal or geographic context.

In spite of this ahistorical emphasis in much of his work, both some of his texts and the language used in relation to the hierophanies suggest an underlying historical or evolutionary schema (perhaps similar to the history of religion mentioned above). This is perhaps most clearly developed in *The Myth of the Eternal Return* (1955) in which his discussion of the role of myth and sacred space in conquering temporality culminate in a view of Christianity as the final stage in mythological development. His use of the terms 'simple' and 'higher' or 'supreme' in relation to hierophanies, with 'simple' usually relating to indigenous religions (which he considers 'primitive') also suggest at the very least a non-temporal sense of progress.

Eliade's work also develops an essentialist definition of religion. Religion is based on a universal experience of the sacred and is common to all human beings at any time or place. This definition underlies his rejection of the use of other methodologies in relation to religion. In this as in many other respects, Eliade seems to be developing the methodology and theoretical presuppositions to their logical extreme. Whereas many of the other phenomenologists skirt around the essentialist implications of their approach, Eliade is willing to make it the cornerstone upon which all his fantastic edifices are constructed.

One additional area of Eliade's analysis needs to be addressed; his categorisation of the religious consciousness of people from earlier cultures. Eliade presents a somewhat more complex discussion of 'primitive religion' than found in many earlier analyses. He suggests that there are four principles useful for understanding religions, including both 'primitive' and modern. First, he suggests the distinction between the sacred and profane and the paradoxical incarnation of the sacred in a natural object, which is the basis of a hierophany. Second, Eliade argues that this feature is common to all religions, albeit developed in different forms. Third, every religion is composed of both simple and complex forms of hierophany. Fourth, 'primitive' religions are not merely constructed from these hierophanies; rather, the hierophanies are part of a systematic whole that includes a wide range of other traditional material. Alongside these aspects of similarity between religious forms and complexity within forms, Eliade does distinguish 'primitive' religion from that which we find in modern societies. The primary difference, he argues, is that 'primitive' peoples live their organic life as a sacrament, whereas modern people do not (Eliade, 1958 [1949]: 31). In these societies everyday acts of eating and sexuality become means of communing with 'ultimate reality'. This distinction has similarities to Jung's view that 'primitive' people live entirely in the realm of the unconscious, and is influential on the theory of primal religion, which believes that individuals in primal religions experience the world in a very different way to modern people.

Eliade's argument also includes an additional factor that is central to his understanding of religion as a whole. He suggests that practitioners of religion understand these everyday sacraments, like all other rites, as repeating archetypal events, events which are understood to be outside time. Through the enactment of these rites, including eating and sex, 'primitive' people put themselves out of time and connect to eternity. This notion of the problem of temporality and the need to conquer it through ritual repetition is a feature of most of Eliade's analyses.

Joseph M. Kitagawa presents a clear statement of the presuppositions that are shared by both phenomenologists and historians of religions that moves in a very different direction to that of the interpretive model developed by Eliade. Although he claims that these presuppositions do not form a definition, he does suggest that they can be used to define in certain phenomena, for example, Buddhism, or define out other phenomena, for example, communism. Thus the presuppositions seem to function as a definition even if they are not so defined.

Kitagawa highlights three areas of agreement, many of which are closely associated with the work of Joachim Wach (discussed above in Part I).

The first of these, which we have seen is a significant feature of the phenomenological arguments, is 'religious experience', which as clearly stated in his discussion is experience of some external power or force. In connection with this essential element, Kitagawa reiterates the rejection of any form of sociological analysis of religion – quoting Eliade he states, 'it misses the one unique and irreducible element in it – the element of the Sacred' (Kitagawa, 1967: 40). The second common element is that religion is not reducible to its constituent elements. It is a 'total orientation' whose main focus is some form of salvation. Religion is ultimately about how to transform either the world or the self. The third area of commonality is that religion is composed of three constituent parts: 'theoretical', 'practical' and 'sociological' (Kitagawa, 1967: 41). The theoretical refers to the shared beliefs, the practical to the practice of the religion and the sociological to the social structural elements.

Kitagawa also discusses the differences between the two forms of *Religions-wissenschaft* (the Science of Religion). These include the 'structural' and the 'historical'. The structural is equivalent to the phenomenological approach. It tends to analyse religions in an ahistorical manner; it attempts to discover the 'universal characteristics' of religion through morphological or typological analysis. The historical method is more concerned with the particularities of a particular religion's development through time. They are interested in the factual events of history, looking at religion within its historical context. The two disciplines are thus clearly different, with different foci; they do, however, share common presuppositions and are seen as complementary forms of analysis (Kitagawa, 1967: 42).

A similar position was taken by Raffaele Pettazzoni, an historian of religion whose analyses of the development of particular religious phenomena included an evolutionary basis. Rather than primarily analysing phenomena using a typological or morphological method, he focuses on the contextualised historical developments. Pettazzoni suggests that the history of religion traces religion's contextualised and particular development within its broader cultural context. Phenomenology provides an additional element to the analysis that cannot be provided by the historian, that is the meaning of the phenomena outside the geographic or historical contexts. The two approaches, he suggests, should not be seen as separate sciences, but rather as 'two interdependent instruments of the same science' (Pettazzoni, 1954: 218).

Ugo Bianchi in *The History of Religions* (1975 [1970]), while arguing for the significance of the history of religions as an academic discipline, develops several significant lines of argument that move in very different directions to his predecessors, and in some respects challenge the underlying basis of the independence of the subject and the discipline. His first argument challenges the very nature of religion. He suggests that the term itself needs to be problematised – it does not describe an essential or universal phenomenon, rather it is a term that is meaningful in a particular culture at a particular point in time. Rather than defining in a strong sense, the term can only be used analogically – phenomena in other societies that are similar to what we consider to be religion, a term embedded in our own cultural context, can be considered and analysed as religion by analogy (Bianchi, 1975 [1970]: 1). This argument suggests that the term religion and the definition associated with that term could only be used in a very provisional sense, as a basis for discussion and communication, but not as a term that relates necessarily to a common experience or phenomenological basis. Bianchi suggests that religions are complex phenomena, which are integrated patterns of belief and practice, are variable in content and nature rather than singular.

Although Bianchi does not directly define religion, as a definition would change his problematisation of the category, he does suggest that religion or religiosity is a near universal aspect of the human experience. He does not, however, associate this universality with either an *a priori* or essentialist basis. His discussion of the problem of universality highlights the diversity of religious expression and experience, and concludes that religion does not derive from a single human faculty or experience. He does mention some areas of content that are common features of religion, for example, the 'existence of mysterious or transcendent truths' and 'existential interests' (Bianchi, 1975 [1970]: 31). He also uses the term 'holy' as the foundation of religion. This concept, however, unlike that of Eliade, seems to be relative to the particular religion rather than a common universal basis. Bianchi also attempts to formulate a formal definition:

> At the very basis of religion, we usually find belief in one or more powers, conceived as superior persons older than human beings and independent of them. Man and the human collectivities, adopt an attitude of dependence on these beings, and this is reflected in their conduct, ethical or ritual, and in a belief in the possibility of communicating with these higher powers ... Religion implies a 'breakthrough', in the sense that one of the first characteristics of the religious element may be discerned in the establishment of a relationship with a super-human power which is understood to condition the life of the world and life in the world. (Bianchi, 1975 [1970]: 33)

Bianchi's definition is a slightly weakened substantialist definition. The 'usually' allows for some latitude in application relative to the cultural context. His concept of analogy also relativises the definition.

Bianchi's approach to the material is also more limited in scope than that of many earlier phenomenologists and historians of religion. He suggests that the primary interest of the discipline should be the 'facts and details' of the object understudy, in the same way as these form the basis of any historical study (Bianchi, 1975 [1970]): 3). He thus places broader questions about the nature of religion into a secondary category. Bianchi, however, also emphasises that the aspect of comparative religion is an essential feature of the history of religions. It is the nature of this comparison that makes Bianchi's approach distinctive. He argues that the comparative element must be 'firmly based on historical-positive enquiry', an enquiry rooted in the context and facts of the object being studied (Bianchi, 1975 [1970]: 4). He suggests that the history of religions in its comparative aspect stands as a mediator between 'phenomenological generalities' and the individual and concrete manifestations.

The form of comparison is significantly different from that of most phenomenologists. Bianchi suggests that the usually phenomenological method of examining elements out of context will tend to be 'mis-understood and arbitrarily identified or contrasted' (1975 [1970]: 7). His discussion underscores the significant problems with the phenomenological methodology: that the categories are in some sense arbitrary and thus of little theoretical merit, and that elements out of context lose the meaning as it arises not from the object itself but from the context of structural relations. Bianchi's method of comparison is to create a typology of a system as a whole, both in terms of its synchronic content and in terms of its diachronic development.

As a whole, Bianchi continues in very significant respects the necessary process, introducing a much more contextualised and relativised form of the history of religions. His approach is much more firmly rooted in the empirical data and challenges some of the more intuitive leaps charac-teristic of many of his predecessors. The only significant issue raised by his methodology is the support of the view that religion cannot be properly studied by other disciplinary approaches. With the removal of any essen-tialist or a priori basis for religion, there seems to be little support for an argument that suggests that religion is distinct from other human institutions and must be studied only in its own terms.

Although Wilfred Cantwell Smith is usually regarded as a theologian, several aspects of his approach to religion are related to and built upon similar ideals to those found in Bianchi. Smith suggests that the question of, what is religion? is, due to the huge diversity both within and between religions, an illegitimate question, and one which must be dropped before one can study religions. He states:

> Neither religion in general nor any one of the religions, I will contend, is in itself an intelligible entity, a valid object of inquiry or of concern either for the scholar or the man of faith. (Smith, 1978: 12)

Smith is arguing that both the concept of religion as an abstractable entity and religions, for example Christianity or Judaism, are constructs with little or no meaning or value. He is not suggesting that the objects under study do not exist, but rather that the view that they constitute an identifiable whole is not justified. He points out that the very concept of religion as an identifiable or separable cultural phenomenon is not found in many languages. Thus, the view that they have something separated from other cultural institutions called 'religion' is an imposition of an external and inappropriate cultural model. Smith presents an extended analysis of the history of the term religion, conclusively demonstrating how the term transforms over time in relation to its specific cultural context. He concludes that the only part of the inherited definition that is worth retaining is that of personal faith, the other elements relating to definition of the essence of the term or one religion in relation to others only lead to confusion or misinformation (Smith, 1978: 50).

He suggests that in the place of religion we can identify two separate elements, faith and cumulative tradition. Faith refers to the individual inner aspect of religion and cumulative tradition to the social outer aspect of religion. Faith refers to the relationship with the transcendent reality – and for Smith the transcendent is real and the foundation of faith. Cumulative tradition refers to the historically conditioned cultural inheritance that shapes the expression of individual faith.

Smith's discussion is both a valuable contribution and inherently flawed from the perspective of a social scientist. Its contributions include the deconstruction of the concept of religions and religion. He introduces to the historians of religions the fact that our concept of religion and other religions are cultural constructs, shaped by our own cultural presuppositions. A second significant point in his analysis is the inclusion of both individual and society in his definition. The main problem area is found in the underlying basis of his argument. He emphasises faith, as opposed to the institutional side of religion, for cultural reasons as intrusive as those he is attempting to challenge. His model of faith and cumulative tradition is open to precisely the same challenge as the term religion. Finally, his whole argument rests on the individual relationship with a transcendental other – a phenomenon which must remain the realm of the theologian rather than the social scientist – social science is concerned with human beings, understanding of god, and how one might conceive of relating to such a being; it can not be concerned with god's relation to human beings.

Ninian Smart, in many senses is a descendent of all three traditions, phenomenology, history of religions and comparative religion. Although he accepts the three major methodological premises of phenomenology, his analysis is very different from the traditional phenomenological analyses, and in a sense he further develops the problematisation of the concept of religion found in Smith and Bianchi.

Smart strongly emphasises the elements of *epochē* and *einfühlung*. In *The Phenomenon of Religion* (1973) much of the first chapter is devoted to a defence of these aspects of the phenomenological approach. The element of *epochē* is particularly significant; Smart uses the concept of 'bracketing' to allow the phenomenologist to present without a value judgment in terms of quality or truth the beliefs and experiences of the believer. His discussion suggests that this bracketed presentation would be little different in content or quality to that of the believer. It would, however, have a greater scope than that of a believer, and have a different goal, that is, descriptive rather than testimonial. Smart's understanding of phenomenology moves beyond a purely rational description, involving imagination and evocation as well.

Smart's discussion of phenomenological analyses suggests that there are two main forms, internal and external. The internal aspect focuses on processes that occur within the religion, and external explanations focus on how religion is shaped by cultural elements outside religion, for example, kinship (Smart, 1973: 41–4). In order to understand these two forms of explanation, Smart reintroduces his concept of dimensions of religion, perhaps the most significant aspect of his analysis. In the account found in *The Phenomenon of Religion* he identifies six dimensions; this number is later expanded to eight (for his initial detailed discussion see: Smart, 1971 [1969]: 15–25). These dimensions in their final version include: the ritual, doctrinal, mythic, experiential, ethical, organisational, material and political. These dimensions are not meant to be understood individually; rather they interrelate with each other in an organic model (Smart, 1973: 43). The internal form of explanation focuses on the interrelationships between these dimensions. The external form shows how the dimensions are related to external cultural features.

Due to the two forms of explanation and the complexity of interrelations at all levels, Smart suggests that the study of religions must include the findings and methods of other disciplines, for example, psychology or sociology. He outlines four interrelated methods by which Christianity and Buddhism might be studied by the study of religion. These methods include: first, the history of religions, focusing on the interrelationships between the dimensions within the specific religious tradition; second, historical-dialectical studies, focusing on the external aspect of historical development and particularly the dialectical relationship between religion and culture; third, phenomenological and structural studies, focusing on internal aspects, while also moving into a form of typological or morphological analysis; fourth, dialectical-phenomenological studies, which refers to those methodologies that analyse the phenomena of religion in terms of their wider social and psychological context (Smart, 1973: 45–8). In *The Phenomenon of Religion* Smart rejects Eliade's call for the study of religion to take one additional step, that is, 'the presentation and development of the values of religion through the activity of the Religionist (the student of religions) which would enable men to assimilate the meanings of religion in a new cultural self-understanding' (Smart, 1973: 35). This would, he suggests be a covert form of theologising. He does, however, suggest that the study of religions would have the positive affect of making people more aware of religious pluralism.

Smart's deconstruction of religion into eight dimensions allows a more open-ended definition of religion than found in many other approaches. Although in his early discussions of the dimensions he is more prescriptive about the necessary presence of each dimension, thereby allowing him to reject Marxism as a religion because it lacks religious experience (Smart, 1971 [1969]: 22), his later work suggests that each religion may include different combinations of the dimensions or differentially emphasise them (the internal aspect of analysis) based in part on different historical and cultural trajectories (the external aspect of the analysis). This more open-ended character allows for the definition to include a much wider range of diverse phenomena. In conjunction with the analogical method of Bianchi and Smith's critique of religion as being a culturally constructed concept, Smart's analysis, if loosely applied, allows for a definition of religion that is both analytically useful and responds to the specific empirical context and data.

Both the contributions and the problems associated with phenomenology and its related disciplines are suggested by the three underlying principles, that is, *epochē*, *einfühlung* and the eidetic vision. The principles of *epochē* and *einfühlung* are particularly significant. Many theories of religion looked upon their object of study as inherently flawed or the product of error. These and other approaches often ignored the internal perspective – not even viewing internal explanations as data, let alone possible explanations of the objects being studied. The concept of bracketing and the challenging of external theorising is also important as a means for dialectically testing the theories: are they merely products of one cultural or academic stance rather than being usefully or meaningfully applied? The move in some of the later thinkers away from more essentialist models to analogical models or models based on different configurations of elements are also very useful, provided the analysis moves beyond description of the particular historical development or structural configuration. The role of typology or, more precisely, comparative analysis is also useful. It can provide the basis of a more dialectical definition of the phenomena being studied, with each new comparator problematising the theory or definition.

These principles, however, also lead to several problems. Many phenomenological analyses, for example Smart's analyses of myth, because of the emphasis on the internal perspective as the only authoritative perspective, tend to be overly descriptive, presenting the theological perspective as the only point of view. As Smart himself suggests they are parasitic on theology; they present the theology in brackets but without any alternative forms of explanation. This privileging of the internal point of view can sometimes appear to be an acceptance of the theological propositions as they are the only ones presented – all other approaches are considered to be reductionist and thus excluded.

This problem is exacerbated by the rejection of theoretical models arising outside the religions themselves. This rejection is based on the view that religion is in some sense inherently different to any other phenomena or that it is not epiphenomenal to them and thus cannot be analysed in reference to them. This view can only be maintained if religion is assumed to relate to some experience that is different from any other human experience, that it arises from a unique human faculty, or that it uniquely is a response to a transcendental other. The first two of these would need to be demonstrated before religion should be distinguished in this way: there is no convincing evidence that religion as an essential phenomenon exists; as pointed out by Bianchi and Smith the term itself is culturally constructed and serves an analogical function. The third possibility is a theological statement and thus should be bracketed and not serve as the basis for argument. It relies on data that falls outside the scope of social scientific analysis. It is our contention that religion is a human construct (whether related to a transcendental other or not) and therefore it can and should be analysed in the same way as any other societal construct. Even if religion arises at the same time as other institutions or shapes as well as being shaped by our psyche this does not prevent it from being studied in context with tools associated with sociology or psychology.

A problem which perhaps arises from an over strong emphasis of the empathetic aspect of the approach is the transformation of the discipline from observational to theological. This is particularly seen in the work of Eliade and Otto but is also found in many other approaches. This problem is found on two levels. The first of these has already been touched upon; the view that religion or faith (as in Smith) arise from experience of some type of transcendental other. As indicated, this, by definition, is a theological statement rather than a scientific observation. The second level of theology is found in Eliade's concept of 'creative hermeneutics'. This, and other similar concepts, sees the role of phenomenology as being transformative, leading modern people to a new understanding of the transcendent. While this may be of interest, it can only serve as data for analysis and not part of an analysis. Weaker forms of this view see phenomenology as transforming our views of other religions or inculcating pluralism. While these may be laudable outcomes, they should not be part of the basis of an academic discipline.

The underlying view in many phenomenological approaches – that they are presenting an internal view without imposing an external theory – is undermined by their own typological emphasis. The typologies that they employ are not determined by the empirical data, they preexist any particular set of data and are thus externally imposed by the phenomenologist. The way that a typology is developed, that elements are included or excluded, is based on an external perspective that rests on a stated or unstated theory or definition of religion. In addition, the use of the typology, that is, the expectation that it will reveal some essential characteristic is also theoretically motivated. This problem is particularly true of the phenomenological approaches similar to Kristensen and Eliade; it is also true of the dimensional approach of Smart. Although Smart's model allows for a greater degree of flexibility, the choice of which dimensions to include and the definition of those dimensions is shaped by a predetermined understanding of religion and the content of religion. Smart's definition, certainly, has a greater ability to arise from the empirical data, each religion has a different configuration and thus a different definition, but as indicated by Smart's rejection of Marxism the model can also serve as a straitjacket. The final problem with these approaches is the view that one can approach data naïvely, that is, without any theoretical presuppositions. All descriptions are based on a selection process and thus on a theoretical perspective; it is better from an academic perspective to be aware of the theoretical perspective and to challenge it than to assume that it is not present.

CHAPTER 9

Feminism, Gender and Religion

Feminist approaches have moved in a wide variety of directions, which include: critiques of both religion and religious studies; an attempt to recover women's voices in historical and ethnographic discussions; different attempts to reformulate theologies to express women's needs and values; and in contradistinction to the others, an attempt to revalidate traditional patterns from an internal women's perspective. An additional area, which is touched on, is that of feminist theories of religion and those feminist approaches imbedded in other disciplines that study religion.

Although much of this section treats feminist approaches from a somewhat monolithic perspective, feminist critics of religion vary in regard to their politics and attitudes, as well as the underlying goals of their discussions. The major debates within feminism today are similar to those found in other aspects of religious studies. A major focus of feminism has been on the essentialist side of the debate, arguing for a universal understanding of women and women's experience of religion, based on a view that women experience the world in different ways to men. More recently a non-essentialist trend has developed, emphasising the diversity of women's experiences, and the religions and theologies that arise from them.

In assessing feminist approaches to religion it is important to keep in mind that many of them emerge from the praxis of religion and retain this orientation as an underlying feature of their discussions and critique. Thus, many early feminist thinkers, rather than attempting to redefine religion or develop new methods of analysing religion, attempted to challenge and transform the role of women within religion. This struggle to transform the role of women found its emphasis particularly in the access of women to positions of religious authority and was closely associated with movements on a wider societal level seeking equality for women, especially in terms of politics.

One area, however, which began to challenge the nature of religion as such, is found in early feminist biblical interpretation. *The Women's Bible* (1895) by Elizabeth Cady Stanton challenged the biblical underpinnings of Christianity, arguing that the very language of scripture and scriptural interpretation upheld the systemic exploitation of women. Challenging the use of language and its role in validating patriarchal patterns of thinking is a continuing feature of the feminist critique of religion.

The current feminist tradition, which developed primarily after the 1960s, has been highly and appropriately critical of the androcentric or patriarchal orientation of most discussions of religion. Men have generally written and developed these approaches about men's roles and understandings, answering the questions that arise from a male-oriented perception of religion and culture. Even when women have written in these areas much of their work, or the ethnographic/historical material on which it is based, has been written by and for men.

Feminist critics suggest that the field of religious studies has been both implicitly and explicitly sexist. On one level, studies of religion from almost every discipline have ignored the roles of women within religion and society. Discussions of religion have tended to focus on those agents with power and authority and the related institutional structures, many of which are controlled by and express the aspirations of men. Women's spirituality and religious aspirations, which are often relegated to the private sphere, are rarely discussed or perceived as significant. They also point out that most studies of religion have been highly textually centred. These texts, they argue, are usually written by men and do not express women's understandings or feelings.

Religious studies and other disciplines are also criticised for ignoring the role that religion plays in creating systems of power and hierarchy, models of identity including gender and perpetuating systems of exploitation. Many feminist thinkers suggest that these issues have not been raised and need to be at the very heart of the study of religion.

Perhaps the most important issue that arises from the feminist critique of the study of religion is its challenge of the supposed universality of the definitions and models proposed by the different approaches. Feminist critics argue that since these approaches have ignored the roles and voices of women both in the specific religions and in the very framing of the approaches themselves, their definitions should not be seen as universal. The definitions and the aspect of religion that they study arise from a specific set of power relations and are not in any sense a universal depiction of the phenomena.

This critique also highlights the fact that all social phenomena are made up of a wide range of different interest groups and can only be understood in a relative sense in respect of those interest groups. This aspect of their critique ultimately challenges the universalisation of the feminist critique itself and suggests the need to relativise it through an examination of its particular cultural location as well as its power and hierarchical aspects. This critique also raises questions about the nature and value of any analytical construct, as in some sense essentialist, including that of religion itself.

Rosalind Shaw in 'The Gendering of Religious Studies' (1995: 65–76) raises an aspect of this issue in regard to the history of religions, and particularly the phenomenological school of Eliade (1995: 67). She suggests that although phenomenology moved in the correct direction through its interpretive standpoint that claimed to privilege and empathise with internal experience, the issue of 'whose experience' still remains. She suggests that the object of empathy was still specifically male and therefore the supposed universality was at variance with a feminist approach to the study of religion. Shaw emphasises that there are two problems with Eliade and, by extension, to other approaches to the study of religion. First, in spite of their claim of universality, these approaches are partial. Second, and perhaps even more significantly, these approaches reflect the andro-centric orientation of power and are essentially views from an entrenched power position: in Shaw's terms, a 'view from above', as opposed to the feminist position which comes from the exploited group and is a 'voice from below' (1995: 67).

Shaw's critique of phenomenology thus challenges its two essential theoretical pillars: that it presents a universal understanding of religion and that it presents a shared internal point of view. The phenomenologist's view that religion is in some sense *sui generis*, that it arises from some unique and specific aspect of human nature and thus stands outside any particular distinctions, is challenged when feminist critics demonstrate that both the analysis and content of the analysis arise from a particular gendered point of view. If the feminist analysis is taken into account then, at the very least, the particular phenomenological analyses, if not the whole phenomen-ological enterprise, must be severely challenged. The textual basis of phenomenology, as already indicated, is also highly problematic as it arises from a specific system of androcentric power relations, and thus the view that it is non-gendered and represents a shared cultural consensus, if not a universal basis, is also unsustainable.

These issues lead feminists to suggest the need for a new model for studying religion. At the foundation of this new model is a re-under-standing of the term religion itself. Ursula King suggests that rather than seeing religion as a cumulative tradition, which would tend to emphasise the androcentric nature of those who have selected that tradition, understanding and analysis of religion should focus on the 'experiential and personal', an approach which would validate the experience of both women and men (1995: 1–38). She also suggests that the focus on institutions and texts as the basis of an understanding of religion has also contributed to the absence of women and therefore presented a false picture of religion. A more holistic and individually centred approach would facilitate a positive reconstruction of the discipline.

June O'Connor lists a number of 'moments' that she suggests should characterise feminist critique and study of religion. The first is suspicion of the nature of sources. As mentioned above, texts are seen as arising from an androcentric context. The second is an attempt to recover women's voices, or to recreate those that are lost. The third, mirroring the arguments of Shaw, is the need to challenge notions of universality. The fourth is a more general challenge to the methods of academic scholarship, addressing whether a feminist scholarship would ask different questions or use different methodologies. Finally she cautions against turning feminist approaches into a new orthodoxy (1995: 46).

O'Connor's discussion suggests some ways in which academic scholarship might be transformed by a feminist critique. She focuses on the question of epistemology, that is, how we come to know things. She touches on a number of areas: the extension of 'root metaphors' – arguing that the basic concepts of religion, for example, sin, are created by particular groups with particular roles and power; the political and ethical implications of the root metaphors, as in the implications of a concept of 'God the father'; and the nature of sources, that is what is in them and what is not – she asks, what might these sources be like if they had been written by women? Finally, she challenges the very nature of morality as a diverse or gendered subject. All of these issues ultimately come together in challenging a concept of universality. Not only is religion itself an artificial construct reflecting power structures, so too are the forms of knowing that underlie the academic disciplines which study it (1995: 49–54). The ultimate question, which arises from these challenges to epistemology, is whether men and women have different epistemologies, different ways of knowing? Although many scholars have argued for a single way of knowing, O'Connor highlights the role that the different cultural experiences of men and women, and indeed other groups within society, have in shaping how and what we know.

This deconstruction of an essentialist understanding of knowing is encapsulated clearly in the following programmatic statement:

> Feminist analysis contributes to the scholarly enterprise, the work of critique and corrective, *in order that our observations about human life, our theories about human knowing, and our claims and conclusions about what is good for human beings are informed by a broad data base that takes seriously the diverse ways in which human life is experienced, thought about and lived.* (O'Connor, 1995: 56)

Any claims of universality must be tempered by the recognition of diversity in experience, power and, to some degree, biology.

It is important to note that O'Connor is not only addressing the questions that are asked, but also, and more significantly, the underlying basis of such questions. Many feminist critics of religious studies have argued that women, due to their different life experiences and relations to power do not approach issues of morality in the same way as men. Men's use of concepts like sin and redemption are built on power relations. Women's experience and view of these issues is much more embodied and experiential. This empathic and embodied nature of morality will clearly create a very different range of questions and analyses.

Shaw, following a line more akin to the Marxist critique of society argues that the element of power must be included in any analysis of religion. She states that 'power is "interior to" – not somehow detachable from – their lived religious experience' (1995: 70). Although she is speaking specifically in relation to the phenomenological argument that religion can only be understood in its own terms, her argument is generally applicable to other theoretical perspectives. Shaw, however, is not arguing for a new feminist religious studies; rather she is arguing for a much broader rearticulation of the disciplines in which women play a shaping role. She argues that feminists should not fall into the trap of phenomenology in universalising and essentialising the 'female reality'. Shaw sees this process specifically in theologies and critiques that replace male versions of god with female versions. She argues that the levels of difference and power relations must be recognised within the feminist discourse as in other cultural discourses (1995: 73–5).

To a large extent religion can be critiqued in much the same way as the study of religion. Religious texts and institutions have tended to reflect the interests and values of men. They also, and perhaps most significantly, play a significant role in the perpetuation of systems of hierarchy and power that validate patterns of exploitation. This critique works on several levels. It examines the way that practices and institutions relegate women to subservient positions, the ways in which religion enables the constructions of models of gender that shape women's perceptions of self, and men's perceptions of them, and how religious symbols and language are used as vehicles for creating a gendered understanding of reality. A key aspect of the critique is that religion in part creates false consciousness – creating a way of understanding and conceiving the world that traps women within the system of exploitation.

The critique of the study of religion, and indeed that of religion itself, shares many theoretical presuppositions with the Marxist analysis of religion and society. This theoretical inheritance is best seen in the work of Mary Daly. She emphasises both the issues of alienation and false consciousness respecting women's relationship to religion. Religion as the ideological tool of patriarchal systems provides a means by which women's alienation is covered up and women come to accept their position as inferior. Daly's discussion, like the Marxists, moves beyond analysis of an exploitative system; it argues for a need to overturn that system and the symbols that support and validate it. Daly's criticism regarding both alienation and false consciousness should also be extended to the study of religion. As indicated, as an academic discipline, religious studies is as much part of the androcentric ideological structure as is religion itself. Thus, it also forms part of a system that validates or naturalises (makes seem natural or normal) alienation and thus creates or supports false consciousness.

A second aspect of many feminist critiques of religion is the attempt to reconstruct religion in such a way that it expresses women's needs and values; these reconstructions form the basis of feminist theologies. Although theology is not directly relevant to the arguments analysed in this book, theologies are data for the study of particular religions rather than analysis, many of the issues that they take up are relevant to our discussion of the feminist critique of religion.

One of the most significant patriarchal religious symbols addressed by feminists from many different faith perspectives is god. Feminist critics have pointed out that in spite of the fact that many religious traditions, specifically Judaism and Christianity, have a wide range of gendered symbols for the divine, both masculine and feminine, most traditions give predominance to the masculine symbols, hence the very term god implicitly has masculine gender. These theologians have sought to recover those terms with feminine gender. Aside from the theological implications of their attempt at reconstruction, their analysis of the masculine gendered bias is a significant critique of the role of religion in creating false consciousness. On a simplistic level, it is hard for many people, women or men, to picture the Christian or Jewish god in other than masculine terms; this is due in part to the use of masculine language in relation to god, nouns and pronouns, and the other methods of symbolising the divine in art and other media.

This type of false consciousness is not only created in relation to images of the divine, but also to wider aspects of language and images of men and women. Throughout the liturgies of many religions, for example, the positive actors or agents are depicted as men, with male pronouns being used. This reads women out of seeing themselves or being seen as active or public agents. The images of women are even more problematic. As critics since the nineteenth century have pointed out, biblical images of women, for example, Eve, have created a very negative attitude towards women, associating them with sin. Both men and women internalise these images and thus they support the system of ideology and false consciousness.

Feminists working within specific religious traditions, as mentioned above, have also highlighted the nature of religious texts and their interpretation. These texts have usually been written by and for men, and generally write out women both in relation to active participation in religious tradition and their voices in the creation or expression of that tradition. In many cases feminist theologians have tried to recover women's voices and roles. This has been done by revisiting and emphasising women mentioned in various scriptures and by historical analysis of the role of women in these religious traditions; usually tracing their progressive marginalisation.

Aside from the interpretive and theological aspects of this search, it is a significant and essential feature in new ways of studying religions. In spite of the common emphasis on men's voices in most analyses of religions, the search for women's voices in theology is part of a trend in the disciplines that study religion and culture to try to hear women's voices. This trend, which is discussed in greater detail below, emphasises that despite the fact that women have usually been marginalised, their religious experience is as important as that of men and must be studied in any analysis of a particular religious tradition. This has led to anthropologists and other scholars studying religion to focus on the religious experiences of women and to give them the same status in the understanding of religion as that of men. It has also led historians to try to discover the roles of women buried in the different forms of documentary evidence, as for example, the discussions of women playing leadership roles in early synagogues and churches, based on inscriptions discovered by archeologists.

Part of this trend or process within feminist theology, the recreation of women's voices, provides an interesting insight into the role of reading and rereading history as a means of expressing and validating current theological views and arguments. A recent book, *The Red Tent* by Anita Diamant, although a novel and work of fiction, provides an example of this process. The book retells and recreates stories from Genesis, transforming the narrative focus from the men to the women, particularly the stories of Rebekah, Leah, Rachel, Zilpah, Bilhah and Dinah. The issues that are addressed, particularly those of intermarriage and sexual politics, owe more to current debates than those of the time when the biblical text was created. The text presents an essentialist view of women, with a strong focus on women's reproductive experiences. It also develops ideas of women's use of storytelling and women's rituals, which are highly distinctive and part of current feminist depictions of women. Other books, for example, *Sarah the Priestess* by Savina Teubal, similarly creatively excavate the biblical text to discover women's voices and forms of spirituality that validate current theological or political debates. These books are examples of an ongoing process, which has occurred since authoritative texts began, of creative interpretation and reinterpretation to find in the sources an image of one's own values and perspectives. This process must be regarded as data for religious studies, rather than analysis arising from the study of religion.

The process of recovering the voices of women has thus far focused on the theological implications or applications of this process. It has also been a significant addition to the methodological framework of a wide range of disciplines studying both culture and religion. This is particularly true of anthropology. Although much of the early ethnographic material privileged the experience of men, in the latter third of the twentieth century many anthropologists were increasingly aware of the need to listen to women as well. Initially, many of the anthropologists who moved into this area were almost ghettoised, in feminist anthropology; they have now moved into the mainstream. Most feminist anthropologists today seek to place the experiences of women into the wider cultural context and hear the many voices of a specific community, without necessarily privileging one or other. In some respects the work of these anthropologists is related to that of the womanist movement.

Many of the arguments raised by O'Connor and Shaw discussed above, that challenge some feminist attempts to develop an essentialist view of women and feminism, have been taken up by a group within the feminist tradition who label themselves as womanists. This group receives its impetus from a wide range of Third World women theologians who are aware of the possible neo-colonialist implications of such an essentialist model.

A persuasive presentation of womanist arguments is found in 'Womanist Theology: Black Women's Voices' by Delores S. Williams (1994: 77–87). Williams' use of the term 'womanist' arises from the ground-breaking book by Alice Walker in which she attempts to articulate a uniquely black understanding of what it means to be a woman. Williams argues that like Walker's own approach, a womanist approach to theology must focus on specific cultural codes. These codes are imbedded in the African American community through 'women's activity', that is through practice (1994: 78). The codes include patterns of relationships between mothers and daughters, specifically mother-daughter advice, understandings of the body and food, and the cultural embodiment arising from skin colour. Williams suggests:

> These cultural codes and their corresponding traditions are a valuable resource for indicating and validating the kind of data upon which womanist theologians can reflect as they bring black women's social, religious, and cultural experience in to the discourse of theology, ethics, biblical and religious studies. Female slave narratives, imaginative literature by black women, autobiographies, the work of black women in academic disciplines, and the testimonies of black church women will be authoritative sources for womanist theologians. (1994: 79)

A significant point of the argument is the specificity of these experiences, and the potential variety in feminist understanding which arise from it.

Although part of the womanist agenda is the articulation of specifically black women's cultural codes, and like other forms of feminist theology, the recovery of black women's voices and histories, the womanist agenda is not separatist. Following Walker, Williams argues that just as the womanist approach affirms the loving relationships between black men and women, a womanist Christian theology must ultimately affirm the unity of all Christians.

The womanist approach shares many elements with the feminist approach, but it also clearly distinguishes itself from it. The womanist approach, as already suggested, refuses to be 'guided by what white feminists have already identified as women's issues' (1994: 81). It chooses to follow its own guidance based on the particular nature of black women's cultural experience. The theology that Williams outlines in the following pages emphasises the aspect of community building, but even more, distinctive theological and ethical paths which arise from black women's experiences.

Although Williams' discussion is specifically related to the black women's experience, and develops a unique form of feminism based on that experience, it has wider implications and applications. Like the closing arguments of O'Connor and Shaw, Williams' arguments suggest that women's experience should not be essentialised to the western model, but must be seen within its own cultural context, and therefore have and express its own uniquely feminist aspirations.

This same argument is developed in many of the other contributions to King's *Feminist Theology From the Third World*. Kwok Pui-Lan, for example, reiterates the challenges against feminism, and particularly feminism in Christian theology. She suggests that the feminist arguments have largely been concerned with issues relevant to the first and second worlds and are largely irrelevant to those of the third world. She asks: 'Why should we assume there is a "universal" approach to the liberation of more than half the world's population? Would it not be a kind of cultural hegemony if there should be just one way of doing feminist theology?' (1994: 64). Kwok Pui-Lan's arguments suggest that the essentialist models of feminism in relation to religion are a form of missionising and imperialism rather than giving Asian feminists a voice in their own liberation.

Serene Jones, in 'Women's Experience Between a Rock and a Hard Place: Feminist, Womanist, and *Mujerista* Theologies in North America' (1997: 37–53), traces the relationships and conflicts between a range of broadly theological perspectives, universalising and particularising discourses. The particularising (which includes the womanist) perspectives all arise from a constructivist approach to gender, that is, that it arises in relation to culture and is thus diverse as opposed to being biologically determined and thus unitary. They challenge the essentialist notions of traditional feminism (and religious studies); drawing on the diversity of women's experiences they see the nature of women as being highly diverse. In all cases, aspects of experience are essential in both the understanding of women and women's theologies.

Interestingly, the theologians seem to be divided in much the same way as the theorists of religion. Jones points out a key division in feminist (broadly speaking) theologies. On the one hand (her rock) are the universalising approaches, which present an essentialised depiction of women – these approaches typically use psychoanalytic and phenomenological basis for their arguments. On the other hand (her hard place) are the approaches, as in the womanist, which particularise the experience of women and are non-essentialist. These approaches draw on social anthropology and post-structuralism with its emphasis on the interplay of language and power.

In addition to this form of a womanist approach to religion and society, there is a stronger womanist approach, which not only challenges the possibility of defining a singular model of feminism or liberation, but also denies the possibility of its use, and external analytical models or judgments in relation to the experience of women in different cultural settings. This approach sees the use of such models as another form of cultural imperialism, imposing a western understanding of feminism and western values arising from that model. This imposition sees the other culture as passive, waiting to be analysed and interpreted by western systems of thought, without the means of giving an authentic understanding of itself.

Leila Ahmed's discussion of the veil and its use in the discourse of Islamic oppression of women shares many elements with the womanist approach and moves towards the strong womanist model. Her book, *Women and Gender in Islam*, examines the role of women within Islamic society. In part, her goal is to recover the roles of women in history and to trace the progressive disenfranchisement of women. In one of the concluding chapters she specifically examines the role of the veil in relation to feminist discourse. Rather than focusing on the symbolic valences of the veil in Islamic societies, her discussion traces the way the veil has been used as a means of expressing the control of western colonial systems over Islamic societies. Feminism, rather than serving a liberating role, was used by the colonial masters as a way of expressing contempt for the societies they ruled, and expressing the need for those societies to give up their own ways of being and become westernised. She states:

> The idea (which still often informs discussions about women in Arab and Muslim cultures and other non-Western world cultures) that improving the status of women entails abandoning native customs was the product of a particular historical moment and was constructed by an androcentric colonial establishment committed to male dominance in the service of particular political ends. (Ahmed, 1992: 165)

Not only was the discourse of the veil an external colonialist model, it and colonial feminist concepts ultimately serve an androcentric purpose of domination rather than liberation.

Ahmed is not suggesting that women were not oppressed in Islamic societies. She agrees with the wider feminist perspective that they were oppressed and continue to be oppressed. The models used to articulate that oppression, however, were misconstrued and used for colonial political ends. The Muslim feminist agenda cannot be externally set, she argues, but must arise from the specific needs and understanding of the community itself. The veil has been externally determined to be an object of oppression, rather than internally determined. Ironically, as a response to the association of the discourse of the veil with neo-colonialism, wearing the veil rather than being a statement for or against feminism has become a statement of liberation and resistance from Western cultural and economic imperialism. The veil also becomes a revolutionary vehicle, allowing women access to social spaces which had hitherto been forbidden to them.

Some women commentators from the Islamic world go further than Ahmed. They suggest that the veil, if understood from an internal women's perspective, should be seen as an expression of liberation rather than oppression. Not only is it an expression of resistance against external neo-colonial imperialism, but it also allows women to function in society in a non-sexual way; that is, the veil makes the sexuality irrelevant by covering them from the sight of men.

Some commentators on Orthodox Judaism and its exclusion of women from public forms of spirituality also deploy this form of argumentation. These commentators suggest that the separation gives women a specific status in the home, which is different than that of men, while still being empowering and significant. They also suggest that the private spiritual experiences of women should be seen as just as significant and validated as the public religiosity of the men.

Although these approaches or challenges to traditional feminism as western and culturally imperialist are an essential critique, and emphasise the need to develop a number of feminisms rather than one particular feminist approach, there remains an essential underlying problem. If these approaches deny the possibility of using external models or critiques, then either it is only women from within the tradition who can speak of it, or external observers can only describe and not analyse (as any analysis implies the use of an external critical apparatus). Lack of any analysis would always leave the question of whether the internal view was merely a form of false consciousness based on women unconsciously buying into a patriarchal system. An alternative approach that would bring together both types of feminist thought would sensitively present the internal model, analyse it in relation to the external critique of power and powerlessness, critique the critique from the internal perspective, and ultimately through a dialectical process arise at a new model.

CHAPTER 10

Anthropological Approaches to Religion

Anthropology has been interested in religion since the development of the discipline in the nineteenth century. Nineteenth-century approaches were dominated by different forms of evolutionary theory, some scholars tracing the development of religion from the belief in souls or spirits, and others from specific forms of belief, for example totemism. As anthropology moved into the twentieth century most of these unilinear models were replaced by approaches that emphasised the particular historical development of specific cultures or religions, or those that focused on the particular structures of existing societies, without attempting to speculate about origins. The dominant theoretical paradigms of the latter type of approach were the various forms of functionalism, structural functionalism building on the work of Radcliffe-Brown (see chapter 2) and functionalism building on that of Malinowski (see chapter 2). This consensus lasted until the late 1950s, when the association of functionalist theories to colonialism or neo-colonialism became a source of criticism, and other theoretical models came to the fore.

Although the theoretical approaches discussed in this chapter are highly diverse, for example Spiro's emphasis on Freudian models and Geertz's distinctive theory of symbolic anthropology, there are some elements that are shared by most, if not all, anthropologists. While anthropologists are interested in the individual and individual religious experience, their primary interest is in the social or communal aspects. Thus when examining individual religious experience the anthropologists will attempt to contextualise that experience within its social setting, explaining the way that the experience is socially constructed, the social meaning of the symbols articulated, and the relationship between the experience and other social facts. So, for example, is the experience of possession a means of obtaining or expressing power?

Anthropology is also a comparative science. But, unlike phenomenology, which compares fragments of religious structures out of context, anthropology is very firmly based in the empirical ethnographic data. The emphasis on ethnography is perhaps one of the reasons why many anthropologists have not attempted to construct theoretical models that go beyond their own data.

A final related element that might be mentioned is the holistic approach that is characteristic of many anthropological discussions. While anthropologists may discuss religion, it is never religion separated from other social institutions or constructs. Anthropologists emphasise the interdependence of the different cultural constructs, while also recognising that in many cases the constructs are those of the anthropologist rather than the community being studied. This last point is important as it forces us to confront the relativity of terms like religion and culture. These abstract terms may be of help in discussing a particular set of practices but may purely be constructs imposed by the anthropologist (or for that matter any disciplinary practitioner) on the objects being studied.

Nupe Religion (1954) by S. F. Nadel presents a very good example of a functionalist analysis of religion. Nadel's discussion does not attempt to develop a comprehensive definition of religion, rather it attempts to delineate the object being studied and to examine that object in relation to its social functions. One of the most useful sections of his analysis is found in the discussion of how religion should be defined. Rather than accepting the apparently straightforward definition that 'religion shall here be meant all beliefs and practices implying communication with and control of the supernatural', Nadel problematises the concept of the supernatural and thereby the definition of religion (Nadel, 1954: 3). Nadel suggests that the concept of the supernatural and its implications in respect of science and verifiability are not congruent with the Nupe perspective, thus these distinctions are not useful in understanding what they mean by religion. Nadel attempts to use internal categorisations, based on Nupe terms and distinctions, rather than imposing external models or definitions.

This basic internal definitional approach is the basis for Nadel's selection of data to be studied. Unlike the phenomenologists who in many cases stop at the descriptive stage, Nadel attempts to synthesise his analysis in a formulation of the competences of religion. He suggests that religion has four main competences:

1. The capacity of religion 'to furnish certain supplements to (the) view that the world of experience' which 'our intelligence is driven to demand';
2. its capacity to announce and maintain moral values or, more generally, an 'economic ethic', that is its competence to guide 'the practical impulses for action;

3. its competence to hold together societies and sustain their structure; and
4. its competence to furnish individuals with specific experiences and stimulations. (Nadel, 1954: 259–60)

These competences emphasise the functionalist basis of Nadel's discussion. The first refers to the need for explanation – similar to arguments developed by Weber, the second to maintenance of morality or more specifically the type of economic ethos suggested in Weber's analysis of religions, the third to maintenance of society and social structure, and the fourth to providing religious experiences which support and validate the system as a whole.

Anthony Wallace in *Religion: an Anthropological View* (1966) develops a definition of religion that both harks back to some of the early anthropological definitions of religion and has features that foreshadow some of the more recent theoretical arguments. His discussion is built around a very simple substantialist definition that harks back (like that of Spiro discussed below) to that of E. B. Tylor who suggested that a minimal definition of religion is a belief in supernatural beings (1871). Wallace states:

> It is the premise of every religion – and this premise is religion's defining characteristic – that souls, supernatural beings, and supernatural forces exist. (Wallace, 1966: 52)

Thus religion can be recognised by the inclusion of these specific elements.

In addition to this basic definition, Wallace also suggests that religion will include a set of practices – these practices are similar in status to the dimensions of religion posited by Ninian Smart (discussed in the section on phenomenological definitions of religion) and look forward to the polythemic definition of religion suggested by Southwold (see below). He differs from Smart due to the inclusion of a substantialist definition alongside these practices, and from Southwold due to both the definition and the view that all the characteristics are necessary. The thirteen practices include: prayer; music; physiological exercise – practices meant to induce a religious experience; exhortation by one person, for example a priest, on behalf of the divine; myth or scripture; simulation of significant objects or events; mana – passing on power through touch; taboo – the prohibition on touching; feasts; sacrifice; religious meetings; inspiration or other forms of revelation; and use of symbols. Each of these practices can occur on their own or more commonly in combination with other practices in the form of rituals.

Wallace suggests that rituals are religion's most significant instruments. They are the means by which religion 'accomplishes what religion sets out to do' (Wallace, 1966: 102). In relation to his discussion of rituals and their function Wallace refines his definition, adding a functionalist aspect to the substantialist basis:

> Religion is a set of rituals, rationalised by myth, which mobilises supernatural powers for the purposes of achieving or preventing transformations of state in man and nature. (Wallace, 1966: 107)

The functionalist aspect is found in the 'transformations of state'. These transformations overlap with the functions assigned to religion by a wide range of different theoreticians including Durkheim, Weber, Malinowski and Radcliffe-Brown (see the discussion of functionalism above) as well as a wide range of ethnographic material from highly diverse sources. Wallace lists a number of different types of ritual, each of which serves a different functional role.

Wallace's discussion makes several points, which are useful in understanding religion from an anthropological perspective. In spite of the substantialist aspect of his discussion, his development of the thirteen dimensions of religious practice opens interesting avenues of analysis that are more open ended. The emphasis on practice, that is behaviour, is an important counter balance to those approaches that overemphasise the cognitive aspects of religion. His approach, however, has some substantial flaws. For example, it is difficult to see how the different elements fit together in terms of a comprehensive theory. The different dimensions, the various forms of religion, the functions assigned to the different forms of ritual all seem to come from different theoretical discussions and do not present an holistic model for the understanding of religion; such an holistic model is appropriate because many of these elements are presented as being necessary features of any religion. A second problem is found in relation to his basic definition. He does not present any convincing argumentation for the inclusion of the supernatural in the definition – it can be seen as included because it is a seemingly self-evident element of Western religious models. A similar question can be raised in regard to the thirteen practices; there is no logical or argumentative reason why they are necessary to religion. On the whole Wallace's discussion raises many interesting questions but resolves none of them in a convincing manner.

Clifford Geertz's 'Religion as a Cultural System' (1968) presents one of the most influential anthropological discussions of religion. It moves in a very different direction to the essentially functionalist definition proposed by Wallace, while also retaining certain functionalist elements. Geertz suggests that his analysis of religion focuses on its cultural dimensions. Geertz's model of culture focuses on the transmission of symbols – embodied meanings – that convey a community's worldview. Geertz's analysis there focuses on religion as a cultural or symbolic system which embodies and conveys these patterns of understanding.

Geertz's model brings together the aspects of ethos and worldview. He states:

> In religious belief and practice a group's ethos is rendered intellectually reasonable by being shown to represent a way of life ideally adapted to the actual state of affairs the worldview describes, while the worldview is rendered emotionally convincing by being presented as an image of an actual state of affairs particularly well arranged to accommodate such a way of life. (Geertz, 1968: 3)

Geertz's model suggests a circle of interrelated elements with the two key aspects, ethos and worldview, being validated mutually and validating each other. He adds two additional elements to this circle. On the one hand, the mutual validation naturalises the worldview, that is, it presents it as part of the natural structure of the universe. It thereby suggests that it is the only possible and natural way of acting in and viewing the world. On the other hand, through religious or emotional experience, it validates the ethos and worldview.

Geertz brings all of these elements together in his now classic definition of religion:

> Religion is: (1) a system of symbols which acts to (2) establish powerful, pervasive, and long-lasting moods and motivations in men by (3) formulating conceptions of a general order of existence and (4) clothing these conceptions with such an aura of factuality that (5) the moods and motivations seem uniquely realistic. (Geertz, 1968: 4)

This definition presents an open-ended model of religion in which although a set of specific elements are included, that is, worldview (conceptions of a general order), ethos (motivations) and experience (moods), the content of each of these categories is left open.

In order to clarify the exact meaning of this definition it is helpful to look at each of its five elements separately. The first element, a system of symbols, is particularly important to the definition due to Geertz's emphasis that both religion and culture are ultimately systems of communication. Geertz defines a symbol as a carrier, for example, a word, action or object, which embodies a conception. A conception can be as simple as the direct association between a number of objects and a numeral, or as complex as an object of religious veneration. His discussion takes this definition one step further by broadening the material embodied by symbols to include feelings and other non-conceptual content. He also adds the caveat that the anthropologist is not interested primarily in the individual understanding of the symbols but rather in their meanings and uses as articulated in 'cultural acts' (Geertz, 1968: 5).

Geertz suggests a further distinction within the concept of symbol, or more precisely complexes of symbols, that is, symbols or models *of* and *for*. A 'model of' is a symbolic system that represents or depicts something external to it. Thus a map, as a description or a depiction of space, can be seen as a model of that specific area of geography. A 'model for', on the other hand, is like a blueprint that is used to build a building – thus it structures reality rather than depicting it. It is important to note that, although this distinction is useful for analytical purposes, the two types of symbolic systems overlap. Thus a map can also be a 'model for', if it is used to create or support the ideology behind a political entity. Equally the blueprint can function as a 'model of' if it is used to illustrate or depict the building once it has been built. If we examine this dichotomy in relation to Geertz's initial discussion of religion, the worldview can initially be seen as a 'model for', it shapes and gives form to experience. Though the process of naturalisation the perception of the worldview is transformed into a 'model of', it is seen as depicting reality rather than shaping it.

The second element of Geertz's definition centres on moods and motiv-ations. Moods seem to refer to the experiential aspect of religion. They are like a fog, short-lived and ephemeral. Moods are essentially emotional experiences, ranging in different ethnographic contexts through all poss-ible emotional responses. Geertz uses terms like 'reverential' and 'solemn' as well as 'exultation' and 'self-pity' to encapsulate the variability of this element. The significant feature of these moods is that the very experience of them transforms one's perception of self and reality. It is important to note that Geertz is not associating this feature with any specific experience or emotion, depending on the ethnographic context any experience or emotion could be placed in this category. Perhaps the one feature which religious moods share is that in the context of the experience they are seen as 'totalistic', encompassing all of reality (Geertz, 1968: 11). Motivations are closely associated with Geertz's concept of ethic. They are a long-lasting directional aspect that arises out of religious experience, creating a dis-position to act in a certain way. Although moods and motivations are very different phenomena, the two are closely interrelated. On the one hand the types of moods and motivations found in a specific ethnographic context will be closely related, with the mood leading to a model of reality and the motivation the related model for reality. On the other hand, they will also be closely related to worldview, with moods validating worldview and motivations shaping action in response to worldview.

Moods and motivations and their relation to worldview lead us to the third element of Geertz's definition, that is, conceptions of a general order of existence. The key feature of Geertz's argument is that the symbols that underlie the moods and motivations are the same as those that underlie the element of worldview. This aspect is already indicated in a discussion of moods and motivations, the system presents a comprehensive and totalising understanding and experience of reality precisely because all the elements share the same symbolic structures and mutually validate each other. Geertz uses the example of golf to indicate the relationship between the elements and the definition of religion:

> A man can indeed be said to be 'religious' about golf, but not merely if he pursues it with passion and plays it on Sundays: he must also see it as symbolic of some transcendent truths. (Geertz, 1968: 13)

This quotation both illustrates the connection between the elements, particularly the need for there to be a connection between the experience and the ethos with the worldview and illustrates the potential inclusive quality of Geertz's definition. The aspect of worldview as a system of ordering reality or giving meaning to reality is further emphasised by Geertz, who quoting Salvador de Madariaga, suggests that the minimalist definition of religion is 'that God is not mad' (Geertz, 1968: 13).

Geertz further defines the religious worldview, suggesting that it substantially deals with three issues or problems – places where interpretation of meaning seems to be absent. The first of these existential problems is the problem of explanation. He suggests that human beings are unable or willing to retain gaps in understanding. Any gaps in knowledge create an existential crisis which must be resolved. The second area of existential angst is the 'problem of suffering'. This problem refers to the human need, according to Geertz, to find a resolution to the existence of suffering as part of human experience. Religion provides the symbolic framework for resolving this problem, sometimes by denying the existence of suffering or in others, like Buddhism, making it the central religious fact of existence. The final problem is that of evil; it refers to the inability to 'make sound moral judgments' (Geertz, 1968: 21). This refers to the perception of a disjunction between the way the world is and the way that we believe it should be; in other words, why do bad things happen to good people? The totalising worldview resolves or provides a meaning for each of these areas of existential crisis. This aspect of Geertz's argument shares affinities with his teacher Talcott Parsons (see above) and through him to functionalist argumentation and to the work of Max Weber (see above) on worldviews and particularly the problem of meaning which becomes in Geertz's argument the basis of the religious worldview.

The next element of Geertz's definition moves from the question of the content of religion to that of the mechanisms with which religion is able to inculcate this symbolic system into the believer. Geertz suggests that we do not accept religious frameworks based on our direct experience of the world. Geertz traces our acceptance of these systems to different forms of authority: 'persuasive power', authority arising out of mystical experience, that is, the power associated with the experience, and the power associated with the personality of a charismatic leader. The significant source of authority, however, arises for Geertz in the context of ritual. The ritual brings together ethos and worldview, and through the interaction of the two creates a powerful feeling that makes both the ethos and the worldview uniquely significant and meaningful.

This brings us to the final element of his definition, that is, making the moods and motivations seem uniquely realistic. This aspect of his argument brings together the elements of religion and the commonsense everyday way of being. The power of religious symbols is that they become the model of reality that shapes (or attempts to shape) other models of reality. Through the processes discussed above, particularly the experiences engendered by ritual, the individual is changed such that the religious worldview and the feelings and ethos associated with it are privileged as uniquely reflecting the natural order of existence in a totalising way. Any other way of being, particularly the commonsense perspective is relegated to being a partial depiction of reality; it becomes part of the religious perspective rather than in competition with it.

In *Islam Observed* (1968a) Geertz further expands on the relationship between religion and the commonsense perspectives. It should be noted that commonsense, like any other way of perceiving the world, is culturally constructed; there is no universal commonsense. Like any other cultural perspective it gains authority by being perceived as natural, that is, taken for granted as the way things are. Geertz emphasises that both are ways of conceiving the world rather than one, the commonsense perspective, merely being an instrumental way of living in the world. The commonsense perspective precedes other perspectives; the other perspectives emerge because commonsense, as suggested above, is not sufficient as a totalising worldview. Geertz suggests that the study of religion should include an analysis of the commonsense perspectives from which religion emerges and the dialectical relationship between the two perspectives; as a totalising perspective religion revisits commonsense and transforms it in light of its way of conceiving the world.

Geertz also takes up the issue of secularisation and the relationship of that process to his model of religion. He suggests that in general people's relationship to religion has changed with the advance of modernity and particularly the scientific worldview. Geertz presents a dichotomy in religion that can be seen as analogous to Weberian ideal types: one side of the dichotomy is 'religiousness', the second is 'religious-mindedness' (Geertz, 1968a: 61). The first type of religion, religiousness, is that which characterises non-industrial societies. These societies are characterised by a high degree of conformity and pressure to conform. People by and large accept their religious symbolic systems and live within them. They can be described as being held by their religions. In industrialised societies a new form of totalising worldview has arisen that challenges the religious worldview leading to 'religious-mindedness'. Geertz presents this struggle as 'a struggle for the real' (Geertz, 1968a: 104). The distinction presented thus far is identical to the secularisation theses of sociologists like Steve Bruce (see the section on sociological theories). The effect of this challenge to the religious worldview leads to a change in the way people are religious. In many cases religion, rather than being lived, becomes an ideology – people are no longer held by their religions, they hold them. He suggests that the rise of 'scripturalism' in Islam (popularly called Islamic Fundamentalism) is an example of this process through which religion is transformed into ideology. On one level religion becomes a means of taking a particular stance against modernity and neo-colonialism; it becomes an expression of opposition.

Talal Asad in *Genealogies of Religion* (1993) develops a highly critical yet constructive analysis of Geertz's model. Asad critiques Geertz's analysis on both theoretical and technical grounds. We shall only develop the main theoretical critiques in this discussion. Asad challenges the underlying basis of Geertz's analysis, the view that religion is essentially a conceptual system. He suggests that while this is significantly true of modern Western religion, this understanding cannot be maintained from an historical perspective. He demonstrates that this 'self-evident' aspect of religion is historically situated; it was developed during the Enlightenment and it differs significantly from the earlier idea of religion, that is, religion moved from being understood as a 'concrete set of practical rules attached to specific processes of power and knowledge' to 'be abstracted and universalised' (Asad, 1993: 42). Thus, even in a European context, Asad argues that there can be no trans-cultural/historical definition of religion.

Asad suggests a related challenge to Geertz's discussion of religious meaning. He suggests that Geertz ultimately limits religious meaning to the problem of 'disorder', a limited space for meaning that has much to do with the privatisation of religious belief. Geertz's model also suggests that religious belief precedes knowledge rather than being based on knowledge.

This understanding of the basis of belief is also a product of the modern marginalisation of religion, with other discourses taking over the area of knowledge. In the Middle Ages, Asad asserts, 'Christian belief would have been built on knowledge' (1993: 47). The fact that belief in these two periods is built in a different way, and built out of different life experiences, suggests that the belief so constructed would differ in each case. This undermines Geertz's view of a 'distinctive mental state' that can be considered religious (Asad, 1993: 48).

Asad's conclusions bring out additional aspects of his critique in a very pointed manner. He poses Geertz a number of questions, each of which highlights a different problem in Geertz's analysis. The questions focus on the problems associated with the apparent independence of significant aspects of Geertz's definition of religion from the life experiences of the believers and perhaps even more importantly the relationship between particular elements of religion and the authority structures that authorise them. Asad emphasises that the particular experiences of religion and ways of understanding religion must be historically and culturally situated; it is these contexts that produce and authorise their particular forms of religion and religious experience. The conclusion of Asad's argument is that there is no one definition of religion. Each definition is culturally and historically situated, and cannot and does not extend beyond that specific context.

Melford Spiro in 'Religion: Problems of Definition and Explanation' (1968), while sharing some common elements with Geertz's discussion, particularly functions related to the problem of meaning, moves in a very different direction. His analysis of religion brings together psychological and sociological analysis of religion, and he develops a substantive definition of religion that has its roots in Tylor's nineteenth-century definition of religion, that is, a belief in supernatural beings (1871).

Spiro opens his discussion by raising the problems associated with different forms of definition. He suggests that many definitions of religion, for example, that of Durkheim, that seek to define religion in terms of essence have two related problems; the essence itself is both vague and non-empirical. He suggests that a significant problem with this definition is that it is impossible to define something in terms of its essence if there is no agreement about what should be included in the object so defined – if we can't agree on what is religion, how can we determine its essence? He also suggests that these types of definitions tend to be too overly broad to be academically useful.

Similar problems are found, he suggests, in functionalist definitions of religion. The only difference between a functionalist and an essentialist definition is that the essence is replaced by a function. The two are similarly circular. He also emphasises that the main problem with functionalist definitions is that other social institutions that are clearly not religion will usually fill the functions that they attribute to religions. Thus, like essentialist definitions, functionalist definitions are too broad to be useful.

Spiro suggests that a substantive definition is the only form that properly defines the boundaries of the object under study and thus both presents a narrow range of phenomena useful for study and comparison and does not have the logical circularity of either the essentialist or functionalist definitions. Such a definition, he suggests, is necessary when studying, as it delineates the object to be studied. If the ethnographer does not have a consciously articulated definition, he or she will rely on an implicit definition to determine what is or isn't to be included in the category of religion.

One of the major problems in defining religion has been its applicability over a wide range of different cultural phenomena. Hard cases, like Buddhism, have consistently challenged attempts to define religion by content, specifically belief in the supernatural. Spiro suggests that, although any definition of religion must have some degree of cross-cultural applicability, if some phenomena are defined out that should not pose a problem for the definition, rather it should be seen as an opportunity for further analysis. Alongside cross-cultural applicability, Spiro suggests that any definition must have 'intra-cultural intuitivity', that is, it must not be counter intuitive to people who use the term (Spiro, 1968: 91). The presence of 'superhuman beings' is one such element, the absence of which would be counterintuitive. For Spiro this becomes the essential differentiating characteristic that defines religion in relation to other social phenomena. As we shall see in the discussion below, a second and perhaps more significant reason for the inclusion of superhuman beings is Spiro's use of the Freudian paradigm that sees religion as emerging from a child's projection of his parents, particularly his father.

On the basis of these arguments Spiro suggests the following formal definition of religion:

> An institution consisting of culturally patterned interaction with culturally postulated superhuman beings. (Spiro, 1968: 96)

The substantive element in the definition is the limitation of religion to cultural systems that include 'culturally postulated superhuman beings'.

In order to clarify exactly what Spiro means by this definition it is useful to unpack some of the terms. The term 'institution' relates to the social aspect of the institution. It emphasises the anthropological interest in the behaviour and systems developed by groups rather than individuals. As

Spiro suggests, he is following in the tradition of Durkheim's distinction between church, that is religion, and magic (Spiro, 1968: 97). The term 'interaction' refers to patterns of behaviour. Spiro divides these into two types. The first type of behaviour refers to the value system embodied in the superhuman beings. This value system will form part of that of the group, and be the basis for some of their actions. These actions are understood to be following the will of the superhuman beings. The second form of behaviour is that designed to influence or propitiate the superhuman beings. Spiro introduces a concept of symbolic action in relation to the overlap between these two types of behaviour. He suggests that symbolic action is that which is not seen as pragmatic when viewed by the anthropologist. Those actions that serve a spiritual or religious, but not a pragmatic, end are defined symbolic action or ritual. Like religion, religious rituals are cultural actions rather than those created by an individual. The term 'superhuman beings' is a broad term meant to include anything more powerful than a human being. Each group develops a belief system around these beings, though the beings may not be the primary object of the religion. Thus, his definition includes a defining substantive element as well as three elements that constitute any cultural institution, that is, a belief system, an action system, and a value system (Spiro, 1968: 98).

After defining religion Spiro takes up several questions relating to the existence and persistence of religion as a social institution. Spiro suggests that there are two primary forms of explanation that are used to explain the continued practice of religion, that is, causal and functional. A causal explanation details the historical process that necessitated the development and continuation of an institution and a functional explanation elucidates the persistence by reference to the object's social role. Spiro suggests that the type of explanation used will depend on the aspect of religion under discussion; his discussion develops two of these aspects: the reasons why people accept the beliefs of religion as true; and the reason why people continue the practices of religion.

As we have suggested above, one of the significant features of religion in Spiro's definition is the system of beliefs, that is, religion as a cognitive system that people believe to be true (1968: 101). The question arises as to why people continue to accept these ideas as true. Spiro suggests that the social nature of these cognitive systems explains why we believe what we do, but not why we continue to believe them. Spiro argues that the explanation for the persistence of belief can be found in a Freudian causal explanation. Freud had suggested (see above) that in the face of the chaotic world children projected an image of the 'all-powerful' father onto the universe in order to give it meaning and order. Spiro suggests that although

Freud's emphasis on the father is ethnocentric, the need to project an all-powerful parent in order to give structure to the universe provides a clear psychological basis for the development and persistence of the beliefs of religion. It is perhaps unsurprising, as suggested above, that Spiro's formal definition includes the substantive element of superhuman beings, an element essential to this Freudian explanation.

In relation to the second aspect of religious persistence, that is, practice, Spiro deploys a functionalist mode of analysis. He bases this on a view of human action that regards all practices as being in some sense instrumental, that is, fulfilling some type of need either sociological or psychological (Spiro, 1968: 106). Following Merton (see above) he divides function into latent – unintended and unrecognised – functions and manifest – intended and recognised – functions. However, he further develops this by suggesting that there are also functions that are unintended but recognised and those that are intended but unrecognised. This final type, as discussed below, is associated with his Freudian model. These functions are unconsciously intended and therefore are unrecognised.

Spiro divides the different needs addressed by religious practice into three areas, some of which overlap with the elements of worldview developed by Geertz. The first area is that of 'cognitive' needs (Spiro, 1968: 110). This area relates to the problem of meaning on two level: meaning as why and how. Spiro encapsulates this function in the following proposition:

> Religious beliefs are held, and are of 'concern', to religious actors because, *in the absence of competitive explanations*, they satisfy this desire. (Spiro, 1968: 110)

Religious belief therefore resolves the psychological need for explanation when no other form is available.

The second area of need is 'substantive' (Spiro, 1968: 112). This area of function refers to the recognised and intended outcomes of ritual practice. Thus if a religious actor is asked why they are performing a ritual and they respond 'to bring rain which is desperately needed', this desire is the substantive need which is fulfilled by the practice. Spiro summarises this area of functionality as:

> In the absence of competing technologies which confer reasonable confidence, religious techniques are believed to satisfy these desires. (Spiro, 1968: 112)

Thus, religious practices serve as a symbolic means of acting upon the world when there are no alternative forms of technology.

The final area, the 'expressive', deals with the intended but unrecognised functions (Spiro, 1968: 114). This area of functionality provides a mechanism for reducing 'painful drives', that is, all sorts of unconscious needs and motivations that are culturally problematic or forbidden. This form can be encapsulated in the following statement:

> In the absence of other, or more efficient means, religion is the vehicle – in some societies, perhaps the most important vehicle – by which, symbolically, they [painful drives and motivations] can be handled and expressed. (Spiro, 1968: 115)

Spiro's discussion of these elements mirrors the Freudian concept of the unconscious. Thus, for example, he explains evil superhuman figures as objects upon which individuals can project repressed hostility that cannot be openly or otherwise expressed.

He concludes his discussion with a summary of the 'real' functions of religion. As in the rest of the argument the psychological aspect is presented as the most significant. He suggests that religion as a social institution, by providing a means of dealing with 'repressed motives', provides society with a psychologically well-balanced set of individuals, protects the community from disruptive unconscious desires, and provides a common goal in the shared projection of the superhuman beings (Spiro, 1968: 121).

Spiro's definition and analysis of religion has both technical and theoretical problems. The most significant problem is found in his definition. He claims that the basis for the inclusion of 'superhuman beings' rests on two factors, that is, the need to distinguish religion from other social phenomena and on 'intra-cultural intuitivity'. The second of these elements is particularly problematic. It privileges the cultural perspective of the anthropologist, for what else is 'intra-cultural intuitivity' and imposes that perspective on the material analysed. There seems to be little good reason to assume that our society's understanding of religion, which emphasises the aspect of the supernatural, should serve as the basis for a definition that is used cross-culturally. While the first element in his argument is more convincing, it argues for a definition that can set clear boundaries rather than the need to arbitrarily choose one substantive aspect as its basis.

Spiro's introductory discussion of different types of definition presents a clear argument against the use of both essentialist and functionalist forms of definition. Yet if we examine Spiro's arguments as a whole, his discussion of religion, and therefore his analysis of religion, includes all three forms of definition. In fact, his preferred form of definition, the substantialist does not stand independently of the other two. Thus, for example, the primary substantialist element of his definition, the cultural belief in 'superhuman beings' rests in reality on an essentialist argument, that of Freudian psychoanalysis. The remainder of the definition and the role that religion plays in relation to the needs articulated by the Freudian argument lead us to a functionalist rather than a substantialist form of definition.

An additional problem area is found in the rather ethnocentric form of argumentation. This is particularly seen in the definition of religious symbol. A symbol is anything that the anthropologist cannot understand and does not perceive of as serving a practical purpose. The ethnocentric aspect is also seen in some of the discussions of functionality in which religion is seen as a form of defective scientific explanation or psycho-analytic analysis.

Martin Southwold takes up aspects of Spiro's arguments, particularly respecting whether Buddhism should be considered a religion. This issue, as suggested above, had been considered by Durkheim, leading him to develop a definition of religion based on the sacred, and in the case of Spiro, the argument that in spite of theological statements to the contrary Buddhism includes superhuman figures, for example, the Buddha. Southwold argues that Spiro's contention does not fit with the ethnographic material; he suggests that some forms of Buddhism do not include these figures or consider them to be part of the sacred. Nonetheless, in spite of the absence of any form of theism necessary for substantialist arguments like that of Spiro, he suggests that Buddhism is 'uncannily' like a religion. Thus, 'theistic definitions of religion are shown by Buddhism to be wrong' (Southwold, 1978: 367).

Southwold argues that Buddhism is a system of religious practice that does not include supernatural powers; this, he suggests, demonstrates that this aspect is not an essential feature of religion. It is one element that might but need not be present. Southwold suggests that this element may in fact only be a derivative element.

Southwold suggests that a new definition of religion needs to be developed that can adequately include religions that do not have a theistic component. Following the work of Rodney Needham, he suggests that a different form of definition be used, that is, a polythetic definition. This form of definition while including in it a 'bundle' of elements, allows each specific example to include some but not all of the elements (Southwold, 1978: 369). Each form of religion would have a different set of elements from the same 'bundle'.

Southwold outlines a set of tentative elements to be included in this 'bundle':

1. A central concern with godlike beings and men's relationship with them.
2. A dichotomisation of elements of the world into sacred and profane, and a central concern with the sacred.

3. An orientation towards salvation from the ordinary conditions of worldly existence.
4. Ritual practices.
5. Beliefs which are neither logically nor empirically demonstrable or highly probable, but must be held on the basis of faith …
6. An ethical code, supported by such beliefs.
7. Supernatural sanctions on infringement of that code.
8. A mythology.
9. A body of scriptures, or similarly exalted oral traditions.
10. A priesthood, or similar specialist religious elite.
11. Association with a moral community …
12. Association with an ethnic or similar group. (Southwold, 1978: 370–1)

This polythetic definition provides a means of including any social phenomena that share some of these elements. It allows for comparative analysis, examining how and why different elements are present or absent. It also, he suggests, challenges the view that religions have a common basis, as each religion is built from a different set of these elements with some elements being differentially emphasised. In some respects this definition can be seen as similar to that proposed by Ninian Smart (see the section on phenomenological analyses of religion). The significant different between the two is that Southwold's definition is less prescriptive about the elements needed if the phenomena are to be defined as a religion.

Southwold's definition, although a clear advance on previous substantialist definitions, is still essentially a substantialist definition and retains the problems associated with that form of definition. Any set of contents, however flexible, if it is determined by the anthropologist in advance of the data creates a circular form of analysis; it is merely a demonstration of what has been stated already in the definition. This form of definition is also potentially ethnocentric – what is the criterion for inclusion or exclusion of specific elements? The definition also contains a degree of ambiguity. If only one element is needed to be considered a religion, then almost any social institution could find its way into the definition.

In *Conceptualising Religion* (1993) Benson Saler outlines the most significant polythetic definitions of religion and suggests a variation on them, which he labels a 'prototypical' approach. Like the polythetic approaches he sees religion, as an abstract term, including a 'pool of elements'. The members of the category of 'religion' are based on a principle of analogy. Saler argues that we need to build from a prototypical example. Based on that example, other phenomena are examined and if their elements are considered to be analogous to the prototype they are added into the category. He uses the term 'family resemblances' to indicate the nature of these analogies. The aim of his model is not to set boundaries for the concept of religion, but to establish an analysis of greater or lesser typicality. In his summary of the model he states, respecting the inclusion of phenomena into the category:

> Those instantiations, called religions, include the Western monotheisms, our most prototypical cases of religion. They also include whatever else we deem to participate in the pool of elements to the extent of resembling the Western monotheisms in significant respects. And how do we establish what is significant? By cogent analytical arguments about elements that we deem analogous to those we associate with our reference religions, the Western monotheisms. (Saler, 1993: 225)

As Saler himself acknowledges this approach is potentially ethnocentric – it depends on a choice of prototype and a selection of the significant elements of that prototype and a judgement of what is or isn't a significant analogy. The advantage of Saler's approach is that it moves some distance away from the enumeration of elements, however flexible, to a model that allows for a less predefined and predetermined analysis.

Thus far we have examined theories of religion as opposed to theories of culture that by their nature include religion. It seems appropriate to discuss one such theoretical approach, that is, structuralism. In the discussion of Radcliffe-Brown in the first section we touched on the structuralist implications of his analysis of myth. His analysis of the myths of Andaman islanders demonstrated that the symbolic systems depicted in the myth shared an underlying structure. Evans-Pritchard's work on the symbolic systems of the Nuer also indicated an underlying structural pattern. In the Andaman material this underlying structure was triadic, based on the sea, the land and the treetops; in the case of the Nuer the structure was dyadic, based on spirit and earth. A significant aspect of the analyses was the association between the structures of the symbolic system and the social organisations of the respective cultures.

The implications of this approach were particularly developed by Claude Lévi-Strauss and the associated school of French Structuralism. Although much of Lévi-Strauss' work has focused on mythology it also has broader implications relating to other areas often included in religion, for example, ritual and symbolism. He brought together the structuralist implications the work on structure found in the Structural Functionalists and the developing concepts of structural linguistics. His analysis focused on the underlying structural relations or patterns, rather than on the specific meaning of the objects being studied. Thus, using a simple linguistic analogy, Lévi-Strauss examined the grammatical rules, which allow us to construct meaningful sentences, rather than the meaning of the specific sentence. His approach is in two respects significantly different to that suggested by the analogy. He believed that the underlying structures were at some level universal, whereas the rules of grammar are language specific, and he also argues that the underlying structures are unconscious rather than conscious.

Based in part on the linguistic aspect of his approach Lévi-Strauss emphasises the communicative aspect of myth. Rather than focusing on the content of the myth, that is the narrative, he suggests that myth communicates underlying structure. Underlying structure can be seen as the process of categorisation and the ways that these categories are related one to another. Thus, in effect, what myth is communicating is a way of organising and relating to the world as it is conceived of and experienced by a particular group. Although the way a particular group utilises underlying structure may be specific to that group, Lévi-Strauss argues that the basic structuring principle is biological and shared by all human beings.

In terms of this analysis the conceptual aspect of religion, its mythological system, ultimately communicates, or embodies, structure rather than any particular theological content. Lévi-Strauss' approach to this material can be seen as one of the most thorough going forms of reductionism. Rather than reducing religion or the content of religious symbolism to another aspect of society, for example, economics or social structure, Lévi-Strauss suggests that all of these social institutions can be looked at as different ways of exemplifying the same underlying structural relations. Lévi-Strauss' approach, therefore, presents a coherent model for looking at religion in the same way as any other social institution. Lévi-Strauss' analysis clearly has an essentialist basis, that is, the biological underlying structure. The essentialism, however, is different to that proposed by other thinkers. It does not provide a distinctive basis for a single human institution; rather it provides a basis of all human institutions. It points to the essential unity of human cognitive processes rather than suggesting the unity of a single type of institution. The capacity for structuring can be seen as the definition of being human rather than the definition or unique basis of religion.

Within this cultural model of underlying structure, is there a structuralist definition of religion? Although Lévi-Strauss does not offer a comprehensive definition of religion, it is possible to construct a definition from his discussion of myth; myth can be seen as highly structured narrative. Myth is different from other forms of narrative in that its structures are more clearly articulated. On a wider level we could define religion as highly structured patterns of belief and practice. Thus the content of religion is not fixed; each community will have a different set of beliefs and practices that are highly structured. The significance of religion then, is that it is the most significant social institution for the communication of underlying structure.

In Lévi-Strauss' original formulation, myth and ritual were seen as serving different societal purposes. Following the line established by Durkheim, ritual was seen as a means of unifying a community while myth was seen as a more centripetal or divisive phenomenon. While it is possible that the two aspects might have these differing social effects, we are not at all convinced that they do and indeed in some of his writings Lévi-Strauss seems to see them as, at the least, complementary; both myth and ritual are vehicles for conveying symbolic and structural information. They may use different ranges of symbols, but if structuralist theory is correct, they will structure this different symbolic content in the same way and therefore communicate the same underlying structure. Analysis of Israelite myth and ritual supports this view that myth and ritual are structurally similar (see Kunin, 1998).

Lévi-Strauss' model of structuralism has been criticised in several respects. Two of the most significant of these are verifiability and agency. Many critics have suggested that structuralist analyses are idiosyncratic, with each structuralist proposing different structures for the same objects of study. While this objection has some validity, there are several responses to it. The fact that different scholars propose alternative structural analyses does not challenge the validity of the theory; it merely challenges the application of the theory. Recent applications of the theory have also attempted to introduce a degree of predictability, particularly in respect of mythological traditions that have existed over long periods of time.

The issue of agency is more significant. Underlying structure is by definition unconscious. It is understood to be a determining factor in shaping cultural objects, thus there seems to be little room for individual agency or choice. Some new developments in structuralist theory have introduced individual agency within a more complex underlying structural pattern. Agency becomes the conscious realm in which individuals and groups can both emphasise certain aspects of underlying structure or push the structure in new directions. This element also introduces an aspect of dynamism into structuralism that seemed to be missing from the more static original form.

Mary Douglas and Edmund Leach are two other anthropologists who have developed aspects of structuralist theory, particularly in relation to ritual practices and mythological systems. Mary Douglas' work on purity and food rules, examined in the final part, has been a very influential attempt at trying to understand the underlying structural relations within a system of symbols, and perhaps more significantly in relation to ritual practice, whether it relates to food rules, purity or sacrifice. Her arguments are particularly significant on several levels. They demonstrate convincingly the way that categories work in different cultural settings, particularly focusing on the relationship between categories, rather than the specific symbols that are included in the categories. She also demonstrates that symbolic objects that are in some sense uncategorisable, that is, that do not fit properly into any category, are anomalous and raise some of the most significant issues addressed by systems of religion. Her argument also demonstrates that the structural patterns found at one level, that is, animals, can also be found respecting the relationship between different cultural categories. Thus, for example, the Israelite model of humanity is seen to be structured in the same way as their understanding of the natural world. One key area that distinguishes Mary Douglas' work from that of Lévi-Strauss is the goal of analysis. Mary Douglas does not seek to discover elementary structures that are common to all humanity. Her work illustrates the way that different structural patterns are found in different cultural contexts.

Mary Douglas develops her structuralist model in a slightly different way in her discussion of embodied symbols in *Natural Symbols* (1970). She suggests that bodily control and social control are structured in the same way. Her analysis focuses on the way we use different bodily symbols to express different levels of control. In the third part of this volume we discuss her analysis of the use of hair as a symbol for control or lack thereof. She presents a general rubric, the 'purity rule', which argues that there is a direct relationship between the individual's control of their body and societies' control of the individual. In structuralist terms, this rule can be expressed as:

individual:body::society:individual
[in this equation, ':' means 'is to' and '::' means 'as'].

Her analysis is particularly significant regarding religion. It provides a model for analysing the structure and nature of religious experience (see the third part). The purity rule suggests that in those societies where society has a weaker control over the individual, the individual will have a weaker control over their bodily actions and therefore be more likely to have more active forms of religious experience.

Edmund Leach's analysis of myth and ritual both develops aspects of French Structuralism, as in his analysis of biblical myths, and addresses the issue of symbols and communication. Leach distinguishes between ritual, which is symbolic behaviour, and behaviour that arises out of an actual emotional state. Thus mourning practices in many cultures are conventional rather than reflecting individual or real psychological states. Leach suggests that myth and ritual are about communication rather than affective experience. At different points Leach focuses on different forms of communication, but his primary argument is that the structure of myth and ritual communicates social structure.

In an article dealing with the structural logic of sacrifice, 'The Logic of Sacrifice' (1985), Leach presents a fascinating discussion that links models of ritual practice, particularly rites of passage (see the discussion of Turner and van Gennep in the third part). His analysis examines the different categories that are brought into relationship through sacrifice. His argument emphasises the area of mediation, the place where the categories meet, for example the space joining this world and the other world. He suggests that it is through the mediatory or liminal aspect of this space that ritual can link the two very separate categories. He also suggests that this aspect of mediation in sacrifice can also be directly linked to a process of transformation in which the sacrificial act and space provide the means through which the initiate is transformed. Thus, like Mary Douglas, Leach's emphasis focuses on the elements between categories rather than the categories themselves. In Leach's case, however, these mediating elements are essentially positive rather than anomalous.

At the outset of the chapter we highlighted several commonalities to the anthropological approach; we might add an additional common feature articulated by Durkheim and even more clearly by Evans-Pritchard:

> He is not concerned, *qua* anthropologist, with the truth or falsity of religious thought. As I understand the matter there is no possibility of his *knowing* whether the spiritual beings of primitive religions or of any others have any existence or not, and since that is the case he cannot take the question into consideration. The beliefs for him are sociological facts, not theological facts, and his sole concern is with their relation to each other and to other social facts. (Evans-Pritchard, 1965: 17)

Like the phenomenologist, anthropologists have bracketed the beliefs they are studying, and for either observational reasons or cultural relativist ones, they have not attempted to judge qualitatively the beliefs. This does not mean that they have not attempted to show how the beliefs and practices may relate to other social facts; even if a belief has a social function this is not a denial or an affirmation of whether it is true. In a recent publication James Lett has argued that anthropology should be used to evaluate and challenge the truth of religions. He goes further, clearly stating that 'no religious belief is true' (Lett, 1997: 116). We do not agree that it is the role of anthropology to make such determinations, particularly ones that assume that there is a position from which such a truth can be determined, and which already seems to have predetermined the outcome. Lett argues his case on the basis of supposed rationality; if anthropological studies have taught us anything, rationality and logic are cultural constructs and therefore relative rather than absolute.

In this discussion we have examined some of the significant approaches to religion developed by anthropologists in the course of the twentieth century. As can be seen through comparing these approaches, anthropologists have developed and deployed a wide range of methodological and theoretical approaches in studying religion. If any themes or trajectories can be seen in the development of theory, there seems to be a general attempt to develop theories of religion that are more comprehensive, in which the theory provides a methodology for studying the phenomena rather than predetermining what the phenomena are. The work of Asad particularly challenges the attempt to create a universal definition. It reminds us that all definitions and all practices are historically and culturally contextual, and of the need to be aware of the authorising processes at work in these different cultures and contexts.

CHAPTER 11

Some Final Words

In this section we have examined some of the significant thinkers in the social scientific approaches to religion. The discussion in the chapters has focused on the nature of the definitions used by the various theoreticians. In this final chapter we would like to briefly take up a few broader themes that arise from a view of the chapters together. The discussion here centres on four basic dichotomies: insider/outsider, the irreducible/reductionist, religion/religions and the related world religions/primal religions. The last of these dichotomies is somewhat different than the others. In the first three cases the dichotomy is between sets of methodologies and theories that are in debate with each other. The final dichotomy is one proposed by a set of approaches to religion. This dichotomy is between two types of religion rather than approaches to religion. Each of these dichotomies raises several very significant analytical questions; we can do no more than skim the surface of these discussions.

Although the insider/outsider dichotomy raises issues particularly between the phenomenological approach and that taken by the other disciplines, it also reflects a debate with anthropology. The essence of this debate rests on which understanding of, or perspective on, religion should be privileged, the view taken by the believer or the external view taken by the scholar.

The essence of the debate can best be seen in the use of two terms that were coined by Kenneth Pike: emic and etic. These terms were taken from the terms used in linguistics, phonemic and phonetic. The first term refers to the sounds used in a language in their own terms, while the second refers to the signs devised by linguists to analyse and compare the sounds (McCutcheon, 1999: 15). Pike himself uses the terms 'discovery' and 'creation' to characterise the two different approaches (1999: 29). The emic approach is seen by Pike as being that of discovery, presenting an internal view of the object being studied. The etic perspective is that of creation. It is an 'alien view' created, Pike suggests, by the scholar and imposed on the object of study (1999: 29). It should be apparent from the language used by Pike to describe these two approaches that he considers the emic approach to be preferable. The other emphasis is found in the work of Marvin Harris (see above). In *The Rise of Anthropological Theory* (1968: 568–92) he presents a detailed discussion of the relationship between emic and etic analysis. While he recognises that the emic approach makes important contributions to anthropological analysis his discussion privileges the etic. He suggests that it is only the etic approach that allows scientific predictability and the possibility of falsification. He also suggests that the actor can know what they believe but they may not be able to know why they believe it; it is through etic analyses that this can be determined. As suggested above, Harris' own explanatory or etic model is that of cultural materialism, using economic or materialist explanations that would be very different from those of an internal point of view.

Regarding the theories discussed in this section, particularly those of the phenomenologists who emphasise the emic point of view, the question can be legitimately asked whether such a point of view is either possible or even desirable? The internal perspective as a methodological tool can be divided logically into two: the description of the religion by an actual insider, usually understood as theology; and the attempt of an external observer to depict the position of the believer. The theological statements of believers are clearly adequate depictions of how they perceive their reality; if this is the goal of the depiction, then there is no need for an external observer to mediate their position. Thus, if the phenomenologist is merely parroting the internal position then they are, as some of them admit, parasitical on the community they are depicting. Such a depiction, however, whether by the theologian or phenomenologist should not be seen as analysis (unless the phenomenologist is suggesting, and several do make this suggestion, that an analysis that depends on having one's own internal faith position is the only possible explanation).

The question arises as to whether such an emic position is possible when the material is to be presented to a context different from the believing context – a context that often has different presuppositions about the world and different languages. In this case the internal position is transformed on at least two levels, the linguistic and the conceptual. The depiction of the insider must be translated and in doing so interpreted, as there is no possibility of literally translating one language into another – each choice of words implies an interpretation by the observer. There is also a wider conceptual transformation; terms like supernatural, sacred or religion have very different meanings and their use or the use of other terms involves an interpretation of concepts from one realm of discourse to another. Thus, an external believer explaining another religion in these terms would still be imposing an external model, his or her mode and understand of belief. Even if an internal believer is making these transformations, the fact that they possess the languages of the other cultural context and its conceptual apparatus suggests that his/her position will no longer be the same as a naïve believer (should such a person actually exist). We are not suggesting that it is unimportant to try to depict the internal point of view; rather we are suggesting that it is important to be aware of the limitations of this attempt, and of the fact that even such an attempt will involve the use of an external point of view.

The suggestion that any depiction involves an etic perspective also functions on an additional level. All observations and descriptions depend on a selection from the objects of perception. When a scholar describes a religious system, the scholar selects those elements that he or she considers to be significant. This selection is both conscious and unconscious. On the conscious level we make choices based on the questions we are addressing. On the unconscious level we may take certain things for granted or omit certain things because they are outside our conceptual range. While aspects of our perceptions will always be outside our conscious control, it is important to be aware of the underlying perspectives or theories that shape our selection of those aspects which we include or exclude. At the simplest level, how we define religion may shape the elements that are depicted, it is thus important to be aware of our theoretical perspectives, because it is only by such awareness that we can challenge our theories rather than be led around by them.

Since a pure internal or emic perspective is probably impossible, should we then privilege the external point of view? This question leads us to the apparent conflict between theology and scientific approaches to religion; if we privilege the external perspective we deny the possibility that the internal view may be a possible or adequate depiction of reality.

The two points of view look to very different sources of knowledge. In one case religion and religious phenomena are often explained in terms of some type of transcendental other and in the other by recourse to forms of humanistic explanation (we shall take up the related issue of reductionism later in this chapter). Most of the various social scientific approaches to religion, with the exception of the phenomenologists, have argued that since the 'supernatural' is by definition not an observable social fact it is not relevant to social scientific analysis. Thus external forms of analysis have looked to other factors to explain the existence and persistence of religion. The acceptance of the latter point of view might then be seen as a rejection of the former.

It is our contention that scientific analyses of religion must analyse the object of study using the forms of evidence available to them. Thus they must analyse it as a human construct; examining and determining the way this construct relates to other human constructs. Such an analysis must include a discussion of the emic point of view and perception of reality. Thus, while the insider view cannot be the end of the discussion, it forms an important and essential part of the discussion – this is particularly necessary to prevent the easy abstraction of elements as the internal view provides the context and elaboration of these elements and often emphasises their uniqueness.

On a second level, the emic and the etic perspectives can be seen as two hypotheses that need to be tested. It would be equally incorrect to consider the etic perspective to be proved in advance of the analysis as it would to accept the emic as proved by definition – this latter position seems to underlie many phenomenological arguments that assume the existence of the sacred prior to their analysis rather than as a result of it. In any case, a humanistic approach to religious phenomena does not, as many objectors would have it, necessarily deny the possibility of a transcendent; it merely examines the way that religion as a human institution works both in relation to the individual and society. The existence or non-existence of the transcendent cannot be the object of study, such a study belongs to a different set of discourse, that of the theologian. Although the theologian may use the findings of social scientists and social scientists may analyse the work of theology as data, the two sets of discourses are and should be mutually exclusive.

The dichotomy between analysing religion as irreducible and from a reductionist is closely related to the insider/outsider dichotomy. The view that religion is an irreducible phenomenon and thus must be studied separately from other social phenomena has been strongly upheld by both theologians and phenomenologists. The reductionist position has recently been defended by a number of scholars most notably Robert Segal (see for example 'In Defence of Reductionism' [1999]).

The term reductionism has been used in a number of ways. In general, phenomenologists have used the term to criticise any approach to religion that uses a humanist form of explanation. They suggest that this form of analysis privileges the humanist explanation, that is, the explanation that denies the possibility of the supernatural. Scholars taking this approach suggest that the reductionist model has an *a priori* rejection of the insider's understanding and explanations. On a more narrow level the term has been used in relation to those theories that explain religion (or other social phenomena) in terms of a single causal explanation, for example, economics or social structure. This form of critique has also been deployed against psychological, sociological and anthropological approaches to religion. Against these humanistic or scientific approaches, the arguments posed by those who see religion as irreducible often deploy the insider point of view, which sees religion through the eyes of belief and thus as something distinctive and unique and therefore irreducible.

In the course of the discussions of phenomenology we have touched on some of the arguments against reductionism. One of the arguments most commonly deployed is that religion is a distinctive institution and deserves its own science on the analogy of the separation between psychology and physics. This approach suggests that reality can be divided into related categories; while these categories are related one to another they would not be reducible into each other (Ryba, 1994: 35). They argue that the reduction of religion to any other explanatory system would be analogous to analysing all of psychology through explanations provided by physics. One of the arguments deployed to support this conceptual categorisation is that religion is a comprehensive domain, which can not be understood, from an holistic point of view, by reducing it or subsuming it to any other theoretical perspective. The approach makes the *a priori* assumption that religion is necessarily a distinctive phenomenon. While it is possible that this may be the case, this should be the end result of analysis rather than the foundation of the analysis. It seems just as likely that religion is a social institution that can be analysed in the same terms as other social institutions. It is also arguable that an holistic analysis that examines the interrelations between the full range of social institutions will lead to a more comprehensive understanding than one which examines a particular phenomenon out of its wider social context. Other arguments ultimately rely on the acceptance of the theological explanation of religion, that is, that it has its basis in a transcendental source. Whether this source is God, the Holy, or the Sacred, this presents a theological presupposition rather than a scientific argument. An interesting concomitant to this form of argumentation is the suggestion by many theological scholars, for example Otto and Eliade, that only a believer can understand religion.

In many phenomenological texts it is possible to discern an additional motivation for the rejection of so called reductionist models. This rests on the fact of disciplinary distinctiveness. Many phenomenologists see their analyses as primarily descriptive, rejecting any forms of explanation either in terms of function or origin; Kristensen explicitly states this view. The approaches that they reject as reductionist challenge the very basis of their disciplinary independence. Thus the rejection of alternative approaches is not grounded in theory but as a means of maintaining their disciplinary unity (see, for example, Edwards' discussion in 'Religion, Explanation, and the Askesis of Enquiry' [1999]).

There are a number of arguments that have been deployed to support various different forms of reductionist analysis. The reductionist or scientific approach to religion poses a question; in its most developed forms it asks whether the phenomena can be understood in human terms and if so how? Unlike the alternative approach it does not assume that religion has a particular status. A good reductionist analysis produces a reductionist explanation after, rather than prior to, the analysis. A reductionist analysis also examines the data that is available – we can only analyse, from a scientific perspective, social facts and from that same perspective explain them in relation to other social facts. This process does not mean that we will exhaust the phenomena being explained. There might be features that are explained by other theoretical perspectives, either those from other disciplines or perhaps the insider perspective. Reductionist theories explain phenomena using terms and variables that we can observe and test; they do not rely on additional variables that may not be needed to explain the phenomena.

Ivan Strenski in 'Reduction Without Tears' presents a clear analysis of different models of reductionism and their benefits for the analysis of religion. He emphasises the positive role that reductionism plays in developing or challenging paradigms. It is precisely because scientific approaches apply different models to the same phenomena that knowledge can be developed and advanced. If religion can never be explained in any other terms than the insider view, then there is no possibility of change or development of conceptual frameworks (Strenski, 1994: 97).

Two problematic aspects of reductionist approaches are their claim to be able to test the truth of religious propositions and to exhaust the meaning of religious propositions and practices. While reductionist explanations can provide an analysis of how and why a religious proposition works and examine the nature of that proposition in relation to our model of reality, its determination of truth can only be a relative determination. There seems no necessary reason to privilege our model of truth over other models of truth. Reductionist theories, like that of Freud, also claim to provide the full or real meaning of the objects they study. As suggested above, social phenomena are highly complex and work on a number of levels simultaneously. While a particular analysis may highlight specific meanings, that are implicit in the proposition or practice, these implicit meanings do not necessarily replace the explicit means as understood by the religious practitioners.

The third dichotomy is that of religion or religions. In the course of our discussion of the different approaches to religion we touched on a range of theorists who view religion and the history of religion as standing in some sense outside the particular instances or histories of religions. This view is closely associated with that of the irreducibility of religion and shares many of its presuppositions. As stated above the theological underpinning of this position cannot, in the context of the academic analysis of religion, replace academic argumentation. While it is possible that religion has a singular history, this view cannot be assumed in advance of empirical data – as far as we can see no such data exists.

There are, however, more serious issues in connection with this dichotomy. These issues are found on at least two levels, the theoretical approach to the topic and the object of study. On the theoretical level the question relates to whether religion is in any sense a singular object. As suggested above, in the conclusion of the final part to the discussion of anthropological theories of religion, we follow Asad's critique of theories, seeing religion as a much more culturally and historically specific phenomenon. Any understanding of religion, whether internal or external, is culturally and historically situated and closely interrelated with systems of power and ideology. Thus, as there is no one theory or definition of religion, there is no singular phenomenon that can be called religion. The term, as any similar abstract term, can be used to identify phenomenologically analogous phenomena, which then must be analysed in their own terms, rather than pigeonholed into a predetermined definition. This process can then serve to challenge dialectically the understanding of religion in its abstract sense.

The second level relates to the specific object of analysis. Thus far we have challenged the attempt to essentialise the theoretical concept of religion (as opposed to seeing essential aspects to human beings). A similar process of essentialisation is found in respect of the specific religions being studied – thus scholars speak of Judaism or Christianity in an essential and monolithic sense. If, however, we examine a religion in terms of its practice, we find that there is no such unity. There are many different Judaisms. This multiplicity is found in respect of the predefined divisions, for example Reform or Orthodox Judaism; it is also found within these sub-divisions. In some sense each community has its own defined variation on what Judaism means, both in terms of practice and belief.

Some theorists have attempted to resolve this dichotomy between religions as they are practiced and as they are conceived (by some central authority). Distinctions like great tradition/small tradition or philosophical/practical religion have been offered as a way of relating these two levels of religion. Many approaches to religion have emphasised one aspect or the other. Thus, for example, phenomenologists have tended to emphasise the great tradition level, and anthropologists the small tradition. In part these emphases are due to the objects that these different disciplines have analysed. Phenomenologists have tended to focus on the texts produced or authorised by the centre, while anthropologists have tended to look at religion as local communities practice it. Although on one level it is clear that any analysis should take into account both levels, religion as a social institution does not exist in some ideal sphere – what is important is how local communities use and understand what they believe to come from the centre, not an idealised version which has little or no resemblance to the practices and beliefs as they are found in their almost infinite variety. It is important to examine the processes of power and authority that seek to create or authorise a unitary model as well as the countervailing cultural processes that militate against this. In part, the argument against essentialised religions is related to our argument against essentialised definitions. If religion, as Asad would have it, is culturally and historically contextual, then so too must all religions be contextualised by the many different cultures and subcultures in which that are instantiated. Thus, just as we would problematise the definition of religion as a unitary phenomenon, we would also problematise the view that religions are unitary.

The final dichotomy to be touched on is that between 'primal' and world religions. This distinction is found in texts of many different areas of religious studies. A clear discussion of the concept of 'primal' religions is found in James Thrower's volume, *Religion: The Classical Theories* (1999). Thrower suggests that the term is used in the place of 'primitive' due to the ethnocentric implications of that term. Nonetheless, the term 'primal' itself has clear implications. While it is used for religions that still exist, it suggests that these religions share elements that are foundational to all religions, and were the basis of all religions existing today, even those that are no longer to be included in the category. Thrower suggests that whatever the context, historical or geographic, of these societies, they share 'a common worldview' (1999: 11). The primal worldview is understood to be composed of a number of shared elements. These elements include: religion of a single ethnic group or community in which religion and culture are not distinguished one from the other: the world is perceived not as an object but as a subject, filled with personality; and these cultures are generally confined to oral transmission.

There are a number of problems associated with this description. On the methodological level, the discussions of so called primal religions often move from ethnography to ethnography, selecting elements that fit their analysis and ignoring the elements that might challenge it. Thus, for example, Thrower uses examples from Malinowski's discussion of the Trobriand islanders, ignoring the fact that Malinowski specifically argues against the view that people in the Trobriand Islands experience the world in a very different way from modern people. Arguments for this approach tend to take on the excesses of the phenomenological approach in decontextualising elements on the basis of a pre-existing argumentative structure.

The discussion relating to primal religions is also flawed on the basis of empirical data. The theory is clearly harking back to Lèvy-Bruhl's distinction between rational and pre-rational patterns of thinking. All reliably ethnographic evidence suggests that there is no difference in the deployment of rational modes of thinking or viewing the world from an objective perspective between complex and less complex forms of social organisation. In all forms of society people utilise different modes of experience depending on the individual and the context. Thus, there is no reason to assume that the subjective experiencing of the world is in any sense the property of one form of society.

These elements, along with that of being non-literate, make a clear opposition between primal religions and the modern religions, which have been called by some scholars world religions. The model suggests that world religions are qualitatively distinct from primal religions – at a minimum they perceive the world in a different way, are spread beyond ethnic or cultural borders, and are literate. The model also suggests that primal religions in some sense precede the world religion – suggesting a unilinear model of evolutionary development. Unilinear models of evolution have been shown to conflict with empirical evidence, and thus have generally not been deployed in anthropology since the beginning of the twentieth century. The dichotomy between world religions and primal religions suffers from the same fundamental problem – they are both ethnocentric models. In each case a hierarchy of development is established, with the form of religion of western society being seen as the more developed form. Even if one seeks to return to the primal ways of perceiving as suggested by Eliade, this does not remove the problematic valuation that is implicit in the model; this form of false nostalgia can be seen as a form of Orientalism, in which we idealise our religious aspirations and use other societies as a means of expressing those values or desires. In terms of the issues of literacy and size of a particular religion, these elements do not provide a convincing basis for distinguishing between types of religion.

It seems more useful to reject this dichotomy and to examine each set of religious phenomena in their own terms, without attempting to suggest that one form is evolutionarily prior. The emphasis on supposed commonalities is also a mechanism for ignoring the significant differences that have been observed in religious phenomena, both within single religious traditions and even more between distinctive religious traditions. In a sense the concept of world religion is an idealisation of religious phenomena, where as in practice each community has its own variation on that tradition, a variation that is analogous to those phenomena found only in a single community.

PART III

Taking the Discussion in Different Directions

Introduction

In the first two parts of this book we have examined a wide range of theories of religion. In the course of the discussion it has been suggested that the concept of religion as a definable category needs to be problematised. Critical analysis of the theories suggests that the main types of definitions of religion, particularly the essentialist and substantialist variants, raise a wide range of different logical and empirical problems that necessitate moving to a new way of looking at categories like religion.

The discussion raises some aspects that might be part of this approach. First, it suggests that the approach to defining needs to be relativised. This aspect of relativisation works on several related levels. It argues that definitions or categorisations within culture are highly contextualised. Thus in the case of religion, whether it is distinguished from other categories or whether practice or belief is emphasised changes over time and space, and thus the internal understanding of what might be called religion and what is significant in it changes. The aspects of power and authorising process within a culture must also be included. This element addresses both the ways in which definitions of religion or its content are socially constructed and manipulated, and it also leads us into an examination of the complexity within communities in which religion may be highly contested. These elements must also be part of the understanding of our own models of religion. These models, like the internal categorisations, are relative to our context and shaped by identical process. This is particularly significant respecting the ideological use of definitions. All of the definitions of religion discussed in this volume arise from particular systems of power and reflect a variety of ideological bases that shape how and why religion is defined in the way it is.

Second, in relation to this understanding of the relativity of our conceptual models there is a need to move to a more analogical rather than definitional method. Rather than using definitions in a strong sense, any definition should provide the basis for examining material that is related by analogy. Analogy suggests similarity at one level but is clearly not identity. If this aspect is taken seriously then it forces the analyst to examine each phenomenon in its own terms without assuming that it shares a common essence, substance or function with material that is analogically related to it. The analogy provides the basis for a field of study; it does not predefine the nature of the material to be included in that field. The concept of analogy also suggests a greater degree of provisionality. As one moves from object to object the analogy is changed and stretched in different directions.

Third, it also suggests the types of theoretical approaches that might be most useful. One of the significant issues seen in many of the approaches is that theory, rather than being analytical, is based on content. Thus, the theories or definitions state in advance of the empirical data what religion is, what its content is, or what its function is, and then examines (or selects) material that fits that definition. There are significant logical problems associated with this type of argumentative strategy. It seems more useful to develop theoretical approaches that provide methodologies for analysing the data without prejudging either what it is or what it does. A relativised and more dynamic version of Geertz's model is a move in this direction. It does not limit religion to any specific content or role, but provides the conceptual tools for determining what religion is in any specific ethnographic context. From another perspective a structuralist analysis also provides an analytical methodology that allows for a diversity of content and possibly functions. Although it does have an essentialist basis, in the structures of the human mind, this foundation is sufficiently generalised and potentially open ended – at its most coherent, structuralism argues for a universal structuring principle rather than universal structures.

In this part we take these principles and suggest that they are applicable not only at the level of religion, or other abstract analytical entities, but also to more specific elements that are usually seen as being constituent parts of religion. Like religion, these analytical categories are socially constructed and authorised; and, similarly, the definitions used and the valuation of those definitions needs to be problematised. We are suggesting that all definitions relating particularly but not uniquely to comparative discussions need to be both relativised and seen as provisional stages in a dialectical (but not evolutionary) process in which the definition is constantly in process, recreated by setting it against the empirical data.

This part examines three main areas: ritual, symbol and myth. In each area specific examples are examined using the approaches of different anthropological theorists. The range of theorists selected is based on two criteria, that is, that they exemplify some of the major theoretical perspectives, and they take the argument or analysis of the same element in different though related directions. There is no intention to cover all areas of interest to the study of religion; rather specific examples are chosen to illustrate the methodologies and issues.

CHAPTER 12

Ritual

Ritual has usually featured as one of the significant features of most definitions of religion, and to a large extent, its definition suffers from precisely the same problems as definitions of religion. Catherine Bell's (1992) analysis of the history of such definitions and the approach that she advocates moves in a similar direction to that presented here.

Bell suggests that most definitions of ritual have included two elements; they have argued that ritual is a unique category of human action and have attempted to define that category on the basis of universal qualities (Bell, 1992: 69). These forms of definitions have aspects of both the essentialist and substantialist aspects. The essentialist aspect is found in theories that see ritual as arising from some intrinsic aspect of the human personality or of the human experience. The substantialist aspect is more common and is found in those theories that define ritual on the basis of specific elements. As Bell points out, this second aspect is particularly problematic as almost by definition each ethnographic situation forces the definition to include provisos or exceptions. The uniqueness of ritual as a social category rests on the elements used to define the practice. These elements do not hold up to ethnographic scrutiny and are often at odds with the insider perception of their own practices.

Bell also suggests that the view that ritual is a unique category rests on a dichotomy between different types of action, often between ritual action and technical or instrumental action. In this model actions are defined as ritual if they are not perceived by the observer to have some practical purpose – they are therefore symbolic rather than practical. This distinction ignores the possibility that within the ethnographic context there is actually no distinction between the two realms of action, both may be understood to be equally symbolic and equally practical. It is the ethnocentric evaluation of the observer that distinguishes between the two (Bell, 1992: 70).

Alongside this approach to ritual we also find theories that see ritual as part of all social action. One example of this type of argument might suggest that ritual is the symbolic or communicative part of all social action. The major flaw in this type of theory, Bell suggests, is that it does not provide a clear basis for analysis; by embracing all human action the term itself loses any analytical value.

Bell provides a resolution to the problems posed by the earlier theories of ritual by focusing on the concept of 'ritualisation' (Bell, 1992: 74). This is a process within specific cultural contexts through which different social actions are differentiated from one another. Her approach suggests that there are social practices that generate distinctions between actions, and at different times based on those processes privileges one set of actions over another. Bell suggests that there are no specifically predefined areas of ritual, nor are all social actions ritualised; rather, on the basis of the distinguishing social practices, some actions are significant and others are quotidian or everyday actions.

We can agree with Bell's formulation to this point. In effect it suggests that ritual should not be seen as a content-full category, rather ritual is a category defined by a specific social practice that can relate to any area of social action. Unfortunately, however, Bell includes two other elements in her definition, that such action creates a distinction between sacred and profane and distinguishes a category that is associated with things thought to transcend the human realm. Through including these two elements Bell moves back towards a substantialist argument and thereby limits the application and use of her definition.

Ritual as a category of practice can be defined partially as patterned behaviour, which is privileged or highly structured. Due to the structure, which is imbedded in the practice and mirrors or relates to other social practices, rituals contain both affective and communicative elements. As suggested by Bell's work, different rituals will emphasise either the affective or communicative aspect or both aspects, but these elements are secondary to the ritual practice itself; ritual is not essentially about feeling or ideas. In some contexts rituals are highly communicative, working with a range of symbols for which detail exegesis is provided, in other contexts very little exegesis may be present and the affective or experiential aspects may come to the fore. In some cases neither of these elements is consciously deployed. An example of this is found among the Dorze as described by Dan Sperber in *Rethinking Symbolism* (1975). He describes a number of rituals that although seemingly full of symbolic material to the ethnographer are left uninterpreted by the Dorze themselves. The symbols are deployed and discussed as elements of the social practice. Sperber's own analysis suggests that underlying these practices it is possible to discern a clear structure of interrelations between the symbols and symbolic categories. Thus the practice may gain significance and be distinguished as significant because it is highly structured, rather than through any specific message or feeling that it might convey. It is also important to emphasise that most social practices identified as rituals utilise the body. Such practices are clearly effective on a wide range of levels, because these practices have an immediate and direct impact on both mind as both are directly are involved in the practices.

– RITUAL PROCESS –

As we have suggested, there is no necessary sphere of ritual action, nonetheless certain aspects of formal structure often characterise privileged highly structured areas of practice. Arnold van Gennep suggested one model of these formal structures in his classic work of 1909, *Rites of Passage*. He suggested that rituals, particularly those relating to transformation, had a common tripartite structure: the separation phase, the liminal phase and the incorporation phase. The separation phase included a set of practices that separated or removed the initiate from their original status or social position. The liminal phase, or the threshold phase, represented the point between the two statuses; it was seen as the primary transformative aspect of the ritual. Practices included in this phase often emphasised ambiguity or danger. The incorporation phase centred on practices associated with returning the initiate to the community in their new status or role.

Victor Turner's discussion of ritual builds on van Gennep's model; he emphasises the liminal stage. Turner sees the liminal phase as the most significant aspect of the ritual process and suggests that its most salient feature is the creation of *communitas* – an experiential state in which boundaries between individuals are dissolved, status distinctions are removed, and a sense of unity or community is created. *Communitas* is understood to be anti-hierarchical and thus there is a direct relationship between the level of *communitas* and that of hierarchy. Turner extended the model of rites of passage to include pilgrimages, which he saw as the paradigmatic example of *communitas* and ritual, which allowed individuals to move beyond the normal cultural structures and hierarchies.

Colin Turnbull's descriptions of rites of passage among the BaMabuti and the Bantu villagers, presented in *The Forest People* (1993), provide a useful test case for both van Gennep's and Turner's models. The BaMabuti are a hunting and gathering people who live in the Ituri Forest of the Congo. They interrelate on a number of levels with Bantu villagers who live and farm on the edges of the forest. It is important to note that these two communities are very differently structured; while the BaMabuti have very little social differentiation, the villagers have a much more hierarchically structured society. The two communities have both economic and ritual patterns of interrelation, and share a set of common rites of passage. In spite of the fact that they perform some of these rituals together, the two communities have a very different understanding of the nature of the rituals.

This difference in perception is particularly noticeable respecting the *nkumbi*, that is, the initiation ceremony for boys. The villagers controlled the *nkumbi*, and to a great extent the *nkumbi* was a village ritual in which the BaMabuti chose to participate. For the villagers it was a very serious ritual that transformed the boy into a man. If the ritual were not performed then the boy would never achieve that status. The transformation was also seen on a wider level; it joined the boy to the village ancestors and thus socialised him into continuity with the past and the future. It was so important that it was sometimes performed for boys who had died prior to the ceremony. In relation to the BaMabuti, the villagers saw the ritual as creating a patron/client relationship between the boys and the participating BaMabuti. This relationship was an important aspect of the economic relations between the two groups.

The BaMabuti understood the *nkumbi* very differently. They do not see the ritual as transformative; a boy remains a boy, in spite of going through the ritual, until he has killed his first game and participated in the ritual initiation for girls, that is, the *elima*. The BaMabuti choose to undergo the ritual for purely pragmatic reasons; the tie created with a villager is economically very useful. It provides both resources and employment which are not available in the forest.

If the *nkumbi* is examined in terms of van Gennep and Turner's models we find that it works well in relation to the villagers but less well in relation to the BaMabuti. For the villagers all three stages are present. The ritual begins with a separation phase. The children are removed from their homes and taken to a special site near the forest. Their heads are shaven, symbolising the end of childhood. The liminal phase occurs in the encampment. It is an ambiguous period, filled with prohibitions and restrictions. The initiates are tortured and made to go through physical ordeals. The liminal phase culminates in circumcision. The ritual concludes with the incorporation phase. The transformed initiates are returned to the village as men. The *nkumbi* is thus a classical rite of passage described by van Gennep. It also fits Turner's model, particularly the elements found in the liminal stage. The aspect of *communitas*, however, does not seem to break down the barriers between the villagers and the BaMabuti. It is possible, however, that this might occur; unfortunately the ritual observed by Turnbull only included BaMabuti boys.

For the BaMabuti, the ritual does not function as a rite of passage; it is merely a necessary stage in defining their relations with the villagers. This difference is seen clearly in the description of the ritual that Turnbull observed. Turnbull discusses a particular example in which no village children were present, and due to the rule of the ritual no villagers could be present during the nights. While the BaMaButi followed the restrictions and rules during the day when the village men were present, during the night they ridiculed the taboos and indicated clearly the lack of meaning of the ritual for them.

As suggested above, the BaMabuti had no specific rite of initiation for boys. A boy became an adult through killing game. This suggests that unlike the villagers who strongly emphasised liminality, the liminal aspect of the ritual being the most important aspect, in the BaMabuti case there appears to be no liminal period; the boy is a child until he kills the game and becomes an adult, in effect, upon doing so. It seems likely that due to the lack of hierarchy and structure in BaMabuti society there is less need for anti-structural elements and thus less need for liminality.

The comparison between the villagers and the BaMabuti suggests that the model of rites of passage as proposed by both van Gennep and Turner needs to be relativised. Their models cannot be seen as prescriptive; rather they should be seen as the basis for discussion. The ethnographic data suggests that liminality is not a necessary element of rites of passage; its presence or degree of emphasis is interrelated to other social facts, in the specific ethnographic examples to degrees of hierarchy or social structure. These are not the only possible variables.

Ethnographic work on Jewish rites of passage, for example, suggests that they too do not have or emphasise liminality. Jewish communities unlike the BaMabuti, however, are socially structured and hierarchical. In Judaism's case the operative feature is the attitude towards transformation. Judaism does not like movement between categories and thus rejects transformation. Without transformation there is no need for or acceptance of liminality. Thus, while it is clear that the traditional models of rites of passage need to be modified, particularly by seeing them as analytical tools rather than definitions, by highlighting the issues they allow analysis of both differences and similarities without creating a false sense of universality.

– RELIGIOUS EXPERIENCE –

Religious experience is closely related to issues of liminality and *communitas*. Anthropological research has demonstrated that these types of experiences are culturally constructed and closely interrelated to other aspects of social structure. The ritual process provides a common setting for religious experience, and in many respects shapes the type of experiences that will occur. The liminal phase is particularly well suited for the construction of religious experience as it moves individuals and groups out of their normal social settings and relations, and *communitas* can be understood as one form of it. Clifford Geertz has pointed out that religious experience also serves a broader role as a means of validating and supporting worldview.

Although one might commonly see religious experience as referring to ecstatic experiences like trance or spirit possession, the term refers to a much wider range of phenomena. At one end of the scale it might be the feeling of connection or community, at the other, it might be the loss of all bodily control in a case of spirit possession or trance. The type of experience found in a particular ritual or occasion is not spontaneous or haphazard, but is closely related to cultural expectation and context.

Mary Douglas in *Natural Symbols* (1970) argues that ritual practices and religious experiences can be understood through two interrelated models. The first of these propositions, the purity rule, suggests that there is a close relationship between the degree to which society controls the individual to the degree to which the individual controls their body. This rule can then be worked out in the second model, that of grid and group. The model of grid and group indicates the relationship between the individual and society expressed in the purity rule. Grid refers to the level of control over a person's thoughts by some aspect of society. Group refers to the level of control over a person's actions by some aspect of society. A high level of grid means that people are expected to share a common set of beliefs, and strong group means that behaviour and use of the body is highly conventional and formalised. In relation to religious experiences this suggests that in communities which exercise a high degree of control, both in respect of grid (thought), and group (action), the individual will not lose control of their body. Thus, religious experience will be highly controlled; the individual will remain in control of their body – limiting the experience to a pervasive mood or feeling – and the interpretation of the experience will stay within the acceptable understanding of that particular group. As the control of the group is lessened, the individual's control over their body will become weaker and allow more active forms of religious experience. In tandem with the lessening control over the body, the control over ideas also plays a significant role in shaping the experience; the higher degree of control over the interpretation of the experience.

The model of religious experience presented here is also applicable to religious experience in various contexts within our own societies. Thus, within the Christian context a number of different types of religious experiences can be identified: the sense of community or communion, speaking in tongues – either privately or publicly, being slain by the spirit, the Toronto Blessing and prophecy. Each one of these kinds of experience can be associated with particular religious structures. Thus, in those contexts that are highly structured and hierarchical we would expect to find only the weaker types of religious experience, whereas in those contexts that are much less formally structured the more active forms of religious experience will be found. Similarly, where an inappropriate form of spirit possession intrudes, it may be interpreted as negative, demonic possession rather than positive possession by the holy spirit.

I. M. Lewis in *Ecstatic Religion* (1971) adds an additional level to the discussion of religious experience. He suggests that religious experience can be a means of challenging aspects of hierarchy and social structural relations. It provides a method by which disempowered individuals or groups can take a more active role in society. This form of spirit position is commonly, though not uniquely, found among women. A good example is found in Islamic Somalia. The society examined had a strong hierarchical distinction between men and women, with women having little or now public power. Women's positions were made even more precarious through the practice of polygamy, which created a high degree of tension within the family unit. This social setting provided the context of possession of women by malevolent demons called *Sar*. When possessed, women would act in ways which were normally inappropriate or prohibited. They would demand luxuries or food, and use forms of language usually reserved for men. Husbands would provide the luxuries and food demanded by the demon. The possession could only be resolved by feeding the demon, and ultimately by hiring a women shaman.

This example clearly illustrates Lewis' association of this form of possession with powerlessness. The possession provided a means of challenging the system without actually overturning it. From a functionalist sense it can be seen as a valve for releasing societal tension. Although the challenge to the system is controlled and ultimately the system is restored, the possession did allow women to gain a measure of real power – only women who had been possessed could become the shaman necessary for curing this form of possession.

Lewis also distinguishes between peripheral and central cults of spirit possession. The cults are those that challenge traditional values or roles within a society. As in the example from Somalia, these cults are found among the socially oppressed. They include both an aspect of protest against dominant structures and a means for temporarily relieving pressure within the social structure. Central cults of possession are those which support society and its norms and values. Very often the spirits found in peripheral cults are perceived as being demonic, from outside the culture, while those associated with central cults are often ancestors or spirits perceived of as being within the community. In central cults possession is used as a means for legitimising or maintaining patterns of hierarchy and authority.

Lewis' model provides an interesting addition to that of Mary Douglas. In a sense most of the forms of possession described by Douglas, and fitting into the purity rule can be seen as centralised cults of possession. Thus being taken by the Toronto Blessing was not a sign of being dispossessed, but rather an affirmation of the community and its values. In the same social context, being possessed by Satan might be seen as an example of a peripheral form of possession and reflect power structures within a particular community. Mary Douglas' model also adds a greater degree of flexibility into Lewis' model which seems rather black and white – with the different possible variations on grid and group, a wider range of forms of possession than suggested by Lewis are possible.

CHAPTER 13

Symbolism

Symbols are often seen as one of the significant components of religious constructs, whether in the context of myth, ritual or artifacts. Symbols have been discussed in a number of contexts in the previous sections of this volume. Three different trends can be traced. The first trend sees symbols as those cultural aspects that are not pragmatic or rationally verifiable. Thus, the tracing of an alligator around a seed being planted is symbolic, because from the observer's perspective it has no pragmatic role in making the tree grow, while placing a fish at the roots is seen as a pragmatic act and therefore not symbolic. This approach is problematic on several levels: it ignores the possibility that both acts may be understood in the same way by the observer; and it is essentially ethnocentric in creating a dichotomy between science or pragmatic acts, that is, those acts the observer considers to be rational, and symbolic or religious acts, which the observer considers to be irrational.

The second trend sees symbols, that is, their meanings, as having a common root in some aspect of human nature. The work of Jung and Freud are good examples of this approach, providing comprehensive systems for interpreting all symbols wherever they might be found. Although, as suggested above, symbols may have their roots in the unconscious, ethnographic data does not support the view that symbols mean the same thing regardless of cultural context. In spite of this caveat, some anthropologists continue to deploy elements of this narrow universalistic, or essentialist, approach to symbolism (see for example the discussions of hair by Leach and Obeyesekere discussed below). One aspect of the psychological approaches that is also common to many other discussions of symbolism is that of decoding. These models assume that the process of interpreting symbols is purely one of replacing the symbolic elements on a one to one basis with their referents. While at one level this might give some indication of what the symbols are doing, there are significant problems associated with this simplistic approach. Many anthropologists and other scholars have observed that symbols are multivocal, that is they communicate a wide range rather than one single concept of proposition, thus any decoding would be an artificial selection from the range of possible meanings. Decoding also assumes that there is no individual or personal content that is brought to the symbol. It also raises the question of why, if the information only needs to be decoded, do cultures and communities go to such efforts to create symbolic systems as they do not seem to give any added value? Thus, it is arguable that decoding theories are not sufficient explanations or interpretations of symbolism.

The third trend is illustrated in the work of Geertz, which focuses on the role of symbols in communication and particularly in structuring our experience of and interpretation of the world around us. Geertz's model provides a methodology for examining how symbols work within a cultural system. He does not qualitatively judge the role that symbols play, nor does he impose on them any specific meaning or content. It is this type of more open-ended methodological approach that is examined below.

Anthropological studies of symbolism have tended to focus on what symbols are, how they work and how they can be interpreted from both the internal and external perspectives. In this section we touch on three approaches to symbolism, that of Victor Turner, Raymond Firth and Dan Sperber. The three approaches, while moving in very different directions, all attempt to move away from discussions of specific meaning or kinds of meaning, rational or irrational, and to examine from a methodological perspective how symbols come to mean and how they work within different cultural contexts. We then examine how different approaches to symbolism have been applied to two symbolic fields, hair and food, both of which have been features associated with many religious traditions.

Victor Turner's analysis of symbolism is found both within his ethnographic studies and in more specifically theoretical discussions. One of the clearest presentations of the main elements of his approach is found in an introduction to a symposium on symbolic action published as 'Forms of Symbolic Action' (1969).

Turner suggests that one of the primary features of ritual symbols is that they are 'multivocal' (1969: 8). Multivocal means that rather than having a single meaning, symbols have many different levels of meaning at the same time. This multivocal aspect distinguishes a symbol from a sign. A sign is univocal while a symbol is multivocal. This multivocal character contains a variety of elements including the 'physiological' qualities of the object, ideological and ethical referents, as well as other forms of cognitive referents (Turner, 1969: 9). These referents are divided into two poles, the sensory and the ideological. Symbols, unlike signs, will develop both poles of meaning. A symbol is an object (in the broadest sense of the term) in which all of these levels of meaning are condensed.

In addition to being multivocal, Turner suggests that symbols have three dimensions: 'exegetical', 'operational' and 'positional' (1969: 11). The exegetical level of meaning is the interpretation by the insider. This aspect of meaning has a number of different forms. A symbol can be explained through a myth or a ritual, or it can be explained by a wide range of individuals each with different types of knowledge – this will include the specialist knowledge of a ritual practitioner and the unspecialised knowledge of a layperson. The operational level is that which is perceived by the observer. It is the meaning or explanation of the symbol as the people within the community use it. This level of meaning may be very different to that of the exegetical level; people may use a symbol in a very different way than they speak about it, and in some cases they may not provide an exegesis for a symbol. Turner suggests that the affective aspect of symbolic performance is an important addition to the understanding of the operative level of meaning. The positional level is perhaps the most important of the three. It refers to how a symbol relates to other symbols. It recognises that a symbol very often gains its meanings by association rather than merely on its own terms.

Turner also subdivides the exegetical level into three additional levels: 'nominal, substantial, and artifactual' (1969: 13). The nominal element refers to the name used for the symbol. The derivation of the name can point to one level of meaning. Thus, Turner uses the example of the mukula tree, from his ethnography of the Ndembu. This tree was used in rituals connected with birth and menstruation. Its name was understood to be derived from the term for maturation, which in women was associated with the onset of menses. The substantial refers to the selected natural properties of the object. In the case of the mukula tree, the tree exuded a red gum; the gum was associated with menstrual blood. The artifactual element was found in the use of a piece of the tree in the figure used in the ritual.

Turner's model develops many important issues in relation to the study of ritual symbols. However, rather than explaining how the process of symbolising works, Turner provides a model for analysing how symbols are used and how they can be interpreted within a specific cultural context. It is significant that Turner's model does not relate to issues of rationality or impose any specific content or interpretation. It provides models for the different levels of interpretation rather than imposing a predetermined interpretation.

Several aspects of Turner's model need to be clarified or refined. His three levels of interpretation do not clearly distinguish between the types of interpretation. Thus all three, the internal, the external and the structural are all seen as potentially equivalent analyses of the symbol. While at one level, this level is useful in that it suggests that no one level is privileged above the others, it does not clearly indicate that an analysis of symbolism must use the internal exegesis as data as well as a form of explanation. Alongside the other uses of a symbol in ritual or other religious constructs, the explanation is also a use of the symbol, and must be analysed as such. Dan Sperber suggests that Turner's model also over emphasises the concept of meaning, which is taken as analogous to the meaning of language. Sperber suggests that the linguistic concept of meaning should be avoided, in part because the meaning may be absent or itself be symbolic; Turner's own view of the multivocal nature of symbolism implicitly supports this argument (Sperber, 1974: 33).

In *Symbols: Public and Private* Raymond Firth develops a second and equally significant aspect of symbolism, the nature of and the relationship between public and private symbols. Anthropologists had long distinguished between these two realms of symbolism. Private symbolism was understood to be symbols created by individuals, motivated by individual experiences and feelings. Public symbolism was created by and for a group. The latter was essentially communicative and was conventional both in expression and interpretation. Private symbols were usually seen to be the domain of psychologists, while anthropologists sought to discover the public aspects of symbolism. This distinction underlies Leach's analysis of hair discussed below. Firth takes up this distinction and argues for an analysis that sees a close interrelationship and movement between the two forms of symbolism.

Firth's definition of symbolism is foundational to his discussion of the public/private dichotomy. His definition focuses on the way that symbols are used, primarily as 'instruments of expression, of communication, of knowledge and control' (Firth, 1973: 77). Symbols are seen fundamentally as objects of expression. While they can express a wide range of different types of concepts, political and religious symbols are seen as primarily expressing values, that is, means of shaping and directing behaviour. They are also objects whose task is to communicate, and in a sense to be a shorthand in communication. By bringing together a number of concepts and abstractions in a single object, the material is condensed in and communicated by that object. Firth emphasises that although a symbol may have many different levels of interpretation or meaning, particularly in respect of the knowledge of different interpreters, all levels of meaning from that of the theologian to that of the person on the street are all equally valid interpretations of the symbol. The relation of symbols and knowledge, particularly what kinds of knowledge they relate to has been a difficult question. Firth rejects Eliade's view (see the discussion of phenomenological theories) that symbols are a uniquely real expression of experience of or knowledge of the sacred. Instead, he suggests that it is important to focus on the knower not the known – to look at the types of knowledge that symbols are believed in particular ethnographic contexts to convey, rather than to make a judgment on the veracity of that knowledge. The final aspect of his discussion is that of control. He suggests that control works on two levels: control of overt behaviour and of the structure that underlies that behaviour. Responses to a religious symbol like the cross or a political symbol like the Queen are good examples of how symbols shape behaviour and emotional response. Other symbols can lead us to act according to the values they express. Symbols that work on the structures of behaviour might include the use of male gendered language in religious texts, leading to a particular perception of the roles of men and women, and thereby shaping perceptions and behaviour. The Queen or the British monarchy can also be seen as the second type of control. As a symbol it helps to establish a whole structure of deference and power, which underlies a system of behaviour and values.

Firth closely examines the interrelationship between private and public symbols. He demonstrates that neither realm can be seen as absolutely distinct. The relationship between the two can be most clearly seen in the case of art. The objects created by artists in western society are by definition private symbols. This symbolism, however, cannot be so private that it does not communicate to an audience. It must, therefore, bridge the gap between the two realms and at times move in a strong sense from the private to the public realm. For the artist the emphasis may remain on the private side, while for the audience it may lie in that of the public – though even for the audience there may be a private aspect of their interpretation.

On the one hand private symbolism is shaped by public symbols and discourses. Thus, for example, Firth cites the case of the Kunapipi cult from an indigenous Australian community in which dreams of men connected to the cult were clearly shaped by the ritual structures of the cult (Firth, 1973: 217). The dreams, however, even more significantly transformed and added to the public symbols. These transformations that emerged from individual private symbolism were often taken up and shaped public perceptions of the symbols. Private symbols can, depending on the context, be taken into the public realm. They can lead to action by the individual or the wider community or be transformed into a symbolic basis for action.

The most significant question relating to this move from private to public is that of reception or validation. Which symbols or transformations will be accepted as valid and which will be rejected? At one level, and one which relates to the private aspect of public symbols, the symbol's acceptance relates to the degree to which it expresses or shapes the feelings of the audience. Firth suggests that new symbols or transformations of symbols need to have some degree of continuity or conformity with pre-existing symbolic systems. They also, particularly if they are predictive, need to be able to be interpreted in such a way that they conform to understandings of reality. Firth also includes the element of individual personality, that is, of individuals who are charismatic in the sense described by Weber. This element, however, begs a question: surely it is more likely that they are charismatic precisely because they are able to shape their personal symbols in the ways already indicated? The final and most important element, however, is that of power. Private symbols are often considered orthodox or heretical purely on the basis of religious or political authorisation.

Firth provides a comprehensive discussion of the nature of public and private symbols and their interactions. His analysis does not develop the processes by which symbols are created; this aspect is developed in the work of Dan Sperber. Sperber's *Rethinking Symbolism* (1975) develops a cognitive model of symbolism, which explains the processes by which symbols are created. His model brings together the multivocal aspects inherent to Turner's model and explains the relationship between the public and private aspects of Firth's model. In developing a model that provides a cognitive basis for how symbols work and the structure of symbolic systems, Sperber avoids the problems inherent to many of the earlier essentialist models. While providing an essentialist basis for the creation of symbols, this basis has no specific content, is not limited to any specific realm, and therefore provides an open-ended model that recognises the cognitive uniformity of human beings.

Sperber's model is based on the view that symbols in themselves do not mean anything. Rather, they provide a basis upon which meanings can be attached. At a basic level, his theory suggests a model in which the mind is composed of two main aspects: an encyclopaedic function, which is essentially passive long-term memory, and an active function, correspond-ing to short-term memory. When new information is presented to the active faculty, it focuses, or focalises, on those elements that it is unable to define. It then sends this object to the passive, encyclopaedic function to evoke a definition. Symbols are precisely those objects that resist definition. The encyclopaedic function returns a partial definition, which, however, is insufficient. Thus the process continues with more and more information being sent to active memory; when conceptual information is exhausted other forms of information are returned, including feelings and memories. This process ends up producing a cone of information rather than a specific definition or meaning. The sense of smell is a good analogy for this process. We are not particularly good at defining smells, thus rather than a smell returning a clear definition it tends to create a cone similar to that of a symbol. It is thus no coincidence that smells are particularly good at evoking memories and feelings.

Sperber's model is helpful in a number of respects. It provides a clear explanation of why symbols have no single meaning and are often resistant to meaning. They are precisely objects that are ambiguous and thus evoke a wide range of meanings. These meanings can be both stated and unstated. His model also explains the role of private meanings in public symbols. Although some aspects of the cone created by any symbol will be public, his model suggests that much of the content will also be private, based on the individual's own emotions and memories evoked by the symbol. His model is also contentless. It provides a cognitive basis for the process of symbolising that is shared by all human beings but it does not determine the content or use of the symbols. Sperber's model also fits in well with other cognitive models, for example, structuralism, which focuses on the cognitive processes by which symbols are related one to another. The structuralist model provides a process by which the cones, through their relation to other cones, are limited in scope. The cone of a single symbol can be seen as potentially unlimited, by relating it to another symbol some aspects of its contents are limited because they are defined in relation to that other symbol, based on the underlying structural model. Mary Douglas' model of grid and group (see above) is also helpful in thinking about the relationship within a cone of private and public aspects of symbols, and suggests a process by which these different aspects can be developed; thus in a low grid low group situation the private aspects of the cone can both be expanded and externalised.

– HAIR –

In order to illustrate some aspects of the symbolic process, and more particularly theories deployed in relation to specific symbols, we will examine two areas of symbolism: hair and food. Both hair and food have attracted a good deal of anthropological interest and are commonly found in systems identified as religious. In a classic essay, 'Magical Hair' (1958), Leach takes up the issue of interpreting symbolic behaviour particularly in relation to hair. He suggests a distinction in symbolic behaviour between the 'pragmatic' and the 'communication' content of the symbols (Leach,

1958: 147). The pragmatic aspect refers to the effect that the symbol may have, perhaps in terms of creating some kind of emotional response; while the communication aspect refers to the information or concepts conveyed by the symbol. He further relates these two realms to the distinction between private and public. By definition the communicative aspect of a symbol must be public, as it must be shared in order for communication to occur. The pragmatic content is private as it relates to an individual emotional or affective response to the symbol. The issue that Leach addresses in his analysis is the relationship between these two aspects of symbols.

As a means of examining this issue, Leach takes up the psychoanalytical discussion of hair, particularly that of Dr Charles Berg in *The Unconscious Significance of Hair* (1951). In brief, Berg argues that in all societies the cutting or manipulation of hair is highly symbolic behaviour. This symbolic emphasis is due to the fact that the head and hair are symbols of the genitals. Thus, the cutting of hair is psychologically equivalent to castration. Berg establishes the universality of this thesis on the basis of ethnographic examples. Leach suggests that although much of the ethnographic material used by Berg was outdated, there nonetheless seems to be a very common association between hair and sexuality. Thus, for example, he cites Fortune, who states that husbands and wives took care of each other's hair, and if another man cut a woman's hair this would be a public statement of adultery (Leach, 1958: 150).

In spite of this apparent association, Leach challenges one of the major premises of Berg's approach. He argues that the psychoanalytical model is based on the assumption that the use of a symbol reflects some underlying psychological state. Thus the use of phallic symbolism relates to an actual psychological issue relating to sexuality. Leach argues that this assumption is confusing the public and private aspects of symbolism – because a public symbol is used to communicate something, does not necessarily imply that it represents the individual's internal psychological state.

In order to demonstrate this distinction Leach takes up Berg's use of Malinowski's ethnography. Malinowski had described a practice among the Trobriand islanders of shaving the head during the mourning process. Berg interpreted this act as representing the internal feeling that the death was equivalent to the feeling of castration. Thus Berg is assuming that the act of shaving reflects, or is a response to, an internal feeling. Leach, however, points out that the shaving of the head is not due to individual inclination or feeling; rather it is a ritualised behaviour that is done due to social convention and expectation, and that the actual people who shaved their heads far from being loved ones, actually had no love for the deceased.

This distinction between the public and private, however, does not necessarily suggest that Berg's thesis has no basis. Leach proposes that in both cases the meaning of the act can be the same. In the case of the public symbol, it is a statement about a particular feeling, whether that feeling is felt or not, and in the case of the private, it is also a statement about that same feeling. In one case the statement may or may not be true, and in the ethnographic example it is not true, and in the other it is a true expression.

Leach suggests that if we keep this distinction between the pragmatic and communicative aspects of the symbols in mind, then we can accept the main point of Berg's thesis. He suggests that wherever hair is ritually used it has this phallic significance. He summarises the ethnographic uses of hair in the following equation:

> Long hair = unrestrained sexuality; short hair or partially shaved head or tightly bound hair = restricted sexuality; close shaven head = celibacy. (Leach, 1958: 154)

The significant point for Leach's argument is that these uses of hair are a public statement relating to these sexual meanings; they are not necessarily statements of an actual psychological state of affairs. Leach also argues that far from being unconscious, as supposed by the psychoanalytical approach, these sexual associations are usually consciously known and manipulated. He argues that in a sense the two approaches move in opposite directions. For the psychologist, the hair, the representation of unconscious drives and emotions, make the rituals which use it powerful, whereas for the anthropologists it is the ritual setting that creates the emotions that make hair powerful.

A final aspect of Leach's discussion is the association of the dichotomies of long hair/short hair; uncastrated/castrated and profane/sacred. He suggests that one defining element of the sacred is the abnormal, and part of the process by which individuals are transformed from the sacred to the profane is through becoming abnormal. The cutting of the hair, if it is seen as castration, is a transformation from normal to abnormal and therefore from profane to sacred. This highlights Leach's main argument. For the anthropologist the use of a symbol like hair is ultimately a public symbol reflecting and perhaps transforming public status.

C. R. Hallpike challenges both the ethnographic and theoretical basis for Leach's arguments. Hallpike observes that hair is a part of the body that has great 'manipulative potential' (1979: 100). Thus, due to its ease of use, he suggests that it would be surprising if it were not commonly used in rituals.

Hallpike takes up Leach's contention that hair is a common feature of mourning rituals and Leach's somewhat tentative agreement with Berg that it symbolises the feeling of castration, if not actually being an expression of that feeling. Hallpike suggests that there is no necessary reason why we should see this practice as a symbol of castration. He points out that in many societies women as well as men shave their heads – what, he asks, 'does it mean to talk of female castration'? (Hallpike, 1979: 101). Hallpike also points out that in many societies alongside cutting of hair other forms of bodily mutilation are performed – these mutilations are often on parts of the body not usually seen as phallic by psychoanalysts; thus cutting of hair may be a bodily mutilation rather than a symbol of castration.

He also further challenges Leach's arguments by using ethnographic material to illustrate other associations and uses of hair that have little to do with sexuality. Hallpike suggests that it is necessary to be aware of the variation in the use of hair (or other symbolic objects) before any attempt can be made to explain them. This observation is directly relevant to the argument being developed in this section. In order to properly analyse different religions or elements thereof it is necessary, at least in the initial stages of the analysis, to work on the basis of variability and to be highly sceptical of any approach that seeks to provide a unitary explanation.

Despite this emphasis on the need to be aware of variability and an awareness of the diversity within the ethnography, Hallpike argues for a unitary model based on social structural rather than psychological considerations. He argues that rather than seeing length of hair being associated with sexuality, it should be associated with social control. He suggests that long hair = outside of society or social control; and short hair = returning to society or being under social control.

Hallpike defends this hypothesis with rather generalised examples. Thus the tonsure of a monk would reflect social control and being part of a very controlling community, while the long hair of a hippy might reflect a rejection of society and social control. He also uses examples from the biblical text to illustrate these points. Thus, for example, he cites Jacob and Esau (Genesis 25). Jacob is described as a smooth man and Esau as a hairy man. While Jacob is connected with the tents and herds and therefore society, Esau rejects society and is a hunter and therefore outside society. Another example deployed by Hallpike is that of Samson. Although all of these cases do support Hallpike's characterisation of long hair and short hair being related to social control, they also all relate to sexuality. Thus the monk and hippy represent celibacy and free sex, Jacob and Esau represent controlled sexuality (marrying the correct people) and uncontrolled sexuality (marrying the wrong people), and in Samson's case extreme uncontrolled sexuality – all of his wives were forbidden in Israelite law.

Thus, it is possible to see Leach and Hallpike's arguments as complementary rather than conflicting characterisations, at least in terms of the biblical material. It is perhaps unsurprising that Berg, Leach and Hallpike are all working within the same symbolic universe as found in the biblical text, and that their attempt to generalise this symbolic universe can be associated with the dominance of Western intellectual and social models. On a broader level, however, each empirical case has to be interpreted contextually, and, as suggested by some of the detail of Hallpike's discussion, in many cases different models of explanation may be appropriate.

There is, however, one important difference between Hallpike's arguments and Leach's model. Whereas Leach's model deals with the level of meaning, Hallpike's model moves towards the area of function. Leach's model is limited because it assumes that the symbol or set of symbols will always have the same or essentially the same meaning. Without the unconscious basis (which Leach rejects) there seems no logical reason why hair should be associated necessarily with sexuality. It may be, but it need not be. Hallpike's arguments do not have this problem as they do not necessarily rely on meaning; cutting of hair can be an expression of social control rather than mean social control.

This association between cutting of hair and social control is developed in a much more comprehensive manner by Mary Douglas in *Natural Symbols* (1970). We have already touched upon Mary Douglas' 'purity rule' in the chapter on anthropological theories. The purity rule suggests that individuals' control over their bodies is directly related to societies' control over the individual. Thus the higher the degree of social control the higher the degree to which the individual will keep their body, including their hair, under control. Thus in a community like the army or prison, where there is a high degree of social control, the individual's hair is kept very short, whereas in a group where there is little control, like the hippy movement, hair will also be uncontrolled. The strength of Douglas' argument is that it is not tied to a specific symbolic element like hair. The purity rule would also relate to the use of the body sexually. In communities where there is strong control, the individual's sexuality will be controlled and the opposite will occur in communities in which there is little control. Thus Douglas' model provides an argumentative basis that brings together and explains the association between the observations of Leach and Hallpike.

Mary Douglas' argument is also more successful in respect of the issues of variation and meaning. The purity rule does not focus on any particular bodily behaviour. It can be contextualised to any ethnographic situation. The concept of control or lack of control can be determined by the context, and thus it is not limited to seeing short hair as a sign of control and long hair as a sign of lax control. This disassociation between the model and specific instantiations of the model also resolves the problem of meaning. All meaning is contextualised, while the model provides a methodology for analysing the use of symbols rather than assuming in advance of the data what the symbols might mean.

Gananath Obeyesekere's *Medusa's Hair* (1981) takes up some of the issues raised by Leach as well as issues relating to more general theories of symbolism. His work, unlike that of the three anthropologists discussed earlier in relation to hair, is based directly on a specific ethnographic context; a Buddhist pilgrimage centre in Sri Lanka. He addresses issues relating to the distinction between public and private symbolism, and argues for a return to an essentially Freudian explanation of rituals connected to hair – both specifically in relation to his own ethnography and more broadly.

One of the main issues that Obeyesekere challenges is common anthropological understanding of the distinction between public and private symbolism – this distinction played a key role in Leach's analyses of the psychoanalytical approach to hair. As suggested in the beginning of this section, public symbols are understood to be essentially conventional, with no necessary relationship to underlying psychological states or emotions. Because they are observable and shared, public symbols have been the major focus of anthropological research. Private symbols, that is, symbols created and used by individuals, reflect psychological and emotional states, but since they are not shared and belong to an individual, they have tended to be analysed by psychologists rather than anthropologists. The major thrust of Obeyesekere's critique is the assumption that public symbols do not contain, or in a sense arise from, internal psychological states. He argues that, at least in respect of his own ethnographic data, the public symbols are motivated not only by conventionality but also more importantly by underlying and unconscious psychological states. In order to bridge the gap between public and private symbols, Obeyesekere introduces the concept of the personal symbol. He suggests that personal symbols are the psychological and emotional content that individuals invest in public symbols, and which lead individuals to unconsciously deploy the public symbols.

It should be noted that we are not addressing at this point the origin or creation of a symbol. Many symbols clearly do emerge from the private and move to the public, as for example the symbols found in a painting like *Guernica*. Obeyesekere is addressing the issue of recreation rather than creation. Unconscious states lead individuals to unconsciously deploy shared symbols that reflect the unconscious issue or problem.

Obeyesekere suggests that this theoretical approach arises from his interaction with the ethnographic data relating to hair. He examines the symbolic use of hair by a number of female ascetics who develop highly matted hair, which resembles, at least from the perspective of other individuals in the society, fleshy protuberances. These protuberances are also associated with snakes, both by the anthropologist and the ascetics themselves. To the extent that the type of ascetic represented by these women had this type of hair, it can be seen as a public symbol.

If Leach's arguments were correct, then the use of hair by these ascetics would be a reflection of a conventional behaviour, meant to communicate but not to represent an individual psychological state. Leach might also suggest that the phallic symbolism of the hair would not be unconscious, but would be consciously deployed as part of the communicative aspect of the symbol. Additionally, in line with the argument that lack of care of hair means a rejection of interest in sexuality, their hair would communicate the ascetic aspect of these women's role.

Obeyesekere challenges Leach on several levels. First, through the use of life histories, Obeyesekere demonstrates that the growth of these protuberances was not a conscious decision by the women. Each of the women he analyses went through some type of sexual trauma that led her to develop unconsciously psychological problems with sexuality. These unconscious states then led the women to develop this particular use of hair, which Obeyesekere suggests represents a rejection of human sexuality by an embrace of divine sexuality. Thus the women, through an unconscious process, recreate the public symbol, which thereby gains its power by having its roots in the unconscious. Interestingly Obeyesekere links also the communicative aspect and the public response to the symbol to the unconscious. He describes his own initial response to the hair as being one of revulsion, which, after some reflection, he determined was due to an unconscious association of the hair with the phallus. He suggests that his own unconscious response might be similar to that of the individuals within the culture, and thus the power of the symbol for them is also essentially personal rather than the simple public communication suggested by Leach.

Second, Obeyesekere argues that for Leach to be correct, the phallic aspect of the hair needs to be consciously perceived by the people deploying the symbol as a means of communication. If it was not perceived then communication as described by Leach could not occur. Obeyesekere suggests on the basis of his ethnographic data that neither the ascetics nor the community was aware of the phallic aspects of the symbol. The community described the hair as fleshy protuberances attached to the head and some of the ascetics as snakes, both of which can be seen as phallic symbols, yet neither group associated the hair directly with sexuality. Thus the only way to bring together the women's stories and the symbol is to assume that the phallic association was unconscious rather than conscious.

On the basis of these and other arguments, Obeyesekere suggests that the hair is an unconscious symbol of sexuality. The hair is publicly associated with ascetics. Women ascetics, however, unconsciously develop this use of hair, and thus recreate rather than deploy the public symbol. Both the ascetic and the community in which she lives share the unconscious aspect. We can also draw from Obeyesekere's arguments an acceptance of Freud's concept of the unconscious and a general acceptance of Freud's interpretation of specific symbols, for example, that of hair.

Obeyesekere's analysis adds several important elements to the understanding of symbolism, particularly its deconstruction of the dichotomy of public and private symbols. It demonstrates that public symbols are motivated by private psychological states and emotions in the same way as private symbols. It also explains why the use of these symbols can have an affect on the user and thus adds to Mary Douglas' analysis. The approach also illustrates a significant aspect of that advocated in this volume, that is, the theoretical material needs to develop in a dialectical relationship with empirical data. There are, however, some significant problems with his analysis. These problems centre on his use of Freudian models of interpretation. One particular problem is found in the assumption of the universality of meaning. He assumes on the basis of Freudian models and his own psychological reaction that the phallic symbolism that he perceives is also shared by the community using the symbol. As this association is not consciously deployed, he can only argue for it on the basis of a shared unconscious understanding. While it is possible that the phallic aspect might be found in this case, there seems little ethnographic support for assuming its universality (either consciously or unconsciously). It seems more useful to assume that symbols, whether conscious or unconscious, are much more culturally specific and thus can not and should not be universalised.

This discussion of the use of hair as an embodied symbol shares interesting similarities to the discussion and definition of religion. Two main strategies for analysing hair can be identified. On the one hand, both Leach and Obeyesekere from slightly different perspectives present an essentialised definition. The specific symbol being analysed, and perhaps by implication other similar symbols have a fixed meaning that transcends cultural or communal boundaries. In the case of Obeyesekere this essentialised definition is fixed by the unconscious, the content of which, or at least the processes that lead to that content, are universal and thus the symbols have a universal unconscious level of meaning. For Leach there is a similar level of essentialisation; in shying away from the unconscious, it is difficult to see the terms upon which Leach builds this commonality – it becomes a commonality allegedly built upon observation of ethnographic contexts rather than any theoretical basis. On the other hand, Mary Douglas' work suggests a non-essentialised approach. It provides a basis for understanding embodied symbols in relation to society, but does not predetermine what or how the symbols will be understood or deployed. Douglas' position is supported by Firth. He emphasises that it is not any specific use of hair that is significant, it is a more generalised use of hair that needs to be contextualised in relation to other cultural symbols. Hallpike, although closely related to Mary Douglas' analysis has a more essentialist basis, specifying a specific universal meaning to specific categories of hair.

– FOOD RULES –

Food is a second symbolic field which is closely associated with the body that has attracted a significant amount of elaboration in many religious traditions. We briefly touch on analyses of the use of food rules in two different ethnographic contexts: the Israelite, as analysed by Mary Douglas, and the Traveller-Gypsies discussed by Judith Okely. Both of these studies employ a version of the structuralist approach to symbolism. They are interested in the way that the communities categorise different foods, the way that these categories relate one to another, and the relationship of these patterns to other aspects of the specific community or culture.

The Israelite food rules have provided a fruitful area of study, with many theories offered to account for why particular animals are prohibited or permitted. We have examined Marvin Harris' arguments, which explained the prohibition on the pig in materialist terms, that is, the pig was essentially not economically viable in the desert and thus its use was prohibited (see the discussion on Cultural Materialism). Other explanations have focused on health or practices of the Israelites' neighbours. Aside from the particular empirical questions relating to each of these specific theories, they all share a common fault, that is, they ignore the fact that the pig is only one element in a much larger system of food rules, and that to understand its symbolic value it must be examined in relation to the system as a whole. While some of these discussions might explain the prohibition on the pig, they do not explain why some other animals are also prohibited and others permitted.

One of the most influential analyses that attempt to look at the system as a whole is that of Mary Douglas. Her examination of Israelite food rules has been developed over a number of years and is found in many publications. One of the most approachable of these discussions is found in 'Deciphering a Meal' (1975). This paper gives a good outline of her theories relating to Israelite food rules and it also provides an interesting analysis of food rules in British society.

Douglas' analysis of food rules emphasises the need to examine the whole symbolic universe. Thus, she examines the food rules in relation to other ways of dealing with animals, that is, in terms of ritual purity and sacrifice. While it might be argued that she introduces these elements a little prematurely, she is correct in arguing that their use of symbols will be closely related to that in the food rules. The pervasiveness of the symbolic structures that she identifies is suggested by the conclusion of her discussion in which she demonstrates that the understanding of self and society is structured in the same way as the understanding of the animal kingdom.

While this is not the place to recapitulate her arguments in full, we shall focus on some aspects of her analysis that both help us to understand the ethnographic context and her theoretical approach. The key element of her approach is her view that the system of food rules is built around conceptual categories of what defines a proper animal. The world is sub-divided into three realms: air, sea and land. Each of these realms has a form of animal that is proper to it. A proper land animal is one that chews its cud and has cloven hooves. Any animal that has these elements is a proper animal and fit to eat and to sacrifice. Any animal that does not have these elements is not proper and is rejected from both the table and the altar. The pig fits into the category of improper animals as it has cloven hooves but does not chew its cud; the pig is thus anomalous and rejected from the table and altar. The pig, as a mediator, including elements from the permitted and rejected categories, is particularly problematic. Its rejection as anom-alous becomes emblematic for the system as a whole. It is clear from her analysis that the pig on its own has no meaning. It gains meaning by being related to other symbols in the system and by being categorised in relation to those symbols. The fundamental basis for the system outlined by Mary Douglas is a classificatory system in which there are two main categories, permitted and rejected – any animal can ultimately be placed in one of these categories.

As suggested above, her analysis also indicates that the Israelite under-standing of self is structured in the same way as their understanding of the animal world. On a broad level the world of human beings and animals is divided into two categories: those under the covenant and those not under it. The Israelites and permitted animals are found in the first category, other animals and nations are in the second category. She also illustrates within the Israelite understanding of self that the hierarchy of Israelite society also mirrors that of the animals under the covenant. While there are some prob-lems of over complexity in the details of her analysis and some empirical problems with the data she employs, it does present a comprehensive explanation of the system as a whole and indicates the way that the system relates to other aspects of Israelite culture.

One of the very strong points of the methodology that Mary Douglas employs is that it provides an open-ended theoretical structure. It is based on a model of cognitive essentialism, that is, that human beings structure their universe as a means of making it understandable, but it does not impose any specific content on those structures. The structure suggested for Israelite society is not seen as universal. Other societies will develop different structural models, as suggested by her analyses of other structural forms in 'Self-Evidence' (1975). The nature of the different structures and the processes of structuring arise from the empirical data – rather than imposing a set structure or a set range of values or meanings.

Judith Okely's ethnographic analysis of the Traveller-Gypsies presents an analysis of symbolism in general and symbolism associated with food in particular that is closely related to that developed by Mary Douglas. She demonstrates a comprehensive model of purity and impurity that organises many aspects of Rom (their term for themselves) life as well as the way they prepare and eat food. She also demonstrates that the underlying structure that organises this purity system is related to a broader definition of self in relation to the wider world. Purity is both structured in the same way as this self-understanding and provides a means of maintaining this self-understanding by creating and maintaining strong boundaries between Rom and Gorgio (non-Rom) society.

The fundamental element in the Rom purity system is the distinction between the inner and outer body. The inner body is understood to be pure, while the outer body is impure. Okely suggests that the inner body represents the Rom; it is that aspect which is kept secret and separate from Gorgio society. The outer body, which is impure, represents the Gorgio. The basis of the system is that these two aspects of the body and society must be kept apart. This distinction underlies relations between the Rom and the Gorgio, marriage rules and the way that a camp is established and maintained.

Based on the association between outer body/impure and inner body/pure, the Rom have a very different understanding of dirt than does Gorgio society. The Rom divide dirt into two categories: *chikli* and *mochadi*. The category of *chikli* includes much of what Gorgio society would consider to be dirt, dust and grime. For the Rom, however, this category is relatively insignificant. *Chikli* does not affect purity and thus can safely be ignored. *Mochadi* is the significant category of dirt; it is the realm of ritual impurity. One of the significant defining features of *mochadi* is that it is associated with the outer body, and can potentially bring the impure outer body into contact with the inner body.

The distinction between *chikli* and *mochadi* is particularly evident in the Rom's system of food rules and food preparation. The boundary maintaining aspects of the system creates a problem for the Rom in relation to the Gorgio – the Rom rely on Gorgio society for much of their food. Food produced by the Gorgio is problematic on two levels; it is impure because it is associated with the Gorgio, and impure because the Gorgio do not understand the need to keep inside and outside apart. The Rom distinguish between different categories of Gorgio food in order to minimise possible contamination. They are usually willing to eat only foods that have been produced in factories and are either tinned or pre-packaged. Although the food from a factory has the possibility of contamination, the impersonal nature of its production minimises this possibility. Even food so produced has to be protected; even a shadow can contaminate food. Bread brought from even a 'clean' baker will often have its crust removed before consumption. Any food that is homemade by a Gorgio would be seen to be contaminated.

Food preparation and the objects used for it are also specified. An object that is used for the making of food should never be used for washing any part of the body. Once a bowl has been so used it is considered to be unclean and can never be used for food. If crockery is damaged or cracked it also becomes prone to impurity and is thrown away. Okely suggests that the Rom are acutely aware that these practices distinguish them from the Gorgio. She states:

> The Gorgios' (non-Rom) failure to make this distinction between inner and outer body is not seen by the Gypsies as merely accidental, but a means of drawing positive ethnic boundaries. A Gypsy is partly defined or defines him or herself by an adherence to these rituals of cleanliness. A Gypsy woman said: 'He's a *real* Gypsy. You wouldn't find him washing his hands in the same bowl as he washes his cup.' (Okely, 1983: 83)

Thus, the symbolic structure becomes a conscious way of articulating the distinction between Rom and Gorgio society.

A similar structural pattern is evident in their categorisation of the animal world. They divide animals into categories of pure and impure based on their behaviour. Those animals that constantly lick themselves are seen as particularly impure because they take their outer body into their inner body – thus the cat is one of the most unclean types of animals; it is directly associated with the Gorgio and death, both negative associations. If a dish or other food object is touched by one of these animals it is destroyed. The type of food animals eat is also relevant. Carnivores are more *mochadi* than are herbivores – thus a rabbit is somewhat *mochadi* because it licks itself but less impure than a cat because it is an herbivore. The hedgehog is understood to be the purest form of animal and seen as representing the Rom, because it is both an herbivore and cannot lick itself. The hedgehog was eaten in certain ritual settings.

Although the underlying structural pattern found in the Rom material is similar to that of the Israelite material as presented by Mary Douglas, Okely's analysis suggests that there are some differences in the ways the categories interrelate. Rather than being two unbridgeable and mutually distinct categories, as in the case of the Israelite system, the Rom's categories have some intermediate stages: on one end is the hedgehog and on the other the cat; in between are different mediating categories with different levels of impurity. It is likely that this structure is also found in their relations with the Gorgio – the Rom can move in the direction of the Gorgio by settling down and the Gorgio that of the Rom by marriage and travelling. Both Mary Douglas' and Okely's use of the structuralist theoretical perspective demonstrates the explanatory power of the theory. It provides a cognitive basis for analysing different systems and based on the empirical data allows those systems to include different content and different structural patterns.

CHAPTER 14

Myth

The study of myth is closely related to that of symbolism, with many of the same arguments being applied. Thus, for example, there is a long tradition of what might be called the semiological approach, which seeks to decode the messages hidden within the myth. A typical example of this type of approach is Freudian analysis, which using a predetermined model of symbolism and of the human psyche, decodes the symbols found in mytho-logical narratives to illustrate how they relate to unconscious psychological complexes, particularly the Oedipus Complex. Like symbolism, mythology is usually understood as a system of communication, with different approaches limiting myth to a specific area of communication or to a specific type of context. Our discussion will suggest that both of these types of approaches are flawed and that a better definition of myth will be found in an open ended cognitive model that does not impose content or function upon the material being analysed but rather provides an explanation for the processes that lead to myth and a methodology for analysis.

Anthropologists and other academics studying myth have developed theories that, for the most part, are either substantialist or functionalist. The substantialist models have defined myth by the presence of specific contents, thus the presence of god, gods or miraculous deeds are common defining features. In many cases these definitions define myth against some other object. Thus myth is often opposed to history. History is defined broadly as being based on the factual depiction of events in the context of an historic chronology, while myth is defined as a fictional depiction of events, often taking place outside historical chronology.

This type of distinction is problematic on several levels. First, the definition is essentially ethnocentric. It takes our model of factuality and uses it as the criterion for classification, with narrative material being defined qualitatively on its basis. The models of past of other societies are often defined as myth because they include explanations based on what we consider to be the supernatural or sometimes because there is simply no documentation to back them up, and our understanding of past is defined as history, and thus in our terms is true.

Second, it is possible to ask why should this narrative element be the defining feature? Is the narrative element so significant that it shapes the nature and use of the story? It seems more likely that such narrative elements need to be contextualised. In some societies or contexts, acts of gods may be appropriate where in others, due to cultural expectations, the big bang might be more appropriate. If stories with or without gods or miraculous deeds seem to work in the same way, there seems no logical reason to give narrative elements the priority assigned to them by such theories.

Third, the selection of this narrative element as significant arises from our cultural context, as a means originally of defining the monotheistic religions in opposition to other polytheistic religions and eventually of defining science in opposition to religion. Myth was used as a term to describe the stories of non-Christian communities, often communities that were seen as preceding Christianity, for example, the stories of the Greek Gods. These stories were seen as essentially false as opposed to the Christian narratives that were seen as essentially true. A similar dichotomy is found between scientific and religious narratives. As the scientific paradigm became increasingly dominant and confident, its narratives were seen as scientific and thus true, while religion's narratives were seen as based on belief, therefore they were myth and false. Both of these dichotomies relate to specific patterns of authority and mechanisms for authorising truth and should not become the basis of a cross-cultural definition of myth. Such a definition should be able to apply the category of myth to all societies including our own, without being based on the ethnocentric presuppositions of one society or another.

Functionalist definitions move from those that are very narrowly defined to those that suggest a more open ended and inclusive model of functionality. Some of the early functionalist definitions of myth were based on a dichotomy between myth and science. Myth was seen as an attempt to explain different natural processes, or aspects of causality in the absence of scientific models of explanation. One example of this type of approach saw myths as explaining the cycle of the year, with death and resurrection myths relating to the movement between the rain and dry seasons. While this interpretation may work in some ethnographic contexts, and even that is debatable, there seems no reason to extend it to all narratives defined as myth. The dichotomy between myth and scientific explanations, if deconstructed, moves us towards a better definition. If myth as a model of reality is seen as doing something similar to science, also a model of reality, then perhaps the distinction between the two is more apparent then real. Perhaps myth, science and history are words describing similar phenomena, mechanisms for creating models of self either in terms of past or in terms of understanding how the world works.

Other functionalist models deal with broader areas of functionality. Thus, for example, the psychological models see myth as resolving issues relating to the unconscious or individual psychological development. The general statement of these approaches is not in itself problematic. It is based on the psychological unity of humanity; for example, all human beings in the Freudian perspective have an unconscious, which creates issues that need to be dealt with, and myth provides a social way of resolving or airing these issues. If the psychological approaches stopped there they would provide an open ended model for analysing myth. Each culture might have its own unconscious issues and different contents of myth relating to those issues. The problem associated with the psychological approaches is that they suggest that there is also a common content to the unconscious (whether in the Freudian or Jungian sense). Thus, rather than interpreting the objects created in different ethnographic contexts, their approach pre-supposes both the content and the specific interpretation of that content.

Some functionalist approaches to mythology are more open ended than discussed thus far. One good example is that of Malinowski, who suggested that myths were charters for social action. This definition provides an inclusive model that can include a wide range of narrative material and does not impose a particular ethnocentric understanding of the phenomena. One aspect that is not explained by a conscious legitimising function is the emotional content that is often associated with myth. This aspect is found in the psychological models, and suggests that the basis of mythology might be found at a deeper level than social legitimisation. Some variations on the structuralist model move in this direction. They see myth as performing as much an unconscious process of legitimising or rationalising as a conscious one. Myths communicate a shared unconscious structure or pattern for organising reality, and thus become the foundation for the way that people understand both the world and themselves. The structuralist model explains the surface aspect of legitimisation proposed by Malinowski as well as seeing myth as serving a more significant organising and cognitive role. There are similarities between this position and the world-creating aspects of Berger's theory (see the chapter on sociological approaches) as well as aspects of Geertz's theory of religion (see the chapter on anthropological theories).

Broadly speaking, myth can be defined as the ways in which human beings construct models for understanding their world and their place in it. Thus, myth can use an historic model or a fictional model; it can also use a scientific model of understanding or one that relies purely on imagination. This definition emphasises a high level of abstraction, focusing on the aspect of worldview; it also, however, includes many other levels simultaneously. Myth works on the conscious level of explaining or justifying institutions or practices, and emerges in inter-relation with them. It also works on the unconscious level of shaping and validating patterns of thinking and categorising our understanding of the world.

This definition of myth brings together essentialist and functionalist aspects. The essentialist aspect is found in the basic presupposition of the definition. Structuralism is a cognitive model that explains how the mind works; it assumes that the human mind is a structuring device, taking experience and other elements and categorising them and interrelating the categories. While the basis for this structuring is biological and therefore an essential aspect of human nature, the structures and the content of the structures are determined at the level of culture. Although the process itself is independent of function, it is merely the way the mind works, it becomes the basis through which we order and give meaning to the world around us. It is important to note that it is the mind that is defined in an essentialist way rather than myth – although myth may be highly structured, all human constructs are structured by mind. The functionalist aspect of the definition is broadly similar to that of Geertz and Berger – through the imposition of structure, cultural experience becomes meaningful.

Sally Falk Moore in 'Descent and Symbolic Filiation' discusses the common motif of brother/sister incest in many different mythological systems. Her analysis primarily relies on the structuralist approach, particularly in its aspect of resolving or clouding contradiction as well as comparing it with the psychological and historical explanations of this mythological feature.

Moore outlines the main features of the psychological explanation of the presence of incest in myth. This model argues that the mythological use of incest is due to the basis of all mythological systems in the Oedipus Complex. While the Oedipus Complex deals directly with the desire for mother/son incest, psychologists see brother/sister incest as a displacement of this universal desire. Moore suggests that while this explanation accounts for the presence of the incest motif, it does not explain why particular forms of incest, for example, mother/son, father/daughter or brother/sister, correlate with particular forms of social structure. Thus social structure must play a role in the shaping of these myths even if the Oedipal desires are the psychological basis of the phenomena.

The historical explanations work in a very different way. They suggest that patterns of behaviour that are depicted in myth reflect actual patterns of behaviour. If these customs are not currently practiced by the society telling the myth, this approach suggests that these practices were once part of the customary behaviour. This model explains the prevalence of the incest motif by suggesting that it reflects practices that were associated with a specific phase in cultural development. They suggest that brother/sister incest was practiced in societies that had matrilineal patterns of inheritance. The only way that a brother could retain right to property was through marriage to his sister. Related arguments are used to demonstrate the existence of matriarchal societies at some earlier point in human history. Moore argues that this approach takes an overly literal reading of the myths, and argues that myths are not essential historical relics, rather they are means by which a community deals with problems and issues relating to their current existence.

Moore, as suggested above, utilises a structuralist approach to examine how the myths relate to issues in the ethnographic present rather than some mythical past. Her analysis both explains the prevalence of incest and indicates why different forms of incest are related to different forms of social organisation. Moore suggests that these myths serve to resolve a paradox arising within certain societies that have two common elements. The first is exogamy, a rule requiring that individuals marry outside a particular group. The second is a creation myth that posits a single creation – and thereby the possibility that the original pair was brother and sister. The contradiction is between the original act of incest, which is implied by common descent, and the requirement of exogamy and its associated rules against incest. An additional aspect of the contradiction is the paradoxical relationship between the specifically delineated kinship group and the rest of humanity. The myth resolves these contradictions by suggesting the unity of humanity and thus, by suggesting that all marriages contain an element of incest, justifies exogamy as an acceptable means of recapitulating the original act. Since different societies have different models of descent, for example, through the male line, the female line or both lines, different forms of incest are used to relate to these different patterns of descent. Moore's model is thus able to explain both the role of mythological incest and the correlation of specific forms of incest with the contemporary social structures in which the myths are used.

As suggested above, Moore argues that one of the significant indicators of the social function of mythological incest is that particular forms of incest are found in relation to particular models of social structure. This is specifically the case regarding societies with either patrilineal or matrilineal modes of descent. In patrilineal societies the mother comes from a different lineage or descent group than her husband and son who are in the same lineage or descent group. In matrilineal systems the father and daughter are part of different descent groups, while the mother and her children, male and female, are part of the same matrilineage. Moore points out that in patrilineal systems mythological incest is often in the form of mother and son, while in matrilineal systems it is between father and daughter. In both cases the sexual act brings together both issues – the sexual act is simultaneously incestuous and exogamous – and thus justifies both the understanding of creation and the need for, or possibility of, exogamy.

The Dogon of the Sudan in Africa are a good illustration of Moore's arguments. The Dogon are a patrilineal and patrilocal society, that is, descent and residence are through the male line. The Dogon have a rule against marrying within the patrilineal group and a preference for marrying one's mother's brother's daughter. The Dogon also specifically associate their marriage patterns with a creation myth.

The Dogon creation myth saw the original creation as being a twin set of placentas each containing a male being; each male was associated with a female spiritual principle. One of the male spiritual beings was born too early and separated from his female half. He attempted ultimately to procreate with his placenta, symbolically his mother. In order to bring creation back into order the proper twins were brought back together and humanity was born.

The Dogon myth thus includes mother/son incest, the form that Moore associates with patrilineal society. In Dogon society a boy is allowed to take liberties with his mother's brother's property, to the extent to having sex with his mother's brother's wife; these elements are symbolically the mother and thus recapitulate the original incestuous act. The circle is complete with marriage to the mother's brother's daughter, who being part of the same patrilineage as the mother is symbolically also the mother. In Dogon society the myth provides a logical link between the two families through symbolic incest and common humanity and therefore justifies the rule of exogamy.

Interestingly one could make a similar argument in relation to endogamous societies, that is, societies that have a requirement to marry inside one's own group. Here the paradox is somewhat different. Common creation and therefore common descent suggest that all human beings are related and therefore possible marriage partners; endogamy, however, limits marriage partners to a very narrow group. In this type of case mythological incest can be used, not to emphasise common humanity, but rather to create models of marrying as closely as possible. This type of resolution is found in Genesis in which all of the ancestors of Israel, a society with a preference for endogamy, have either actual or symbolic incestuous marriages. In both the material analysed by Moore and that of the Israelites incest serves as a way of defining the relation between categories. In the exogamous societies it serves as an explanation for bringing the categories together and in the Israelite, endogamous material for keeping the categories apart.

The significant aspect, therefore, underlying Moore's analysis is that the essential feature of her argument is the way that different categories are related to each other rather than the specific ethnographic details. One problem with Moore's analysis is the over emphasis on social structure as the key to underlying structure. At times her analysis, and other similar studies, seems to suggest that underlying structure can be reduced to social structure. If the cognitive aspects of structure are taken seriously, then the association between myth and social structure is not a causal one; rather, both reflect the same unconscious cognitive patterns. This final point is important; this argumentative move allows structuralism to provide a methodology for analysing cultural constructs like myth and social structure without presupposing the nature of the structures to be found or their functions.

CHAPTER 15

Last Words

In this section we have touched on some of the major constituent elements associated with religion. These elements suffer the same type of problem in relation to definition, as does religion itself. In each of the cases examined one of the fundamental problems was the joining together of theories that both strictly defined the object being studied and then provided the methodologies for that study that presupposed the definition. While this problem is particularly true of the substantialist definitions, it is also found in the functionalist models of definition as well. In order to develop a good working theory of religion, or ritual, symbol or myth, it is necessary to separate these two elements.

The first question to be asked is whether we need to define the object being studied? While it is clear that for the purposes of discussion it is necessary to set boundaries to the object being discussed, it is important, however, to recognise that these boundaries should always be provisional. We should recognise that our definitions are socially constructed and authorised, and thus cannot be seen as prescriptive. Definitions can be used in an analogical sense, bringing together material without forcing identity upon it. Analogy suggests similarity; it also allows for difference and thus retains the essential aspect of particularity. Perhaps the term definition is too strong; other terms like characterisation might be better.

Given that our characterisations are culturally situated they need to be provisional in a second sense; called dialectical in the previous discussions. A characterisation should be seen as a starting place for discussion rather than the conclusion of it. It must always respond and change in respect of the empirical data. We are not suggesting an evolutionary dialectical development in which the characterisation gets better, rather a dialectical relationship in which the characterisation is transformed in relationship to the data.

The second area, a methodology for analysis, is also an important aspect of any attempt to understand. Many such methodologies were presupposed by the definition of the object. We suggest the need for open-ended methodologies that provide a method of analysing without have a predetermined expectation of either the content or result of the analysis. Several methodologies for analysis that fit this requirement have been touched on here.

As a basis for further discussion we would suggests some provisional aspects of a characterisation of religion that is shaped by these issues:

Religion is any shared totalising system of relating to or understanding the world (in a literal or non-literal sense).

The element of being shared is an important aspect of the characterisation. It emphasises the fact that religion, however, characterised is a group phenomenon. This is not to say that individuals may not create totalising systems, rather it is to emphasise the anthropological interest in social facts. The shared aspect also suggests that the totalising feature of the definition is the basis of the shared system, individuals associating with that system need not consistently employ it. The term 'system' is not meant to suggest that religion need be a specifically articulated and defined institution. In some cases religion will be separate from other institutions; in others it will be coextensive with the wider community; and in other cases it might be spread in many different but related institutions. There is also a wide range of institutional structures from formal and hierarchical to informal, fluid and egalitarian. Religion can also be associated with any level of society, from small sub-groups to the community as a whole. The term 'relating to' is meant to suggest practices, which may or may not be accompanied by articulated beliefs. Practices may provide this type of totalising system through instantiating (not communicating) a structural pattern that organises other aspects of lived and perceived experience. In this respect, religion, through the emphasis of these practices can be seen as analogous to the structuralist understanding of myth: religion is a highly structured set of practices. 'Understanding' is meant to include a wide range of cognitive phenomena that may include rational thought or belief or any mixture of the two. It may also refer to the communication of or the unconscious perception of structural patterns, which organise and give meaning to experience.

This definition is not meant to be prescriptive, but rather to serve an analogical function to enable analytical discussion. Elements of it, and the definition as a whole, must be transformable in relation to and response to specific ethnographic situations.

While we have been generally dismissive of essentialist definitions, it is important to keep in mind the cognitive and psychological unity of humanity. Provided that we do not attempt to essentialise culturally specific aspects, as we found in respect of Freud and Jung, it is worthwhile to consider whether there are aspects of humanity that are shared and that shape our social experience. These essential elements may be indicated by two examples: psychological and structural. Although we would not subscribe to the essentialisation of specific complexes, it seems likely that a more contentless structure of our psyches must be shared. Similarly, the structuralist view that the mind is essentially a device for structuring experience, in a purely cognitive sense, may also give an indication of useful avenues of study. Both of these approaches offer open-ended avenues for analysing social phenomena, without either imposing a particular social definition or, if properly done, a particular end result. In both cases they essentialised the human being rather than the cultural object or institution.

Bibliography

Ahmed, Leila (1992) *Women and Gender in Islam*, Yale University Press: New Haven.

Allport, Gordon, W. (1951) *The Individual and His Religion*, Constable: London.

Allport, Gordon, W. (1963) *Pattern and Growth in Personality*, Holt, Rinehart and Winston: London.

Asad, Talal (1993) *Genealogies of Religion*, Johns Hopkins University Press: Baltimore.

Banton, Michael (1968) *Anthropological Approaches to the Study of Religion*, Tavistock: London.

Batson, C. Daniel and Ventis, W. Larry (1982) *The Religious Experience*, Oxford University Press: Oxford.

Bellah, Robert, N. (1964) 'Religious Evolution' in *American Sociological Review*, 29, pp. 358–74.

Berger, Peter (1967) *The Sacred Canopy*, Anchor Books: New York.

Berger, Peter (ed.) (1999) *The Desecularisation of the World*, Eerdmans: Grand Rapids.

Berger, Peter and Luckmann, Thomas (1966) 'Secularisation and Pluralism' in *International Yearbook for the Sociology of Religion*, pp. 73–84.

Bianchi, Ugo (1975 [1970]) *The History of Religions*, E. J. Brill: Leiden.

Biezais, Haralds (1979) 'Typology of Religion and the Phenomenological Method' in Honko, Lauri (ed.) *Science of Religion: Studies in Methodology*, Mouton: The Hague, pp. 143–60.

Bleeker, C. J. (1979) 'Commentary' in Honko, Lauri (ed.) *Science of Religion: Studies in Methodology*, Mouton: The Hague, pp. 173–6.

Bruce, Steve (2002) *God is Dead: Secularisation in the West*, Blackwell: Oxford.

Campbell, Joseph (1968 [1949]) *The Hero With a Thousand Faces*, Princeton University Press: Princeton.

Campbell, Joseph (ed.) (1970) *Myths, Dreams, and Religion*, Spring Publications: Dallas.

Chopp, Rebecca S. and Davaney, Sheila Greeve (1997) *Horizons in Feminist Theology*, Fortress: Minneapolis.

Davis, Kingsley (1948) *Human Society*, Macmillan: New York.

Douglas, Mary (1970) *Natural Symbols*, Pelican: Harmondsworth.

Douglas, Mary (1975) *Implicit Meanings*, Routledge: London.

Douglas, Mary (1975a) 'Deciphering a Meal' in Douglas, Mary *Implicit Meanings*, Routledge: London.

Douglas, Mary (1975b) 'Self-evidence' in Douglas, Mary *Implicit Meanings*, Routledge: London.

Durkheim, Emile (2001 [1912]) *The Elementary Forms of Religious Life*, Oxford University Press: Oxford.

Eliade, Mircia (1959) *The Sacred and the Profane*, Harcourt Brace and World: New York.

Eliade, Mircia (1965) *Patterns in Comparative Religion*, Ohio World: Cleveland.

Eliade, Mircia (1971) *The Myth of the Eternal Return*, Princeton University Press: Princeton.

Engels, Friedrich (1972 [1884]) 'The Origin of Family, Private Property, and State' in Tucker, Robert (ed.) *The Marx and Engels Reader*, Norton: New York, pp. 734–59.

Evans-Pritchard, E. E. (1965) *Theories of Primitive Religion*, Oxford University Press: Oxford.

Firth, Raymond (1973) *Symbols: Public and Private*, Cornell University Press: Ithica.

Freud, Sigmund (1950) *Totem and Taboo*, Norton: New York.

Freud, Sigmund (1961) *The Future of an Illusion*, Norton: New York.

Geertz, Clifford (1968) 'Religion as a Cultural System' in Banton, Michael (ed.) *Anthropological Approaches to the Study of Religion*, Tavistock: London, pp. 1–46.

Geertz, Clifford (1968a) *Islam Observed*, University of Chicago Press: Chicago.

Glazier, Stephen D. (ed.) (1997) *Anthropology of Religion*, Praeger: Westport.

Hallpike, C. R. (1979) 'Social Hair' in Lessa, W. A., Vogt, E. Z. (eds) *Reader in Comparative Religion*, Harper and Row: New York, pp. 99–105.

Hamilton, Malcolm (1995) *The Sociology of Religion*, Routledge: London.

Harris, Marvin (1968) *The Rise of Anthropological Theory*, Harper and Row: New York.

Harris, Marvin (1975) *Cows, Pigs, Wars and Witches*, Vintage: New York.

Hervieu-Léger, Danièle (1999) 'Religion as Memory' in Platvoet, Jan G. and Molendijk, Arie L. (eds) *The Pragmatics of Defining Religion*, E. J. Brill: Leiden, pp. 73–92.

Hill, Peter C. (1997) 'Toward an Attitude Process Model of Religious Experience' in Spilka, Bernard and McIntosh, Daniel (eds) *The Psychology of Religion: Theoretical Approaches*, Westview Press: Boulder, pp. 184–93.

Honko, Lauri (ed.) (1979) *Science of Religion: Studies in Methodology*, Mouton: The Hague.

Idinopulos, Thomas A. and Yonan, Edward A. (eds) (1994) *Religion and Reductionism*, E. J. Brill: Leiden.

Jones, Serene (1997) 'Women's Experience Between a Rock and a Hard Place' in Chopp, Rebecca S. and Davaney, Sheila Greeve (eds) *Horizons in Feminist Theology*, Fortress: Minneapolis, pp. 33–53.

Jung, C. G. (1969 [1959]) *The Collected Works of C. G. Jung, vol. 2*, Princeton University Press: Princeton.

Jung, C. G. (1969a [1959]) *The Collected Works of C. G. Jung, vol. 8*, Princeton University Press: Princeton.

Jung, C. G. (1969b [1959]) *The Collected Works of C. G. Jung, vol. 9, part 1*, Princeton University Press: Princeton.

King, Ursula (ed.) (1994) *Feminist Theology from the Third World*, Orbis Books: New York, pp. 63–76.

King, Ursula (ed.) (1995) *Religion and Gender*, Blackwell: Oxford.

Kristensen, W. Brede (1971) *The Meaning of Religion*, Martinus Nijhoff: The Hague.

Kroeber, Alfred L. (1979) 'Totem and Taboo: An Ethnologic Psychoanalysis' in Lessa, W. A., Vogt, E. Z. (eds) *Reader in Comparative Religion*, Harper and Row: New York, pp. 19–24.

Kunin, Seth D. (1998) *God's Place in the World*, Cassell: London.

Kwok, Pui-Lan (1994) 'The Future of Feminist Theology: and Asian Perspective' in King, Ursula (ed.) *Feminist Theology from the Third World*, Orbis Books: New York, pp. 63–76.

Lang, Bernhard (ed.) (1985) *Anthropological Approaches to the Old Testament*, Fortress Press: Philadelphia.

Leach, Edmund R. (1958) 'Magical Hair' in *Journal of the Royal Anthropological Institute* 88, pp. 147–64.

Leach, Edmund R. (1968) *Dialectic in Practical Religion*, Cambridge University Press: Cambridge.

Leach, Edmund R. (1985) 'The Logic of Sacrifice' in Lang, Bernhard (ed.) *Anthropological Approaches to the Old Testament*, Fortress Press: Philadelphia, pp. 136–50.

Leeuw, G. van der (1986 [1933]) *Religion in Essence and Manifestation*, Princeton University Press: Princeton.

Lessa, W. A., Vogt, E. Z. (eds) (1979) *Reader in Comparative Religion*, Harper and Row: New York.

Lett, James (1997) 'Science, Religion, and Anthropology' in Glazier, Stephen D. (ed.) *Anthropology of Religion*, Praeger: Westport, pp. 103–38.

Lévy-Bruhl, Lucien (1923) *Primitive Mentality*, Macmillan: London.

Lewis, I. M. (1971) *Ecstatic Religion*, Routledge: London.

Luckmann, Thomas (1967) *The Invisible Religion*, Macmillan: New York.

McCutcheon, Russell T. (1999) *The Insider/Outsider Problem in the Study of Religion*, Cassell: London.

McIntosh, Daniel (1997) 'Religion-as-Schema, with Implications for the Relation Between Religion and Coping' in Spilka, Bernard and McIntosh, Daniel (eds) *The Psychology of Religion: Theoretical Approaches*, Westview Press: Boulder, pp. 171–83.

Marx, Karl (1972 [1846]) 'The German Ideology: Part I' in Tucker, Robert (ed.) *The Marx and Engels Reader*, Norton: New York, pp. 147–200.

Marx, Karl (2002 [1844]) 'Critique of Hegel's Philosophy of Right' in Raines, John (ed.) *Marx on Religion*, Temple University Press: Philadelphia.

Maslow, Abraham H. (1964) *Religions, Values, and Peak-Experiences*, Viking Press: New York.

Merton, Robert (1964) *Social Theory and Social Structure*, Collier-Macmillan: London.

Middleton, John (ed.) (1967) *Myth and Cosmos*, Natural History Press: New York.

Moore, Sally Falk (1967) 'Descent and Symbolic Filiation' in Middleton, John *Myth and Cosmos*, Natural History Press: New York, pp. 63–76.

Morris, Brian (1987) *Anthropological Studies of Religion*, Cambridge University Press: Cambridge.

Nadel, S. F. (1954) *Nupe Religion*, Routledge and Kegan Paul: London.

Niebuhr, Richard (1929) *The Social Sources of Denominationalism*, Henry Holt and Co., New York.

Obeyesekere, Gananath (1981) *Medusa's Hair*, Chicago University Press: Chicago.

O'Connor, June (1995) 'The Epistemological Significance of Feminist Research in Religion' in King, Ursula (ed.) *Religion and Gender*, Blackwell: Oxford, pp. 45–64.

Okely, Judith (1983) *The Traveller-Gypsies*, Cambridge University Press: Cambridge.

Otto, Rudolf (1958 [1917]) *The Idea of the Holy*, Oxford University Press: Oxford.

Parsons, Talcott (1954) *Essays in Sociological Theory*, Free Press: Glencoe.

Parsons, Talcott (1976) 'Religious Perspectives in Sociology and Social Psychology' in Lessa, W. A., Vogt, E. Z. (eds) (1979) *Reader in Comparative Religion*, Harper and Row: New York, pp. 62–6.

Persinger, M. A. (1987) *Neuropsychological Bases of God Beliefs*, Praeger: New York.

Pike, Kenneth L. (1999) 'Etic and Emic Standpoints for the Description of Behaviour' in McCutcheon, Russell T. *The Insider/Outsider Problem in the Study of Religion*, Cassell: London.

Platvoet, Jan G. and Molendijk, Arie L. (1999) (eds) *The Pragmatics of Defining Religion*, E. J. Brill: Leiden.

Radcliffe-Brown, A. R. (1945) 'Religion and Society' in *JRAI* LXXV, pp. 33–43.

Radcliffe-Brown, A. R. (1964) *The Andaman Islanders*, Free Press: New York.

Raines, John (ed.) (2002) *Marx on Religion*, Temple University Press: Philadelphia.

Robertson, Roland (ed.) *Sociology of Religion*, Penguin: Harmondsworth.

Ryba, Thomas (1994) 'Are Religious Theories Susceptible to Reduction?' in Idinopulos, Thomas A. and Yonan, Edward A. (eds) *Religion and Reductionism*, E. J. Brill: Leiden.

Saler, Benson (1993) *Conceptualising Religion*, E. J. Brill: Leiden.

Segal, Robert (1999) *Theorising About Myth*, University of Massachusetts Press: Amherst.

Segal, Robert (1999) 'In Defense of Reductionism' in McCutcheon, Russell T. *The Insider/Outsider Problem in the Study of Religion*, Cassell: London.

Shaw, Rosalind (1995) 'Feminist Anthropology and the Gendering of Religious Studies' in King, Ursula (ed.) *Religion and Gender*, Blackwell: Oxford, pp. 65–76.

Smart, Ninian (1971 [1969]) *The Religious Experience of Mankind*, Fontana: London.

Smart, Ninian (1973) *The Phenomenon of Religion*, Macmillan: London.

Smart, Ninian (1986) 'foreword' in Leeuw, Gerardus van der (1986 [1933]) *Religion in Essence and Manifestation*, Princeton University Press: Princeton, pp. ix–xix.

Smith, Wilfred Cantwell (1978) *The Meaning and End of Religion*, SPCK: London.

Southwold, Martin (1978) 'Buddhism and the Definition of Religion' in *Man* 13.3, pp. 362–79.

Spenser, Robert F. (1969) *Forms of Symbolic Action*, American Ethnological Society: Seattle.

Sperber, Dan (1975) *Rethinking Symbolism*, Cambridge University Press: Cambridge.

Spilka, Bernard and McIntosh, Daniel (eds) *The Psychology of Religion: Theoretical Approaches*, Westview Press: Boulder.

Spiro, Melford (1968) 'Religion: Problems of Definition and Explanation' in Banton, Michael (ed.) *Anthropological Approaches to the Study of Religion*, Tavistock: London, pp. 85–126.

Stark, Rodney and Bainbridge, William Sims (1980) 'Toward a Theory of Religion: Religious Commitment' in *Journal for the Scientific Study of Religion*, 19 (2), pp. 114–28.

Sternski, Ivan (1994) 'Reduction Without Tears' in Idinopulos, Thomas A. and Yonan, Edward A. (eds) *Religion and Reductionism*, E. J. Brill: Leiden.

Thrower, James (1999) *Religion: The Classical Theories*, Edinburgh University Press: Edinburgh.

Turnbull, Colin (1993) *The Forest People*, Pimlico: London.

Turner, Victor (1969) 'Forms of Symbolic Action' in Spenser, Robert F. *Forms of Symbolic Action*, American Ethnological Society: Seattle.

Tylor, E. B. (1871) *Primitive Culture*, John Murray: London.

Wach, Joachim (1944) *Sociology of Religion*, University of Chicago Press: Chicago.

Wallace, Anthony F. C. (1966) *Religion an Anthropological View*, Random House: New York.

Wallis, Roy and Bruce, Steve (1984) 'The Stark-Bainbridge Theory of Religion: A Critical Analysis and Counter Proposal' in *Sociological Analysis*, 45 (1), pp. 11–27.

Wallis, Roy and Bruce, Steve (1992) 'Secularisation: The Orthodox Model' in Bruce, Steve (ed.) *Religion and Modernisation*, Clarendon Press: Oxford.

Weber, Max (1958) *The Protestant Ethic and the Spirit of Capitalism*, Scribners: New York.

White, Leslie (1959) *The Evolution of Culture*, McGraw-Hill: New York.

Williams, Delores S. (1994) 'Womanist Theology: Black Women's Voices' in King, Usula (ed.) *Feminist Theology from the Third World*, Orbis Books: New York, pp. 77–87.

Wilson, Bryan (1959) 'An Analysis of Sect Development' in *American Sociological Review*, 24 (1), pp. 3–15.

Wilson, Bryan (1969) 'A Typology of Sects' in Robertson, Roland (ed.) *Sociology of Religion*, Penguin: Harmondsworth, pp. 361–83.

Wilson, Bryan (1982) *Religion in Sociological Perspective*, Oxford University Press: Oxford.

Yinger, J. Milton (1970) *The Scientific Study of Religion*, Macmillan: New York.

Index